Language in Literature

MICHAEL TOOLAN

Language in Literature

An Introduction to Stylistics

A member of the Hodder Headline Group
LONDON

First published in Great Britain in 1998
This impression reprinted in 2003 by
Arnold, a member of the Hodder Headline Group,
338 Euston Road, London NW1 3BH

http://www.arnoldpublishers.com

Distributed in the United States of America by
Oxford University Press Inc.,
198 Madison Avenue, New York, NY 10016

British Library Cataloguing in Publication Data
A catalogue record for this book is available from the British Library

Library of Congress Cataloging-in-Publication Data
Toolan, Michael J.
        p.   cm.
    Includes bibliographical references and index.
    ISBN 0-340-66213-1.—ISBN 0-340-66214-X (pbk.)
    1. Discourse analysis. Literary.   2. Style. Literary.   I. Title.
P302.5T66   1997
808'.001'—dc21

                                                97-17344
                                                CIP

ISBN 0 340 66213 1 (hb)
ISBN 0 340 66214 X (pb)

6 7 8 9 10

Typeset in Erhardt by J&L Composition Ltd, Filey, North Yorkshire
Printed and bound in India by Replika Press Pvt. Ltd., Kundli 131 028

Contents

Acknowledgements

The author and publishers would like to thank the following for permission to reproduce copyright material:

Atwood, Margaret: 'This is a Photograph of Me' from *Selected Poems 1965–1975* by Margaret Atwood. Copyright © 1966 by Margaret Atwood. Reprinted by permission of Stoddart Publishing Company Ltd.

Crampton, Robert: 'Scouse Grit: Jimmy McGovern' by Robert Crampton from *The Times Magazine*, 11 March 1995. Copyright © The Times 1995. Reprinted by permisson of Times Newspapers Ltd.

Heaney, Seamus: 'An Ulster Twilight' from *Station Island* by Seamus Heaney. Copyright ©1984 by Seamus Heaney. Reprinted by permission of Faber & Faber Ltd and Farrar, Straus & Giroux, Inc.

Horsnell, Michael: 'Maxwell fell overboard "while relieving himself", says son' by Michael Horsnell from *The Times*, 21 October 1995. Copyright © Times Newspapers Limited, 1995. Reprinted by permission of Times Newspapers Limited.

Larkin, Phillip: 'Here' and 'Take One Home for the Kiddies' from *Collected Poems* by Philip Larkin. Copyright © 1988, 1989 by the Estate of Phillip Larkin. Reprinted by permission of Faber & Faber Ltd and Farrar, Straus & Giroux, Inc.

Lowell, Robert: 'Inspiration' by Robert Lowell. Copyright © 1997 by Sheridan Lowell and Harriet Lowell. Reprinted by permission of Farrar, Straus & Giroux, Inc.; 'Skunk Hour' from *Life Studies* by Robert Lowell. Copyright © 1956, 1959 by Robert Lowell. Copyright renewed 1987 by Harriet Lowell, Sheridan Lowell and Carolyn Lowell. Reprinted by permission of Faber & Faber Ltd and Farrar, Straus & Giroux, Inc.

Parris, Matthew: 'Speaker chokes on a diet of pickles and beetroot' by Matthew Parris from *The Times*, 25 February 1994. Copyright © Matthew Parris/The Times 25 February 1994. Reprinted by permission of Times Newspapers Limited.

Plath, Sylvia: 'Metaphors' from *Crossing the Water* by Sylvia Plath. Copyright © 1960 by Ted Hughes. Copyright renewed. Reprinted by permission of Faber & Faber Ltd and HarperCollins Publishers, Inc.

Raine, Craig: 'A Martian Sends a Postcard Home' from *A Martian Sends a Postcard Home* by Craig Raine. Copyright © 1979 by Craig Raine. Reprinted by permission of Oxford University Press.

Rich, Adrienne: 'Living in Sin' from *Collected Early Poems 1950–1970* by Adrienne Rich. Copyright © 1993, 1955 by Adrienne Rich. Reprinted by permission of the author and W. W. Norton & Company, Inc.

Stevenson, Anne: 'The Marriage' and 'Utah' from *Selected Poems 1956–1986* by Anne Stevenson. Reprinted by permission of Oxford University Press.

Targan, Barry: extract from 'Dominion', first published in *The Iowa Review*, 10: 2 (spring 1979), reprinted in the *Norton New Worlds of Literature* anthology, ed. Jerome Beaty and J. Paul Hunter, 1989. Reprinted here by permission of the author.

West, Richard: 'Still Dark' book review by Richard West from the *Daily Telegraph* 18 May 1984. Reprinted by permission of the author.

'Awaiting Mandela' from *The Economist*, 6 January 1990. Copyright © The Economist, London, 1990. Reprinted by permission of The Economist.

Every effort has been made to trace copyright holders of material, and those who hold the rights to the reproduction of material. Any rights not acknowledged here will be acknowledged in subsequent printings if notice is given to the publishers.

Preliminaries

The goal of this book is to sharpen your awareness of how language works in texts – particularly, here, in literary texts. Doing this will involve some use of linguistic terms and concepts, and some attention to grammar. While I do not want to resort to technical description any more than seems reasonable, such resort often does seem reasonable to me. Appropriate linguistic terms and descriptions can articulate an inward understanding of the workings of a language, and can situate the verbal technique of a particular text among the range of available repertoires for writing and speaking, and the variety of kinds of text and kinds of language use that exist.

The focus will be on texts – poems, short stories, extracts from novels, advertisements, children's writing, etc. Sometimes those texts may strike you as difficult if not impenetrable, but more often they will not be so hard to understand. So it will not be the case, usually, that we are looking at these texts as problems which, with our sharpened language focus, we can solve. Instead, our general assumption is that these texts are evidently solutions or achievements – often brilliant ones. And we are trying to understand and even explain how those solutions work, and to see just where the brilliance or ingenuity lies, assisted by linguistic terms and ideas and an increased awareness of language resources and language structure. That, in essence, is what I mean by the term (Literary) Stylistics, which is used often in this book (an alternative label for this approach is Literary Linguistics). Stylistics is the study of the language *in* literature.

The basic procedure of the book will be to explain, briefly, some topic in the language structuring of texts, and then to assist the reader to apply that knowhow in analysing particular literary texts. Sometimes this may feel like mere labelling, using exotic linguistic terms to describe familiar material. But the important point is that the labels to be applied are not empty ones: they have content. That is to say, they represent specific and substantiated insights concerning the structure of texts, and the nature of language communication. So although labelling is involved in Stylistics, this labelling is not trivial. The labels are a way of describing the given literary text, and they contribute to an explanation of that text.

For example, you might want to undertake a systematic study of the naming practices in a novel. You could look at whether protagonists are named via a pronoun (e.g., *she*), or by a proper name (*Clarissa Dalloway*) or by various definite descriptions (*the woman*; *the fluttering sparrow*; *the elegantly dressed matron*); you might well want to see how often a protagonist is named in these different ways, and with what kinds of definite descriptions, what kinds of pronoun (e.g. *thou* vs. *you* in Early Modern English texts), and so on. Becoming more sensitive to particular contexts, you might well want to consider any disparities in naming in relation to two or more characters appearing in the same scene. The facts about the text that we separate out in this way, facts about protagonist-naming, are then a usable description of just that aspect of the text: the facts and claimed patterns can be confirmed or corrected, they can be discussed with others, and their significance in apprehending the text as a whole can be debated. So one of the crucial things attempted by Stylistics is to put the discussion of textual effects and techniques on a public, shared, footing – a footing as shared and established and inspectable as is available to informed language-users, who agree that *she* is a pronoun, *herself* a reflexive pronoun, *Clarissa* a proper name, and *the vivacious white-haired woman* a definite description.

The other chief feature of Stylistics is that it persists in the attempt to understand technique, or the craft of writing. If we agree that Hemingway's short story 'Indian Camp', and Yeats's poem 'Sailing to Byzantium', are both extraordinary literary achievements, what are some of the linguistic components of that excellence? Why these word-choices, clause-patterns, rhythms and intonations, contextual implications, cohesive links, choices of voice and perspective and transitivity, etc. etc., and not any of the others imaginable? Conversely, can we locate the linguistic bases of some aspects of weak writing, bad poetry, the confusing and the banal?

Stylistics asserts we should be able to, particularly by bringing to the close examination of the linguistic particularities of a text an understanding of the anatomy and functions of the language. The celebrated Socratic phrase 'the examined life' is often invoked to remind us of our need to subject all our behaviour to rational and moral self-scrutiny; Stylistics nails its colours to an analogous slogan, the need for and value of 'the examined text'. In summary, Stylistics is crucially concerned with excellence of technique; traditionally, its attention has been directed to such excellence of craft in works of literature, but clearly there is no intrinsic reason why it cannot equally be used in the study of excellence of craft (and, conversely, of mediocrity of craft) in other fields such as advertising, political discourse, legal pleading, and pop-music lyrics.

I should stress again that this is a book on topics in Stylistics, and not a comprehensive guide. An attempt at comprehensiveness of coverage of such an extensive tradition would have been sure to fail and, more importantly, would be beside the point. For the chief point of Stylistics is that students learn to apply the methods. This can often be treated as a three-stage activity. First comes the task of understanding the particular language or discourse subsystem under scrutiny. Then one can use this to answer quite specific derived questions concerning the text ('List the number and ways in which the narrative aligned with Mrs Dalloway's point of view refers to Peter Walsh in this scene'). Finally, on the basis of such close studies, one can proceed to answer questions of a broader nature with wider implications: 'Compare and contrast her naming of Peter Walsh with her naming of Hugh Whitbread, Richard Dalloway, Sally Seton, and Sir William Bradshaw'.

The chapters that follow introduce a selection of topics which I have found useful to explore with undergraduate literature students in a relatively short course in Stylistics. The major topics included are: cohesion; naming patterns; modality and evaluation; the structure of simple narratives; the recording of character speech and thought (especially, free indirect discourse); clause processes and participants; the dynamics of dialogue; presupposition; and textual revision.

I should mention at this point two particular textual features you will find in the chapters that follow. One is Time Out boxes: not reviews of current entertainments in London, but brief explanations of grammatical or similar terms which you may not be entirely familiar with: **finite, deictic, degree words**, and so on. These Time Out boxes are sited immediately after such key terms are first introduced. The second feature, tied to the many questions and activities dotted through each chapter, is a series of brief commentaries at the end of each chapter (keyed by number to the earlier question to which they refer). Any question or activity which has an end-of-chapter commentary paired with it carries this symbol: (§). A commentary on a given question is not 'the answer', but a sketch of one way to respond to the question or activity. It should be possible to quarrel with the commentaries as productively as one can quarrel with the questions themselves.

1

Getting started

Let us begin with two rather different poems, written at about the same time, by rather different poets: Philip Larkin's 'Here' and Margaret Atwood's 'This is a Photograph of Me'. We shall take these in order. After Larkin's poem, there are several notes and questions, on the basis of which you should be able to build up quite an extensive stylistic commentary on the poem. Similarly, after the Atwood poem I will raise several questions, and invite you to respond to them by attending to patterns and structures in the text, in much the way that will have been demonstrated in the discussion of 'Here'. As always, these questions and the discussion they trigger are intended to advance our insight into the poet's craft and the poem's effects.

Here

Swerving east, from rich industrial shadows
And traffic all night north; swerving through fields
Too thin and thistled to be called meadows,
And now and then a harsh-named halt, that shields
Workmen at dawn; swerving to solitude
Of skies and scarecrows, haystacks, hares and pheasants,
And the widening river's slow presence,
The piled gold clouds, the shining gull-marked mud,

Gathers to the surprise of a large town:
Here domes and statues, spires and cranes cluster
Beside grain-scattered streets, barge-crowded water,
And residents from raw estates, brought down
The dead straight miles by stealing flat-faced trolleys,
Push through plate-glass swing doors to their desires –
Cheap suits, red kitchen-ware, sharp shoes, iced lollies,
Electric mixers, toasters, washers, driers –

A cut-price crowd, urban yet simple, dwelling
Where only salesmen and relations come
Within a terminate and fishy-smelling
Pastoral of ships up streets, the slave museum,
Tattoo-shops, consulates, grim head-scarfed wives;
And out beyond its mortgaged half-built edges
Fast-shadowed wheat fields, running high as hedges,
Isolate villages, where removed lives

Loneliness clarifies. Here silence stands
Like heat. Here leaves unnoticed thicken,
Hidden weeds flower, neglected waters quicken,
Luminously-peopled air ascends;
And past the poppies bluish neutral distance
Ends the land suddenly beyond a beach
Of shapes and shingle. Here is unfenced existence:
Facing the sun, untalkative, out of reach.

The stylistic mentality is always on the lookout for one or more of the following:

> pattern
> repetition
> recurrent structures
> ungrammatical or 'language-stretching' structures
> large internal contrasts of content or presentation.

And it is not embarrassed about beginning a discussion with broad or vague first impressions, so-called intuitive or subjective responses, and keeping those in mind as the discussion works its way from the general to the specific. What, then, are your first impressions of this poem? It would be useful if you read over the poem again, and jotted down your first impressions and reactions, before reading on.

My own first impressions are that the poem seems to involve a journey, a movement from one place to a different one; that it is highly descriptive, indeed quite packed with mentioned things; and that the final eight lines contrast, in many respects, with what goes before. For instance, they seem both more contemplative and more positive in tone than the earlier lines, or more approving of what they report. These immediate reactions do much to shape the closer language analysis that follows; they are claims that the more detailed attention will now seek to bolster, or adjust. I believe a similar progression, from first impressions to closer study shaped by those first impressions, typically happens *whenever* we encounter a new poem, or new picture – or a new acquaintance for that matter. Influential though they are, first impressions can also be unreliable, which is why the closer look, the analytical inspection, is necessary.

But how does 'analysis' begin? I believe it begins with attempts to answer perhaps the most foundational of 'analytical' questions we can pose of any object:

What do you notice about this object?

This is the first and most basic analytical question that you are likely to be asked, or will ask yourself, when you really look at a particular Rembrandt painting for the first time, or hear a musical composition for the first time. Not 'What is it?'; nor 'Do you like it?': these are not truly analytical questions. But 'What do you notice in this (from among, by implication, all the innumerable things you could notice here)?'. The following comments itemize some of the language-based things that I notice in 'Here', together with attempted explanations of what those noticed features may have been intended to signify.

Activities

ACTIVITY 1

1   Besides the title, the word *here* is used four times in the poem: once in the second stanza and three times in the final one.

> **Time Out: here, a deictic word**
>
> *Here* is a deictic word (deixis is explained more fully in Chapter 2), which means that whatever place *here* is referring to depends entirely on the assumed location of the speaker. Right now, even as I write this, I can refer to the University of Birmingham campus as *here* (it's where, currently, I am); you, on the other hand, unless you too are on this same campus, have a different *here*. What *here* refers to depends entirely on the assumed location of its utterer.

Now an obvious point about the four *heres* in Larkin's poem is that the first refers to one place, a town, while the later three refer to somewhere beyond the town, the seacoast. There is a simple explanation for a text with contrasting *heres*, namely that the speaker's implied location has shifted. Note that the speaker need not have literally moved from, for example, the town to the country: he or she only needs to have shifted their attention (and the reader's attention) from one place to another, and to have given some verbal indications of such an attention-shift. In the case of this poem, what word-choices would you point to as suggesting that the speaker is describing a literal journey from some place to a different one? How might we argue that, however vivid the description of a real journey, it is the speaker's mental or figurative journey that is finally of greater significance? (§)

2   I notice the inordinate length of the poem's first sentence. It runs on until the word *clarifies* at the beginning of the final stanza, a 24-line trek. What are the sentence's subject, and its finite main verb?

In order to answer the latter of these questions, what 'finite main verb' means may need clarification.

Time Out: main verbs

By the 'main verb' I mean the verbal word or phrase which is the state or action upon which the entire sentence hinges. The main verb of a sentence is the verbal hinge or fulcrum of the material which the sentence simply cannot do without. Every grammatical sentence ____ a main verb. Otherwise it ____ incomplete, and difficult to interpret. By 'finite' I mean a verb phrase which gives, in the first word of that phrase, some indication that it is either present or past tense (and that, thereby, the whole sentence is somewhat temporally defined). All main verbs need to be finite.

What, then, is the main verb in the last sentence preceding this box? This was:

In order to answer the latter of these questions, what 'finite main verb' means may need clarification.

That sentence is quite a complex one, with several verb-like chunks: *answer, means* and *may need*. To identify which of these is the 'crucial hinge' of the sentence we must first recognize that the sentence itself is made up of a grammatically dispensable part and an indispensable part. The dispensable portion is

(a) *In order to answer the latter of these questions*

and the indispensable portion is

(b) *what 'finite main verb' means may need clarification.*

The simplest reason for saying this is that portion (b) can stand alone, as a coherent and grammatical sentence, without (a)'s support; but (a) cannot stand alone without support from a clause like (b). Now when it comes to identifying the main verb *within* this main portion, (b), reading aloud is a good policy: for many people, as soon as *What 'finite main verb' means may need clarification* is spoken aloud, it becomes clear that *What 'finite main verb' means* is the sentence's Subject, *may need* is the finite verb, and *clarification* is some kind of Object. But when uncertainty remains, a good next step is to try substituting pronouns or short phrases for the chunks you believe the given sentence to be made up of.

In the present case, suppose you are inclined to think that *means* is the main verb of the sentence. To confirm this, you should be able to find pronouns or short phrases that will substitute for the material which appears on either side of *means*, and that will do so **without wrenching the meaning away from that of the original sentence.**

What 'finite main verb'	*means*	*may need clarification.*
?It	*means*	*?business*

As you can see, neither the material before or after this alleged main verb means can be replaced satisfactorily while retaining the general sense of the original sentence, by simpler phrases or pronouns; there simply are no pronoun substitutes for the chunks *What 'finite main verb' means* or *may need clarification*, because these are not, **on this occasion**, genuine phrases (or 'constituents') in the first place. If, on the other hand, we propose that *may need* is the finite verb, then numerous substitutes, which do not distort the basic meaning of the entire sentence, can be found (including substitutes for the finite main verb):

What 'finite main verb'	*means*	*may need*	*clarification.*
This phrase		*needs*	*explaining.*
It		*requires*	*a gloss.*

In short, the stative or active 'hinge' of the entire sentence is the phrase *may need*. And the first word in that verb phrase, *may*, presents itself as present tense. On the same basis, the finite main verb of the sentence before this current one is *presents*, and it, too, is present tense. Finally, please bear in mind that written sentences can have two or more main verbs; this arises when a sentence comprises two (or more) indispensable parts or 'main clauses', which stand largely independently of each other, almost like separate sentences:

Fionnula walks to work but Iqbal commutes by train.

       m.vb   m.vb

Returning now to the question of the Subject and finite main verb of the first sentence in 'Here', it is evident that both are absent. Instead we are treated to much swerving, in the non-finite progressive form, suggestive of ongoingness without clear beginning or end. And who or what is it that does the swerving? Train, truck, bird, poet? Neither the 'swerver' nor the 'swerved' declare themselves. And yet some individual must be involved in experiencing or witnessing the swerving, for how otherwise could the poem be written? Whoever lays this poem before us, tells us of the swerving and the gathering and final untalkativeness; he or she is reponsible for everything in the poem, all its sharp judgements, and yet includes in the text no impression of him- or herself as a felt presence. Why so? Is it because the poem has 'nothing to do with' the specifics of the speaker's identity and nature? Or because the speaker's is one of those 'removed lives' of which s/he speaks?

3   I am also struck by certain semantic and grammatical patterns in the poem, relating to 'swerving': the 'swerving' in this poem is not quite like swerving in its everyday contemporary uses. Typically, swerving is an act of avoidance: you 'swerve away from' something unwelcome, but without a positive goal. You swerve not so as definitely to meet something, but in order definitely to not meet something. But in Larkin's poem swerving from is complemented by swerving to. In fact the full sequence is

Swerving from . . . swerving through . . . swerving to.

This sequence describes a curved line, but one with a clear endpoint; thus this is not a swerving which is semantically akin to a circular whirling or turning, as in Yeats's 'The Second Coming': 'Turning and turning in the widening gyre, the falcon cannot hear the falconer'. What difference does it make that the sequence of prepositions here is 'from, through, to'? How does that sequence contrast with, e.g., 'through, to, from', or 'to, through, from'? Think about the idea of the order of our language descriptions often matching the actual order in which things are experienced. Do you find B's reply, in the exchange below, awkward?

A: How was your holiday? Where did you go?

B: It was great! We travelled overland to Beijing through Russia from Paris.

Notice too that the same three prepositions are used, in the natural 'purposive' order of 'from, through, to', to describe the residents: they are residents *from* raw estates who push *through* plate-glass swing doors *to* their desires.

4   Lexical congruities and incongruities. One way to analyse this poem into parts is by noting where and on which subjects its vocabulary (or lexis, as this is called by linguists) tends to cluster.

   (a)   There seems to be an extensive use of vocabulary relating to town or urban life, and alongside this a number of words relating to the country. If we treat these – 'town lexis' and 'country lexis' – as two broad groupings, we can go on to consider whether the poem divides into two sections, each section revealing a preponderance of the former and of the latter, respectively. Do you find that these putative sections overlap or merge, or are they rather separate from each other? What might your finding here (i.e., a merging of town and country lexis, or a separation of them) suggest about the speaker's conception of town life versus country life?

   (b)   Stanza 2 is perhaps the most 'thing'-dominated stanza of the four. We can support that claim by counting the number of nouns (some functioning adjectivally, like *barge* in *barge-crowded water*) in each stanza: I count 27 nouns in stanza 2, 21 in stanza 1, 20 in stanza 3, 16 in stanza 4. For reference purposes, here is stanza 2 with those words I would count as nouns rendered in bold:

Gathers to the **surprise** of a large **town**:
Here **domes** and **statues**, **spires** and **cranes** cluster
Beside **grain**-scattered **streets**, **barge**-crowded **water**,
And **residents** from raw **estates**, brought down
The dead straight **miles** by stealing flat-faced **trolleys**,
Push through **plate-glass** swing **doors** to their **desires** –

Cheap **suits**, red **kitchen-ware**, sharp **shoes**, iced **lollies**,
Electric **mixers**, **toasters**, **washers**, **driers** –

If we agree that stanza 2 is particularly 'thing'-oriented, what might this reflect in the speaker's conception of the town and the residents from raw estates? Concerning the town, line 2 says that here cluster domes, statues, spires and cranes. What do these four have in common? Is this particular foursome in any respects an incongruous or unpredictable clustering?

5   Puns and word-play. In line 5, at least two words seem to invoke a double interpretation: *dead* and *stealing*. Give paraphrases of the different senses being brought to mind. In each case, can you 'rank' the two senses attributable to the word, treating one meaning as definitely and deliberately intended by the speaker and the second meaning as only possibly intended?

Time Out: what are 'degree words'?

The words of English are traditionally grouped into a small number of classes, usually called word-classes or parts of speech. These classes are nouns, verbs, adverbs, adjectives, prepositions, conjunctions, determiners, and one or two much smaller classes. 'Degree words' are one of the latter. Each of the word-classes is defined partly in terms of function but very much in terms of where, in a verbal sequence, they can occur. Take the sequence *The ____ filled with water*: a large set of words, all nouns, can fill the blanked slot; no adverbs, adjectives, or determiners normally can (*The casually filled with water;* *The happy filled with water*; *The that filled with water*). In a similar way, there is a small set of words that can acceptably fill the blanks in a sentence like the following:

> *The ____ happy farmer ate the duckling ____ noisily.*

and only that set of words, and no others, can fill those blanks. The words in question include *very, rather, quite, somewhat, way, real, utterly*, and so on (in one dialect of English or another). Functionally, they qualify or indicate the degree to which the following adjective or adverb applies.

If so, is it fair to say that the first and definitely intended meaning is more neutral, less evaluative, while the second and 'deniable' meaning is pejorative, antipathetic, and negative about the residents and their lives?

In the case of *dead*, the double interpretation involves a structural contrast – between treating *dead* as a modifier or degree word qualifying the adjective *straight*, and treating it as a separate adjective.

On the first interpretation of

dead straight miles

the miles are utterly straight (simply); on the second interpretation, the miles are both dead and straight.

What's going on here? Is it an accident, without intended significance on Larkin's part, that phrases like 'dead straight' and 'stealing trolleys', with their double interpretations, crop up here. If not, what was Larkin's purpose?

Incidentally, I have noted that interpreted one way *dead* here is a degree word (qualifying an adjacent adjective by saying 'to what degree' it is true: similarly, *dead clever, real pretty, way cool, rather boring*). Unlike *dead*, most degree words (*very, rather, quite, slightly*) cannot create such an ambiguity as the one suggested by *dead straight miles*. Can you explain why this is so?

6   In the privacy of your own head, try to list a few of your strongest desires. Compare these with those things claimed by the speaker, here, to be the desires of these residents, *c*.1960.

What are the words that might come to mind to characterize, collectively, the 'mentionable' attributes of these residents' desires, particularly *cheap*, *red*, and *sharp*? And what do you think of the sound and rhythm of the final line of desired goods –

Electric mixers, toasters, washers, driers?

What evaluative attitude to the list does the sound of it, particularly as a line in a poem, suggest? (§)

7   Assess the vocabulary (both content words and grammatical words such as prepositions) in terms of spatial orientation.

Specifically, do you find a contrast in the poem between one section in which a horizontal plane is focused on, and another section in which a vertical one is focused on? Annotate this contrast and comment on any implications you feel it has for the poem as a whole.

8   In point 2, I commented on the extended length of the sentence in the early stanzas. How is the final stanza sharply different? How many independent clauses do you find in stanzas 1–3, how many in the final stanza?

Time Out: What is an independent clause anyway?

An independent clause is usually defined as one that could potentially stand alone as a complete sentence. In fact I believe it is more helpful to focus on particular occasions of use, and to define an independent clause as a clause that does stand alone as a complete sentence, on the occasion being examined. Compare the following:

(a) *Why he ever left home.*
(b) *I don't know why he ever left home.*
(c) *She came, she saw, she conquered.*

(a) is a dependent clause, (b) in its entirety is one independent clause, and (c) comprises three independent clauses. It was sometimes argued that what distinguishes independent clauses was that they were or expressed 'a complete and freestanding thought or proposition'. In practice it is difficult to maintain such a strong claim. But it is fair to say that, by comparison with independent clauses, dependent or subordinate ones are significantly more incomplete, in an immediately perceptible way: they 'need' the content of the clause from which they depend in a way that an independent clause does not.

How might you relate the contrast in the frequency of clauses in stanzas 1–3 and in stanza 4 to any thematic purposes of the poem?

9   By comparison with the Atwood poem to be discussed below, which is titled 'This is a Photograph of Me', we could almost re-title Larkin's poem 'This is a Photograph of Them'. Nevertheless, the poem is not only about 'them' but also about the 'me' that tells us about 'them': there is an 'I' buried within Larkin's poem – a sharply occluded speaking 'I'. The speaker is there in the poem in the same way that a photograph not

only records its visible contents but also implies something about the interests of the photographer who chose to record just those contents.

But consider again the question of 'portraying them', which may be a way to get at such issues as whether Larkin's speaker is a snob, or riddled with class-prejudice. The middle section of the poem seems to make unflattering comments on the (Hull) working class, c.1960. And yet one might respect a speaker who comments frankly – and unflatteringly, if necessary – on what he or she sees. If negative comment in itself is not objectionable, what about the question of *fair* comment. Is the speaker unfairly negative about the people of Hull? Are there any words in the poems, associated directly and unqualifiedly with the lower-class residents or by implication not to be associated with them, which make or entail evaluative judgments which seem highly contentious? (§)

10 Genuine oddities or excesses of grammar are almost invariably intentional and authorially motivated. Sort out the grammar of the last three lines of stanza 3 and the beginning of stanza 4: identify the Subject, the Verb, the Object, and any subordinate clauses. How do the similarities between the words *isolate* and *removed* retard rather than simplify the sorting-out? What might be the motivations, then, for the cluster of grammatical complexities, at just this point in the poem, after the relatively simple grammatical structuring (no matter how extended the sentences are) of the earlier lines? (§)

11 Had you noticed that the poem's lines rhyme? The easy flow of (most of) the lines is such that it is easy to overlook how cleverly Larkin has rhymed alternate lines in the halves of some octets, and outer and inner pairs in other halves. But what might you say about the nature of some of these rhymes? Look again at the following rhyming words from the poem,. reproduced in pairs below for easier reference:

shadows	*fields*	*solitude*	*pheasants*	*town*	*cluster*
meadows	*shields*	*mud*	*presence*	*down*	*water*

What *precisely* matches, and is thus the source of our sense of rhyming, in each of these pairs? Do all these rhyme in the same way? Do any feel like better rhymes than others, and do any feel noticeably worse than the others? Why? (§)

12   Comparisons. Find and read Larkin's 'The Whitsun Weddings' (in his collection of the same name, but also frequently anthologized), arguably both his best and most well-known poem (it will be discussed again in Chapter 4). If Larkin's 'Here' involves a train journey in which a participant-observer travels 'swervingly' from London to Hull and beyond, to a clarificatory isolation where the land meets the sea, 'The Whitsun Weddings' is in several respects an answering poem, in which the speaker, in the mid-afternoon (cf. the early hours of the morning, in 'Here'), travels from Hull towards London. While the 'I' of 'Here' is so removed as to be undeclared, and only indirectly inferrable, the 'I' of 'The Whitsun Weddings' is copiously expressed, and increasingly – if reluctantly – absorbed into a 'we': the 'we' of the community of travellers, growing with the addition of more newlyweds at each station. Make notes on other points of similarity and contrast which you find between 'Here' and 'The Whitsun Weddings'.

ACTIVITY 2

Now let us turn to Margaret Atwood's 'This is a Photograph of Me'.

This is a Photograph of Me

It was taken some time ago.
At first it seems to be
a smeared
print: blurred lines and grey flecks
blended with the paper;

then, as you scan
it, you see in the left-hand corner
a thing that is like a branch: part of a tree
(balsam or spruce) emerging
and, to the right, halfway up
what ought to be a gentle
slope, a small frame house.

In the background there is a lake,
and beyond that, some low hills.
(The photograph was taken
the day after I drowned.

I am in the lake, in the center
of the picture, just under the surface.

It is difficult to say where
precisely, or to say
how large or small I am:
the effect of water
on light is a distortion

but if you look long enough,
eventually
you will be able to see me.)

1   If the Larkin poem has deixis in its title, the Atwood title is
    even more sharply situated. Setting aside what the title sen-
    tence means (the meaning seems to be quite straightforward),
    think about its likely occasions of use. That is, in what specific
    kinds of situation can you imagine yourself using the sentence
    'This is a photograph of me'? Answering this question brings
    you to the thematic core of the poem, I think. (§)

2   On what bases might one argue that, structurally, the poem
    falls into two parts? Do you find this claim persuasive?

3   One of the chief challenges that the poem sets us is the task of
    making sense of the following implicit situation: a speaker tells
    you about a photograph of themselves, taken the day after they
    have drowned. 'Ordinarily', we know, such a situation is as
    impossible as a square circle. To make sense of the situation,
    we have to reconstruct it in a way that assumes that some part
    of it is 'non-ordinary': specifically, perhaps this is not an
    ordinary speaker, or perhaps this is not a photograph in the
    ordinary sense, or perhaps no 'drowning' in the literal sense is
    involved – or perhaps all three of these factors are different
    here from the ordinary. Weighing the evidence, considering
    the surrounding text, speculating on what point there would
    be to interpreting these elements in out-of-the-ordinary
    senses, you must decide what seems to you to be the most
    convincing interpretation. But one thing is crystal clear: we
    cannot simply take this poem's words at face value in the way
    that is possible with many poems. The drowned cannot speak,
    cannot share 'photographs' with us. We are obliged to read
    some of the poem's words figuratively, as metaphors, rather
    than merely literally. The speaker here, who says in effect
    'This photograph of me was taken the day after I drowned',
    is challenging our interpretive faculties in a quite different way
    than any of the interpretive difficulties in the poem 'Here':
    nowhere does the Larkin poem state something that, by ordin-
    ary standards, is downright impossible. Some people find this

argument unreasonably dogmatic, but I think it is crucial to the logic by which stylistic interpretation proceeds that it be accepted. The use of words nonfiguratively – with 'photograph' denoting literally and straightforwardly actual photographs, and so on – is such a grounding for our everyday use of language that we should never neglect this literal–figurative distinction. There are substantial differences between drowning in the sea and drowning in a sea of unwritten letters. These points remain important even when, as is sometimes the case, literal usage is quite infrequent by comparison with figurative usage: it is likely that the word 'drown' is only rarely used in situations where actual death by suffocation is involved, just as most people who say they are 'starving to death' are not.

4   At first (to use the poem's own words) you may get the impression that the photograph is a smeared print of blurred lines and grey fleck. You may also get the impression that in the picture there is the branch of a tree, a gentle slope, and a frame house. But in fact are any of these items certainly present? By what linguistic means does the speaker leave the issue unresolved? From the first half of the poem, what can we cite as definitely identified as in the photograph?

5   Turn now to the second half of the poem. What phrases continue or develop the tendencies to uncertainty or vagueness created in the first half? What can the speaker be possibly getting at, in making such vagueness or unclarity so large a part of the experience of the poem? How would you characterize the experience of being shown a photograph of someone, by that person, who then indicates a number of ways in which the photograph is unclear, inaccurate, unreliable, and difficult to make sense of?

6   Assume, for the moment, that the photograph is a standard 6 × 4 inch print. Where do you understand the lake to be, on the basis of the two mentions of it? Discuss any difficulties you encounter.

7   Underline all the verbs or other words to do with perception in this poem, and comment on the cumulative effect they have on how you think about what the poem is about.

8   Conventionally, we think of photographs as objective records, incapable of misrepresenting ('the effect of light on a sensitized surface cannot distort'). The self-photographs we carry around with us, on driver's licences, passports, and other

identity cards, are taken as reliable, direct, needing no 'interpretation' on the part of those who scan them. My facial image is always there, on my US driver's licence, whether anyone is looking at it or not. There is no question of someone only being able to see it 'eventually', as in the poem. Why is it that Atwood's poem/photograph turns out to be so very different? And who, by the end of the poem, is given the responsibility of making the photograph 'work' as an informative representation of its subject?

9   The remark 'this is a photograph of me' makes one imagine one person showing a photograph to another person, with the word *this* denoting the proffered print. Might this be so in the situation of this poem, too? If not, what might be the 'thing' that the word *this* is pointing to? Are there any limits as to what the *this* can be referring to? (§)

10   The text twice refers, in the passive voice, to when the photograph 'was taken'. But who 'took' this 'photograph'? Depending upon the way you interpret the poem, you may come up with more than one plausible answer to this question.

ACTIVITY 3: COMPARATIVE ANALYSIS OF TEXTS

One of the most vivid ways of seeing the effectiveness of a text, in its parts and as a whole, is by considering some of the rival ways it might have been written. Sometimes we can go a step further, when writers' actual drafts or non-final versions of texts are available for scrutiny and comparison with final renderings.

Below are reproduced two poems written around 1960 by a famous American poet. Arguably they are two versions of a single poem. Read each poem through carefully several times first. Decide for yourself what each poem is about. Then, in as much detail as you can, itemize the ways in which the two poems differ. By contrast, in what respects would you argue the poems are similar, even if not identical?

Which of these poems do you prefer and why? What would you pinpoint as its strengths, in terms of phrasing, vividness, clarity, complexity, generality, rhythmicality, subtlety or forcefulness of tone, and so on, by comparison with the partner poem? Are there any points where you feel that the poem you like less is actually more effective? Try to be as specific as possible. (§)

Inspiration

The season's ill;
Yesterday Deer Isle fishermen
Threw Captain Greenwright's wreaths into the channel
And wooed his genius for their race
In the yachtsmen's yawls. A red fox stain
Covers Blue Hill.

Beaten by summer,
I hear a hollow, sucking moan
Inside my wild heart's prison cell;
The slow wave loosens stone from stone
By bleeding. I myself am hell;
I hate the summer,

But cannot move it.
My shades are drawn, my daylight bulb is on;
Writing verses like a Turk,
I lie in bed from sun to sun –
There is no money in this work,
You have to love it.

On a dark night,
My old Ford climbs the hill's bald skull;
I look for love-cars. Lights turned down,
They lie together, hull to hull,
Where the graveyard shelves on the town;
My mind's not right –

It's the moon's search,
All elbows, crashing on a tree,
Downhill and homeward. My home-fire
Whitens deadly and royally
Under the chalk-dry and pure spire
Of a Trinitarian church.

My headlights glare
On a galvanized bucket crumpling up –
A skunk glares in a garbage pail.
It jabs its trowel-head in a cup
Of sour cream, drops its ostrich tail,
And cannot scare.

Skunk Hour

Nautilus Island's hermit
heiress still lives through the winter in her Spartan
cottage;
her sheep still graze above the sea.
Her son's a bishop. Her farmer
is first selectman in our village;
she's in her dotage.

Thirsting for the hierarchic privacy
of Queen Victoria's century,
she buys up all
the eyesores facing her shore,
and lets them fall.

The season's ill –
we've lost our summer millionaire,
who seemed to leap from an L.L.Bean
catalogue. His nine-knot yawl
was auctioned off to lobstermen.
A red fox stain covers Blue Hill.

And now our fairy
decorator brightens his shop for fall;
his fishnet's filled with orange cork,
orange, his cobbler's bench and awl;
there is no money in his work,
he'd rather marry.

One dark night,
my Tudor Ford climbed the hill's skull,
I watched for love-cars. Lights turned down,
they lay together, hull to hull,
where the graveyard shelves on the town . . . .
My mind's not right.

A car radio bleats,
'Love, O careless Love . . . ' I hear
my ill-spirit sob in each blood cell,
as if my hand were at its throat . . . .
I myself am hell,
nobody's here –

only skunks, that search
in the moonlight for a bite to eat.
They march on their soles up Main Street:

white stripes, moonstruck eyes' red fire
under the chalk-dry and spar spire
of the Trinitarian Church.

I stand on top
of our back steps and breathe the rich air –
a mother skunk with her column of kittens swills the
garbage pail.
She jabs her wedge-head in a cup
of sour cream, drops her ostrich tail,
and will not scare.

Commentaries

ACTIVITY 1

1   For my taste, there is enough specificity in the early part of
this poem for me to believe that a real or naturalistic north,
and east, and traffic, and large town, etc., is being described.
Any tourist guide to Hull will confirm that the real, literal
Hull is being alluded to in the middle stanzas. And surely the
'grim head-scarved wives' lose their interest for the reader
unless we understand them to be *real* grim head-scarved
wives. On the other hand, finally – that is, by the last verse
– the speaker doesn't seem terribly interested in the slave
museum or the cranes and spires or other tangible parapher-
nalia. He turns abstract and transcendental, with his references to 'unfenced existence' and similar: you can't point to
unfenced existence the way you can point to a grim head-
scarved wife. When the speaker reports that he is 'facing the
sun', I imagine some hard-to-paraphrase stance, more spiritual
than merely physical, is being asserted. He isn't just sunbath-
ing! He ends glad to be 'out of reach', which is almost a
characterization of metaphor itself: metaphorical language is
language used creatively, in ways beyond the reach of normal
usages (on which see more on pp. 179–81).

6   *Cheap, red*, and *sharp* are monosyllabic, basic or primary terms,
unglamorous, unsophisticated, even derogatory. A dismissive
vocabulary for a simple, dismissed folk? The sequence *mixers,
toasters, washers, driers*, repeats, four times over, the deflating
rhythm in which a stressed syllable carrying the beat is followed by an unstressed one. In traditional terminology, four

trochees in a row and, to add to the dullness, words whose meanings are related and uninteresting.

9   One of the phrasings that seems questionable is the reference to *cheap suits*. It seems reasonable to infer that the speaker is asserting, among other things, that one of the residents' foremost desires is suits, specifically, and, more specifically, *cheap* suits. By implication, their desires run to neither expensive material items nor non-material items. But what is the evidence to justify this characterization of the desires of the residents? How can the speaker *know* that the residents' observable purchases are fairly labelled their desires? In addition, the speaker's use of the word *cheap* may lead us (since there is nothing here to discourage us from doing so) to bring a second, far more judgmental understanding of *cheap* to our reading of the line: *cheap* as meaning not merely the description 'not expensive', but in addition – or even instead – the evaluation 'inferior'. But again, we can ask, how does the speaker *know* that the residents prefer inferior suits (as distinct from buying inexpensive ones since these are all they can afford)?

10 The syntactic complexity of 'Where removed lives loneliness clarifies' occurs at the very point of transition, or removal, from the chaotic jumble of the city to the rural retreat. Perhaps the speaker would have us pause and ponder; the grammar of these lines compels us to do so, as *we* take that extra time to clarify the sense of what is being said, and realize that the subject of the clause, *loneliness*, has itself been 'removed', delayed so as to appear after the object, *removed lives*. This kind of speculation, suggesting that there's a 'fit' between the content and the form, is called 'iconic interpretation'; although it can easily be overdone, it can be useful when applied sparingly.

11 We won't look further at poetic rhythm and metre in this book than the brief comments here. But it's worth noting that, given our English poetic tastes and conventions, many of us regard only the *town–down* pair as a 'full' rhyme, among those listed. And the only other similarly full rhymes in the poem are *wives–lives* and the final one, *beach–reach*. They differ from the rest since only these three are words in which the final syllable is stressed (remember *wives* is monosyllabic: say it aloud), and there is an identical match between just the vowel and following consonants of those final syllables, and nothing

more (e.g., not the consonant before the vowel, or the syllable before that). This is traditionally and sexistly called a masculine rhyme. As the *Norton Anthology of Poetry* (p. 1202) explains the same phenomenon: 'Masculine rhymes, which are the rule [in English poetry], coincide in the vowel and in the final consonant(s) if any, of stressed terminal syllables: *strife, life; compel, bell.*' All the other rhymes in the poem diverge from this pattern, mostly by producing rhymes where all but the initial consonant of the final *two* syllables match, and the penultimate syllable is the stressed one, not the ultimate one: *fields/shields; pheasants/presence.* These are felt to be not so 'strong' or absolute as masculine rhymes and, yup, are traditionally called 'feminine rhymes'. A little further removed from the masculine standard are examples like *shadows/meadows* and *cluster/water;* but these are still rhymes, since readers feel them to be a patterned match to some degree. And almost off the scale is *solitude/mud*, where the only phonological match is the [d] sound; but even here, visually, there is the *-ud-* identity; since the match is primarily visual, this is called an 'eye-rhyme'.

ACTIVITY 2

1   The standard situation in which you say 'This is a photograph of me' is when you are showing a photograph of yourself in which you appear significantly different, perhaps unrecognizably different, from how you look at present. For example, a photograph of yourself when much younger. Otherwise the remark is redundant. In addition, the activity of sharing pictures of yourself when younger and different is usually undertaken only with people who are interested in you, and to whom you particularly want to relate. Much of this network of implications, I think, is brilliantly invoked by the poem's title. A final odd thing to note about the utterance 'This is a photograph of me', as usually used, is that it amounts to saying 'Come and look at this me which is not me'.

9   Any limits to what *this* can refer to? Not in principle, I believe. Imagine that, at the foot of an ash tree in a formal garden, which is on a tiny island, in the middle of a lake, in a suburb, in a city, in a state, is sited a plaque on which is written: 'Whoever reads these words remember: this belongs to us all'. As phrased, there is no way of determining whether the *this* is pointing to just the plaque, or the tree, or the whole

2

Cohesion: making text

In this chapter we shall be examining the linguistic means by which sentences are woven together to make texts, a process called cohesion. The starting-point for such a study is the view that texts are made up of sentences, just as houses are made up of bricks, posts, beams, and so on. But that is clearly not the whole story in either. case. You don't build a house simply by bringing bricks, beams, etc. together; you have to *fasten* or bond them together in a variety of ways. The same applies to texts: sentences must be bound together and cross-linked.

We shall assume that a text is an integrated structure, just as surely as a house is: both need various kinds of fastening devices to hold their parts together. In the case of a house, those devices or binding agents may be potentially visible (nails, screws, brackets, adhesives) while one major means is invisible (gravity). In the case of texts, all the cohesive ties are invisible: they are implicit but palpable connections between words in different sentences. Cohesion thus refers to all the linguistic ways in which the words of a passage, across sentences, cross-refer or link up.

It is important to bear in mind from the outset that we are particularly considering links between or across sentences, and not links within sentences. So we are not considering the link between *Kim* and *she* in the following sentence:

Kim collapsed into the chair because she was exhausted.

You may wonder why we are playing down the very clear connection between *Kim* and *she* in the cited sentence. The reason is that the choice of *she* is so predictable. There is a very strong preference for the 'second mention' of Kim in the above sentence to be via a pronoun (feminine or masculine, to match Kim's gender). There is a very strong 'default' choice, of the pronoun, and we shall treat such a choice as a matter of sentence grammar, not a matter of the textual grammar that is cohesion. In selecting *she* you are constructing a grammatical sentence; but you are not configuring a cohesive text.

But now consider the following:

Kim collapsed into the chair. $\left\{\begin{array}{l}\textit{She was exhausted.} \\ \textit{The poor girl was exhausted.}\end{array}\right.$

The link between *Kim* and *she* (or *the poor girl*) in this situation, we shall say, is intersentential (it crosses a sentence boundary); it is therefore cohesive, and helps to turn the sequence of two sentences into a miniature text. In general, wherever cohesive linguistic devices are used, there is less danger of a piece of writing being a mere collection of unrelated sentences, because cohesion connects sentences to each other. (It is not that single-sentence messages cannot be texts: they often are. It is rather that, via sentence grammar, they more or less *have* to be coherent text; whereas the coherent textuality of multi-sentence passages requires far more conscious effort, using the resources of cohesion.)

The simplest kind of cohesion is the use of pronouns, such as *she* in the second sentence below:

Mary was surprised that the day had stayed fine. She was cooking lasagne.

Here (assuming that the *she* refers to the same individual that the name *Mary* does), the use of the pronoun invites us to forge an implicit link – an invisible dotted line, if you like – back from the *she* to the *Mary*. On the strength of that simple cohesive tie, we feel that the two sentences go together fairly well, and form a single text (about Mary), to a greater degree than, say, either of the following do:

1 *Mary was surprised that the day had stayed fine. He was cooking lasagne.*

2 *Mary was surprised that the day had stayed fine. Steve was cooking lasagne.*

Clearly version 1 is not much of a text. But now consider the following version, in which a new second sentence has been added:

Mary was surprised that the day had stayed fine. She had expected it to rain. She was cooking lasagne.

Now we have two *she* pronouns, linking back to *Mary*. Sequences like this are of course very common in narratives, where there is recurrent reference to a few singled-out individuals; cohesive sequences like this one (*Mary . . . she . . . she*) are called 'cohesive chains'.

But we also have one, and arguably two, *lexical* cohesive links between sentences 1 and 2. The first of these is the word *rain*, which links back to, while contrasting with, the idea of the day staying fine.

being an indirect topic instead; again, no small improvement. Here, arguably, we see the essence of confessional poetry of the Plath–Lowell–Sexton period: a projection of the deeply personal agon of the poet-speaker on to people, situations, and things, so that these more dramatically articulate the sense of absurdity and desperateness which is the poet's obsession.

garden, or the encompassing island, or the entire lake, and so on, up to and including the whole universe.

ACTIVITY 3

The author of 'Inspiration' and 'Skunk Hour' was Robert Lowell, arguably the most gifted poet in the United States in the 1960s. As it happens, only one of these poems was published, to much acclaim: 'Skunk Hour', of which 'Inspiration' is an early draft. But I've shared these poems with enough people who've actually preferred 'Inspiration' to make me reluctant to say 'Skunk Hour' is *obviously* the better poem.

Still, in preferring 'Skunk Hour' myself, I would point to the 'completeness' of the description, in the first two stanzas, of the hermit heiress in all her absurd perversity: she sets the tone for all the later dysfunctionalities, including the gay decorator who is said to prefer to marry, and the speaker himself. By contrast, 'Inspiration' alludes to the Deer Isle fishermen and Captain Greenwright, but who they are and quite why they are mentioned is far less clear; the theme of absurdity is there, in the idea of fishermen engaged in a yacht race, but it's far less focused. I would also point to lines like *I hate the summer,/ But cannot move it*, which read like mere complaint, without suitable resonance or integration with surrounding text. I would also point to seemingly minor adjustments: the way the slightly prosaic *On a dark night* is revised to the starker *One dark night*; and the way the slightly earnest *I look for love-cars* is replaced by the more appropriately predatory *I watched for love-cars*. And how, in the previous line, *the hill's bald skull* is edited to *the hill's skull* – perhaps on the grounds that talk of *bald* skulls is probably preposterous, and only blurs the allusion here to Golgotha, *the place of the skull*, of Christ's passion. Many other such revisions and – in my view – improvements could be cited; but here a final mention must go to the skunks, so much more prominent, purposeful, exemplary or threatening (depending on your interpretation) than in 'Inspiration'. A minor participant in the draft (the ungendered skunk of the last four lines) now occupies the entire final two stanzas, and thus consitutes a much larger presence: first as 'skunks', in stanza 7, then particularized as 'a mother skunk and her column of kittens' in stanza 8 – arguably the only proper family in the poem, and a kind of answer to the heiress and her sheep and her bishop son in stanza 1. But at least as important as the greater foregrounding now of the skunks is the considerable reduction of attention to the 'I' figure, the speaker, whose dis-ease is now confined to stanzas 5 and 6. The speaker and his self-referential pronouns (*I, me, my*) are far less *directly* prominent in 'Skunk Hour',

Although they contrast (*a fine day* vs. *rain*), they go together since they are both about the same topic (weather), in a way that, for example, a fine day has no intrinsic connection with lasagne: there's no cohesive link between the latter two. By which we mean, in effect, that no dictionary, thesaurus or encyclopedia would tell us that these words frequently occur together. So by lexical cohesion is meant any cases where the content words of a passage can be seen to 'naturally' go together, that is, have a fairly high probability of occurring in the same text. The second case here where, arguably, lexical cohesion is involved is the possible link between *being surprised* and *expecting*: both predicates are to do with mental anticipation and prediction and therefore might be judged to co-occur frequently, or be more than randomly connected.

A number of grammarians (most notably, Halliday and Hasan, 1976) have drawn up a list of the various kinds of cross-sentence cohesive links to be found in texts. There are four basic types of cohesion, and I will say more about each of these in order below. The first three types are quite grammatical in nature, while the fourth involves implicit linkage between content-laden vocabulary, and so is called lexical cohesion. The first three types of cohesion concern the use of grammatical items such as pronouns, or versatile words such as *do* and *so* (e.g., as used in *I think so* and *Oh, did he?*), and conjunctions (*and, but, then, so* [when this has a causal meaning], *however,* etc.). These three more grammatical kinds of cohesion are known as reference, ellipsis, and conjunctive cohesion, and various examples are given in the following outline.

Kinds of cohesion

REFERENCE

The first major kind of cohesion is known as reference cohesion. It could as happily be called co-reference or cross-reference cohesion, because it covers all those cases where we use a grammatical word in one sentence in association with a word or phrase in a separate sentence. Typical examples are pronouns and comparative adjectives:

> *Bill and Bob are running for President. I'm going to vote for Bob. Do you know why? Simply because he's older.*

The *he* connects back to both previous mentions of *Bob*; and the *older* connects back to the general mention of both Bill and Bob. But 'connects back' and 'in association with' are vague ways of describing the situation. The real point is that you cannot make sense of either the *he* or the *older* unless you make a mental connection between these items and the material in adjacent sentences which disambiguates them.

Kinds of reference cohesion include:

1   Personal pronouns (incl. *it, its,* etc.), regular and possessive demonstratives (*this, that, these, those, here, there, then*), and the 'subsequent mention' definite article.

   By 'subsequent mention' definite article is meant situations where, after initial introduction of an entity via an indefinite article – *Once upon a time there was a beautiful princess* – subsequent mentions involve a switch to the definite article, in this case *the princess*, so as to indicate that one and the same entity is being recurrently referred to – *But the princess was very sad. It, this* and *that* are particularly versatile, since they often associate with entire clauses (or more) in adjacent sentences:

   A: *Smith is a superb ballroom dancer.* B: *I know that.*
   (or, in some dialects, B: *I know it.*)

2   Comparative constructions involving the following items: (*the*) *same, similar, such, different, other, more, less,* ordinal numbers (*first, secondly,* etc.), *as* + adjective, and comparative & superlative adjectives and adverbs.

   The point about this second type of reference cohesive device is that, when one of them is used, they invariably only make full sense in relation to adjacent text. Consider how *different* is used in the following sequence:

   Iqbal is Muslim. Anil's own religion is different.

   Here *different* is interpreted in relation to *Muslim*: whatever Anil's religion is, it is not Islam (and we would not know this from contemplating the sentence *Anil's own religion is different* alone).

ELLIPSIS

Ellipsis is the second of the four major kinds of cohesion. Again, a point in the flow of text is made sense of by making a mental connection to some adjacent text (called the co-text), but here what characterizes the point in the flow of text is the ellipsis of understood material. Material is left out since its repetition or near-repetition is felt to be unnecessary. Again there are two subtypes:

1   Partial ellipsis. Very often the ellipsis is not total; instead, some 'abridged' or condensed structure is used, to stand in for the

full sequence. This is known as partial ellipsis or substitution, and is very common. It can relate to nouns and nominal phrases, in which case these items appear: *one/ones, the same*. Or it can relate to verbs and verbal phrases, in which case the following items are common: *do, be, have, do the same, do so, be so, do it/that*. Or there can be partial ellipsis of an entire clause, in which case the items *so* (for positive clauses) and *not* (for negative clauses) are used. Here are examples of each:

Kimberley: *Can I look at your watch?*
Martin: *Sorry, I'm not wearing one.*
Kimberley: *You mean you don't usually wear a watch?*
Martin: *I usually do, but today I left it in at the shop to be repaired.*
Kimberley: *Will it be ready by this evening?*
Martin: *I think not; they said come back tomorrow.*

2 Full ellipsis. This is the second subtype of ellipsis, where there is 'full' omission of a second mention of items which can be 'understood' as implicit, because they are retrievable in the given context. In the following dialogue, underlined blanks are my textual additions, and indicate points at which understood material has been ellipted and could be restored. Again, what gets ellipted can be either nominal, or verbal, or clausal in nature, and the items that mark the sites of ellipted sequences, like buoys in a channel, are of distinct kinds. With full nominal ellipses you find *some, one, none, any, neither, each, a few, a lot, many, much, most* and *all* adjacent to the 'gaps'. With full verbal ellipsis you find that various parts of the verbal construction are omitted, being 'understood'. Ellipsis of a full clause is reflected in the use of the polar rejoinders *Yes* and *No*. Examples again:

Martin: *I heard that everyone in the hockey squad had to do extra training this week.*
Kimberley: *A few _____ had to _____, but most _____ were excused _____ .*
Martin: *Oh were they _____?*
Kimberley: *Yes.*

Clausal ellipsis also happens when there is omission of a whole clause where it would otherwise occur after a verb of communication or cognition, as in these examples:

1 Betty: *I've just heard tomorrow is a holiday. Why didn't anyone tell me _____?*

2 Alan: *Don't forget next Monday's a public holiday.*
   Brian: *I know _____.*

The distinction between cohesion by partial rather than full ellipsis is sometimes hard to see, which is why they are best treated as variants of a single phenomenon. Partial ellipsis is the situation where a subsequent re-statement or parallel formulation is replaced by a brief trace (*one, do, so*; etc.) which is interpretable when related to the earlier phrase or clause; while full ellipsis is where re-statement or parallel formulation is replaced by a gap, but a perceptible one (a real but unverbalized trace, as it were).

Ellipsis and substitution cohesion are commonest in two-party dialogue, in which the second party can often customize their responses so as to incorporate the substance of the first party's claim without actually repeating it verbatim:

A: *When I was in Harrods last week I saw Susan Sarandon buying fur coats.*
B: *Did you?* (ellipted: '*see Susan Sarandon buying fur coats when you were in Harrods last week*')

In view of just how reduced our cohesively designed responses are, interesting ambiguities can emerge. Thus if A says *I watched Newcastle thrash Man United on telly last night* and B replies *Why?*, it is not entirely clear how much of A's utterance B is treating as ellipted:

A: *I watched Newcastle thrash Man United on telly last night.*
B: *Why?* ('*did you watch Newcastle, etc.*')
A: *Ach, there was nothing else on and I didn't feel like going out.*

A: *I watched Newcastle thrash Man United on telly last night.*
B: *Why?* ('*did Newcastle thrash Man United*')
A: *Well, a lot of the top United players were on the injury list.*

CONJUNCTION

Conjunction cohesion refers to the use of certain words or phrases, usually at the beginning of a sentence, with the effect of clarifying the semantic or logical relationship of the information that follows with the information that has come before. Cohesive conjunctions thus have a 'semantic signposting' function. The semantic or logical connection may be implicit between the foregoing and following text, but the use of the conjunction makes that connection more explicit. For example, I can tell you:

> *I saw Jan eat three whole pizzas in a row. She was very ill.*

You may feel it is obvious that Jan became ill because of her eating excesses; but perhaps I actually meant that *because* she was ill she ate in that way. If I use a cohesive conjunction I can make the semantic connection much more specific and explicit:

> *I saw Jan eat three whole pizzas in a row. As a result, she was very ill.*

In this case, I have used a conjunction which signposts a 'cause', 'result' or 'purpose' connection between the prior text and the following text. Such conjunctions form a cluster, called causal conjunctions, which is one of five main clusters of cohesive conjunctions:

1   additive (*and, nor, or, furthermore, similarly, in other words*, etc.)

2   adversative (*yet, but, however, all the same, conversely, on the contrary, rather*, etc.)

3   causal (*so, then, therefore, consequently, as a result, to this end, in that case, otherwise*, etc.)

4   temporal (*then, next, first, meanwhile, hitherto, finally, in conclusion, to sum up*, etc.)

5   continuative (*now, of course, well, anyway, surely, after all*, etc.)

There is a very simple and clear way of feeling the cohesive function of these words and phrases (that is to say, their connection to some previous text to which the material that immediately follows the conjunction should be additively, or adversatively, etc. linked). Imagine any of these conjunctions being used *at the very opening* of a conversation, or a letter, or a newspaper article:

> *On the contrary, they played well above their usual standard.*

> *Consequently, the Governor has decided to veto amendment 621.*

> *In other words hi Maria how are you?*

In each case the effect is very strange. Since conjunctions serve precisely to connect up previous material with following material, then to use them where there simply is no previous material, actual or easily imaginable, defies normal logic. (The point about 'imaginable' prior material is added because within literature we commonly find exploitation of this special case: it is part of what enables writers to begin novels and plays with conjunctions, creating the *in medias res* effect.)

LEXICAL COHESION

The fourth and final type of cohesion is in many ways the most obvious: recurrent uses of the same content word, or of related words, conveying a sense of the integratedness of a text. Since such linkage is all predicated on the relations between word uses and meanings, this is called lexical cohesion. Like all the other aspects of cohesion we shall review, the reasoning underlying lexical cohesion is quite straightforward, despite the few technical terms that will be introduced. And as in relation to many other topics in this book, it is often easiest to recognize lexical cohesion by considering cases where it is totally absent. Imagine a text whose content words were just the following, none of which is repeated: *sandpiper, spoke, dot matrix, melancholy, velvet, inscrutable, platelets, paint, comb, diaper, overture.* For example:

> *The sandpiper spoke to the platelets with a melancholy velvet comb.*

I would suggest that such a text displays no lexical cohesion: I can see no familiar or ordinary connection between any of these items; none of them recognizably keeps company with any of the others in ways that might be reported in a dictionary, thesaurus, usage dictionary, or similar record.

Thus what lexical cohesion amounts to is any situation in which we can argue that a word in one sentence of a text is, in the language or culture, non-randomly associated with a word or words in other sentences. Such patterns of lexical association are important since they help us to interpret a text rapidly; they contribute to our sense of the text as coherent. These linguistic or cultural non-random associations may be a matter of sheer repetition or near-repetition, or a case of a more general or more particular reformulation, or instances of familiar idiomatic or usage-based co-occurrence. Take a word like *bacon*: all the following words, in adjacent sentences, would be instances of lexically cohesive linkage with that word: *bacon* (pure repetition); *meat, food, stuff* (increasingly general reformulations); *green streaky* (particularizing reformulation); *rasher*; *pork*; *eggs*; *save*; *crispy*; and so on.

Again, the converse scenario, in which we encounter words in the same text which have no 'inbuilt' tendency to appear in the same context, highlights the reality and importance of lexical cohesion. Thus where the words *bacon, processor* and *dahlia* appear in successive sentences, we have no sense that their appearance in the same text is predictable or unsurprising. We would be inclined to take a close look at sentences in which such disparate items jointly appeared.

The major kinds of lexical cohesion are the following:

1 Simple repetition of a given word: *chair . . . chair.*

2 Use of a synonym or near-synonym: *chair . . . seat.*

3 Use of a subordinate, superordinate or general term to denote a particular entity on a later occasion: e.g., subsequently referring to *my pet rabbit* as *the Angora* (this is a subordinate term, a *kind* of rabbit), or as *the pet* (a superordinate label: the rabbit is here a kind of pet), or as *the animal* (a more general term yet). Note that the most general terms are very general indeed and, although common in speech, are often frowned upon in writing: *thing, stuff, item, person, guy, place, time,* etc.)

4 Collocation: tendency of *rabbit* to co-occur with *hole, hutch, on* – as in *rabbiting on* – and *bunny.*

Activities

ACTIVITY 1

Now consider the following extract from *Through the Looking-glass*, and its many cohesive devices:

> The Cat only grinned when it saw Alice.
> 'Come, it's pleased so far,' thought Alice, and she went on.
> 'Would you tell me, please, which way I ought to go from here?'
> 'That depends a good deal on where you want to get to,' said the Cat.
> 'I don't much care where – ' said Alice.
> 'Then it doesn't matter which way you go,' said the Cat.
> ' – so long as I get somewhere,' Alice added as an explanation.
> 'Oh, you're sure to do that,' said the Cat, 'if you only walk long enough.'

Identify all the cohesive links you can see here. Having read through the text a couple of times, start at its end and work backwards. Use at least two different styles of labelling, to differentiate grammatically cohesive links from lexically cohesive ones (e.g., differently coloured

pens, or linked circled words for lexical cohesion and linked underlined words for grammatical cohesion). For greater detail, since there
are four major kinds of cohesion, you could use four distinct labelling styles. To get you started: consider the *do that* of the Cat's final
rejoinder. To which earlier phrase is it closely tied (so closely that
the earlier phrase could have been used a second time, in the slot
filled by *do that*), and what kind of grammatical cohesion is this?
With reference to the same utterance, you may be wondering about
the word *you*: is it a cohesive item here? The answer is that it is not,
since it is not here 'unpacked' by an earlier textual formulation.
Instead we make sense of the *you* by connecting it not first to some
adjacent text but directly to the situation and the addressee in that
assumed situation. This is an instance of deixis, not cohesion, and is
explained below.

When and only when you have finished analysing the passage, compare your findings with those of Halliday and Hasan, reproduced as a
Commentary at the end of this chapter. (§)

Time Out: is cohesion the same as anaphora?

Those of you who have done an introductory course in
linguistics should see by now that there is some overlap
between what linguists call anaphora (the use of pronouns and other pro-forms in sentences, such as *do*
and *so*) and cohesion. But cohesion is broader than
anaphora (in that it includes intersentential conjunction
and lexical cohesion, besides reference and ellipsis); and
it is more restricted (in not attending to intrasentential
anaphora).

Another question that often gets asked is: 'Are all occurrences of
personal pronouns examples of cohesion, then?' The short answer is
'Certainly not', since a *you* or a *she* pronoun may not in fact link back
to a previous textual naming: it may 'link' directly (and not indirectly,
via adjacent text) to some postulated person assumed to exist in the
situation in which the text is embedded. In such cases the pronouns –
and other items such as *it*, *this* and *that* – are being used **deictically**
rather than cohesively.

Time Out: how is deixis different from cohesion?

The other phenomenon which should be kept separate
from cohesion is deixis. As we have seen, cohesive items
(or, in the case of ellipsis, cohesive 'gaps') invariably link
up with other items in adjacent text (usually preceding
text, occasionally following); and those nearby co-textual
items enable the addressee to interpret or make sense of
the cohesive item itself. For example, going back to our
original 'Mary' passage –

> *Mary was surprised that the day had stayed fine.*
> *She had expected it to rain.*

– we saw that the *She* in sentence 2 is made sense of by
seeing it as tied to the same person that is named and
identified as *Mary*. By contrast, consider the following
mini-passage:

> *She was surprised that the day had stayed fine. She*
> *had expected it to rain. In fact everyone warned her*
> *that it frequently rained here.*

How can we interpret the *She* of sentence 1 here; to
whom does it refer? We have no clues or ties in adjacent
text, e.g., no full noun phrase (*The young woman staying at*
the Four Seasons, or *Ms Maloney*) to which we can relate
it. The *She* just stands there on its own, and can only be
made fuller sense of by knowing or imagining the situation (the nonverbal context) in which it is being used.
Similarly with the *here* in the third sentence. We are given
no adjacent textual language via which we might be able
to disambiguate just where the 'here' is; no reference, for
example, to the clock at Charing Cross or New Street
Station or Pike Place Market. So both sentence 1's *She*
and sentence 3's *here* are deictic and not cohesive.

Deixis (the noun) and deictic (the adjective) are related
to the word 'index': all three terms involve pointing to a
person, place or time, rather than genuinely naming that
person, place or time. It's the difference between me
addressing my son as 'Patrick' (= nondeictic) and 'you'
(= deictic). Relatedly, deictic terms can only be interpreted if you know the situation within which they are
used, and in particular if you know the speaker's position
in space and time.

When words are used deictically, then, they are 'situation-dependent': who, what or where the words refer to, on the given occasion, depends entirely on that situation in which they have been used. Take the following sentence, found typed on a piece of paper in your mailbox:

> *I have your winnings here for you to collect by tomorrow at the latest.*

You assume that you are the 'you' in this message – after all, it is in your mailbox. And now you frantically try to determine who the *I* is, where the *here* is (you very much doubt that *here* means the mailbox; it presumably means some office or residence of the speaker, whoever that is), and – with anxiety mounting – you begin to wonder which final day is meant by *tomorrow*. But of course you cannot interpret these non-cohesive deictic words *I, or here*, or *tomorrow*, without knowing the speaker and their spatio-temporal coordinates. Significantly, just this kind of information, revealing who the speaker is, where they are writing from, and on what precise day, is the kind of information we standardly supply in the top and bottom margins of letters. Compare the following:

Washington State Lottery Bank,
33, Yellow Brick Road,
Olympia WA 99166
9.30.93

Mr Phil Theeleuchar,
Loadsadosh House,
Eureka, WA 98765

Dear Mr Theeleuchar:

I have your winnings here for you to collect by tomorrow at the latest.

Sincerely,

U. Luckydog

Activities

ACTIVITY 2

The following is the first sentence of Ian McEwan's novel, *Black Dogs*:

> Ever since I lost mine in a road accident when I was eight, I
> have had my eye on other people's parents. (§)

Comment on any fleeting difficulties you may have found in understanding this sentence, and particularly in understanding what is being referred to by the referentially cohesive pronoun *mine*. Assuming for the moment that the confusing effect is deliberate on the part of McEwan or his first-person narrator, are you tempted, by the nature of those things fleetingly conflated, to entertain further speculations about the speaker we are just beginning to meet?

ACTIVITY 3

Label the kinds of cohesion between sentences in the following poem by Craig Raine. For example, if you came across the phrase 'such shoes' following the sentence 'Many students wear Birkenstocks' you would label it as 'Reference, comparative'. The locations of cohesive items are marked here for you by underlinings and gaps; the poem has been slightly amended.

A Martian Sends a Postcard Home

Caxtons are mechanical birds with many wings.
Some _____ are treasured for their markings.

They cause the eyes to melt
or the body to shriek without pain.

I have never seen one fly. But
sometimes they perch on the hand.

Mist is when the sky is tired of flight
and rests its soft machine on ground.

Then the world is dim and bookish
like engravings under tissue paper.
Rain is when the earth is television.
It has the property of making colours darker.

Model T is a room. But the lock is inside _____ .
A key is turned to free the world

10

for movement. <u>It</u> is <u>so</u> quick there is a film
to watch for anything missed.

<u>But</u> time is tied to the wrist.
<u>Or</u> ____ ____ kept in a box, ticking with impatience.

In homes, a haunted apparatus sleeps,
that snores when you pick it up.   20

If <u>the ghost</u> cries, they carry <u>it</u>
to their lips and ____ soothe <u>it</u> to sleep

with sounds. <u>And yet</u>, <u>they</u> wake <u>it</u> up
deliberately, by tickling ____ with a finger.

Only the young are allowed to suffer
openly. Adults go to a punishment room

with water but nothing to eat.
<u>They</u> lock the door and suffer the noises

alone. No one is exempt
and everyone's pain has a different smell.   30

At night, when all the colours die,
<u>they</u> hide in pairs

and ____ read about <u>themselves</u> –
in colour, with <u>their</u> eyelids shut.

1 Mark, by circling the relevant individual words and connecting them with dotted lines, all the words in the poem that
   relate in any way to: (a) flight, or (b) colour, or (c) suffering.
   What does each of these lexical networks (a lexically cohesive
   patterning) contribute to the tone and impact of the poem?

2 Read over line 5 again. What, taken on its own, would it
   possibly mean, if the word *one* was interpreted in a non-
   cohesive way, i.e., as *not* linking back to *Caxtons*? (§)
       Highlighting the cohesive links between lines of this poem
   may be useful not merely to get an appropriate interpretation
   of individual sentences, but also so as to derive suitable interpretations of whole clusters of sentences, such as the cluster
   comprising lines 1–6. The scope for misreading and incom-
   prehension comes with the use of daring metaphor: as soon as
   the speaker asserts 'Caxtons are mechanical birds', some inter-
   preters will be confused. Precisely so as to keep such confusion at bay, this cohesion analysis may be useful in its
   unequivocal assertion that the ellipsis after *Some* in line 2

should be filled by *Caxtons*, that the *they* in lines 3 and 6 cohesively co-refer to *Caxtons*, and that the *one* of line 5 substitutes for a *Caxton*. Those are strong and somewhat questionable claims: in the light of what line 1 asserts, there seem grounds for thinking that the *Some* in line 2 could denote *some mechanical birds* or *some wings*, and neither of those readings creates semantic anomaly. More semantically odd, but grammatically permitted, would be reading lines 3–5 as concluding with the statement *I have never seen an eye fly*. So in claiming that all of the opening six lines focus on Caxtons, the interpreter is excluding some plausible variant readings. But he or she is also facilitating interpretation, by the same token: for rather than the poem comprising somewhat disjunct and hard-to-relate propositions (Caxtons are mechanical birds; some wings are treasured for their markings; the markings cause the eyes to melt; I have never seen an eye fly, but sometimes eyes perch on the hand), the poem is being treated as a sequence of comments around the mystery word, *Caxtons*. Hence the interpretive task is considerably more manageable: what thing can it be that can be said to be mechanical, have many wings, be incapable of flight, able to perch on the hand and cause humans to cry and shriek, and might be called Caxtons?

3   Why is the *they* of line 21 not underlined as a cohesive item? (§)

4   Notice how the speaker talks about '*the* eyes', '*the* body', '*the* hand', etc. Why? To what effect? Are these *the*'s textually cohesive here, tying back to some previously mentioned eyes, body and hand? If it is agreed that they are not cohesive in this way, we might classify them in one of two ways: one way would be to treat them as referring deictically to some particular unnamed individual's eyes, etc. Alternatively they may be referring generically to 'anyone's eyes, body, hand'. This is a common enough usage in quasi-factual descriptions – but descriptions in what kind of situation, implying what kind of relation between the reporter and the reported? Cf. 'the lower jaw is studded with a double row of incisors'; 'the torso above the waist is decorated with garlands of leaves', etc. (§)

5   A large part of the 'strange-making' or 'defamiliarizing' effect of this poem comes from unexpected re-namings of what are (to us) quite ordinary things. What are 'our' standard names

for Caxtons, the haunted apparatus, and the suffering mentioned in line 26? This very different way of naming feels so coherent in itself that it may suggest to us that here is not merely an alternative way of naming the same world, but a different naming of a different reality. The poet Wallace Stevens said as much when he remarked that 'metaphor creates a new reality from which the original appears to be unreal.' Raine's re-namings are the most explicit contribution to the poem's reconfiguring of the world, but all the cohesive devices we have examined make a crucial contribution too: just how cohesion is deployed will shape just what kind of text is created.

ACTIVITY 4

Now consider the following passage, from Faulkner's famous story 'The Bear'. At this point in the story, sixteen-year-old Ike has gone into the big woods on his own, in pursuit of Old Ben, the quasi-mythical bear, and spirit of the wilderness, whose defiance of men and dogs and guns is legendary. Ike wishes less to hunt Old Ben than to encounter him. With that intent, he has discarded his instruments of control, his gun and watch and compass, setting these down by a certain tree, and walks on defenceless. But then he becomes lost and, having realized this, sets about trying to find his way back to the tree where he has left his equipment. The text continues:

> When he realized he was lost, he did as Sam had coached and drilled him: made a cast to cross his back-track. He had not been going very fast for the last two or three hours, and he had gone even less fast since he left the compass and watch on the bush. So he went slower still now, since the tree could not be very far; in fact, he found it before he really expected to and turned and went to it. But there was no bush beneath it, no compass nor watch, so he did next as Sam had coached and drilled him: made his next circle in the opposite direction and much larger, so that the pattern of the two of them would bisect his track somewhere, but crossing no trace nor mark anywhere of his feet or any feet, and now he was going faster though still not panicked, his heart beating a little more rapidly but strong and steady enough, and this time it was not even the tree because there was a down log beside it which he had never seen before and beyond the log a little swamp, a seepage of moisture somewhere between earth and water, and he did what Sam had coached and drilled him as the next and

the last, seeing as he sat down on the log the crooked print, the warped indentation in the wet ground which while he looked at it continued to fill with water until it was level full and the water began to overflow and the sides of the print began to dissolve away.

How has Faulkner exploited our expectations concerning the cohesive function of words like *it* and *did*, in the way this part of the narrative is told? How does the use (misuse?) of cohesion here reflect and express Ike's experience of a confrontation between prediction and control, on the one hand, and the unforeseen and uncontrolled, on the other? (§)

ACTIVITY 5

Read over the following passage, which is the very opening of Faulkner's *The Sound and the Fury*, and is narrated from within the mindset of Benjy, a man with the mental age of a young child:

> Through the fence, between the curling flower spaces, I could see them hitting. They were coming toward where the flag was and I went along the fence. Luster was hunting in the grass by the flower tree. They took the flag out, and they were hitting. Then they put the flag back and they went to the table, and he hit and the other hit. Then they went on, and I went along the fence. Luster came away from the flower tree and we went along the fence and they stopped and we stopped and I looked through the fence while Luster was hunting in the grass.
> 'Here, caddie.' He hit. They went away across the pasture. I held to the fence and watched them going away.
> 'Listen at you, now.' Luster said. 'Ain't you something, thirty-three years old, going on that way. After I done went all the way to town to buy you that cake. Hush up that moaning. Ain't you going to help me find that quarter so I can go to the show tonight.'
> They were hitting little, across the pasture. I went back along the fence to where the flag was. It flapped on the bright grass and the trees.

1 We say cohesion is about cross-textual links, while deixis is about referencing directly to people, times, places, etc. which are outside the text, entities we have to assume are in the environment.
   (a) On that basis, state whether Luster's *that way, that moaning* and *that quarter* are cohesive or deictic.
   (b) What effect does this aspect of Luster's talk create?

2   As far as I can see, there is only one instance of true grammatical cohesion in this entire passage. Identify it.

3   The passage has almost no grammatical cohesion. And yet it has plentiful lexical cohesion. What effect would you say this particular combination creates? What *subtype* of lexical cohesion is most apparent?

ACTIVITY 6

Read over the following extract, from Brookner's *A Closed Eye*, which begins right after a couple, Harriet and Jack, on the verge of an affair, kiss. It is Harriet who speaks first:

> 'Do you do this all the time?'
> '_____ Not all the time, no. You could stay, you know.'
> 'Why should I ____?'
> 'Possibly _____ because you want to ____. And ____ because I might want you to ____.'
> 'You?' There was no answer. 'I have to leave, you see. You do see _____, don't you?'
> 'I should expect nothing less of you _____.'
> 'Oh, don't be so . . . so rude _____,' she said angrily.
> They both smiled.
> 'Goodbye, Jack,' she said, holding out her hand. He kissed her again. There was no doubt now about her response. 'That's better ____,' he said. 'I loathe soulful women, with consciences.'

1   In the right or left margin, label the kind of cohesion, and the subtype if you can, involved at each of the blank places underlined (all underlinings are my additions). Comment very briefly on any problematic cases.

2   Look at Jack's final *That*, in *That's better*. Why might we argue that, from our point of view as readers, the word *That* is cohesive; but from the point of view of Harriet and Jack, his word is deictic?

3   Among the 'problematic cases' alluded to in (1) above, the last two underlined 'blanks' are probably prominent. What's missing is nothing so straightforward as a personal pronoun such as *she*, but some kind of comparison. Note that phrases like *so rude*, *better*, and *nothing less* all imply **comparison**, even if the comparison involved has not been spelt out verbally. Each of the sentences used is quite strongly 'latched', by the compara-

tive phrase, to the words and situation that have gone before – as you can see from the odd effect if one of these sentences is imagined *opening* a conversation. Imagine Jack beginning a conversation with Harriet by saying 'I should expect nothing less of you': very strange, precisely because there would be no prior statement from Harriet for Jack's rejoinder to be a latched comment upon. Because of this subtlety and covertness, this is perhaps the most complex kind of cohesion, and we can expect it to be acquired at a relatively late stage by English-speaking children or foreign learners of the language.

ACTIVITY 7

When ellipsis cohesion was being introduced, it was suggested that partial ellipsis of clauses was done by using *so* and *not*, for positive and negative second mentions respectively, while full ellipsis of clauses commonly involved the appearance of a *Yes* or *No*. To confirm this for yourself, think up some plausible dialogue in which the second speaker replies *I (don't) think/believe so* or *I think not* and other exchanges in which the second speaker replies simply *Yes* or *No*.

1 Use your own constructed examples to support an explanation, in your own words, of the difference between the partial and full clausal ellipsis. (You can usefully compare and contrast how we use these with how we use *so* and *not*.)

2 Can you speculate over whether *so/not* ellipsis is more frequent in certain kinds of language use (spoken, written, formal, informal, professional, personal, etc.), while *Yes/No* (i.e., full clausal) ellipsis might appear more in certain other kinds of language use?

3 The famous 'Bill and Ted' deflationary particle, to signal that the speaker intends the opposite of what they have just averred, was *Not*!:

> Chris, sporting a new and truly tasteless haircut, comes up to Wayne.
> Wayne: *Hey Chris! Sharp haircut, dude. Not!*

Is there any good linguistic reason why *Not!* emerged as the put-down of choice, rather than *No*, or the older *I don't think*?

ACTIVITY 8

Notice that in the Martin–Kimberley dialogue about the watch (p.27), Martin used the ellipsis item *one* in his first reply, where he might have used the referentially cohesive item *it* (the issue is also discussed in the Commentary on Activity 4). We often use *it* when we mean 'the very same item just mentioned', using *one* when we mean 'an item of the same kind as just mentioned'. So in a bar Tolly says to the barkeeper that he'll have a whiskey sour and I say 'I'll have one too'; if I said 'I'll have it too' we might be given one drink and two straws. On the other hand in a restaurant if Rosie orders the soup of the day it's quite acceptable for me to say 'I'll have it too', without any sense that we're going to share a single bowl of soup; indeed the ellipsis alternative 'I'll have one too' sounds rather odd, applied to 'the soup of the day', the dish of the day, or whatever. Why might this be so?

Commentaries

ACTIVITY 1

Cohesion in the Alice–Cheshire Cat conversation:

> Starting at the end of the passage, we find the words *do that* occurring as a verbal substitute [partial ellipsis] for *get somewhere*; this in turn relates by lexical cohesion to *where you want to get to* and thence to *which way I ought to go*. The form *oh* is a conjunction relating the Cat's answer to Alice's preceding remark; and in similar fashion the Cat's interruption is related to *I don't much care where* by the conjunction *then*. The elliptical form *where* presupposes *(I) get to*; and *care*, in *I don't much care*, is lexically related to *want*. The reference item *that*, in *that depends*, presupposes the whole of Alice's question; and the *it* in Alice's first remark presupposes *the* Cat, also by reference. Finally both the proper names *Alice* and *the Cat* form cohesive chains by repetition, leading back to the first sentence of the passage.
>
> (Halliday and Hasan, 1976: 30)

Review the places where your analysis of the cohesion in the Alice passage differs from that of Halliday and Hasan, and try to determine whether your understanding of the categories (of grammatical reference, ellipsis, etc.) needs revision. Don't be alarmed if, new to this approach, you didn't see all the links that Halliday and Hasan do. And don't be surprised if you disagree with some of their judgements, particularly concerning lexical cohesion: what counts as a valid lexical tie, of semantic relatedness or frequent co-occurrence, is a tremendously culturally bound issue. For instance if, ten years ago, someone had claimed that *psych!* and *not!* were lexical synonyms, I would not have seen any sense in that suggestion; today, for a sizeable number of English speakers, the claim is true.

So if you question Halliday and Hasan's assertion that *care* and *want* are lexically cohesive, bear in mind the inherent variability of all such associationist judgements. Nevertheless, many will agree that *care* and *want* are lexically associated: can you list some ways in which their relatedness can be displayed? Consider their use in invitations: note down some interactional situations where they can be near-substitutes for each other.

ACTIVITY 2

If there is any exercise in this book which has no single 'correct answer' then this must surely be it (and, of course, virtually all the exercises are free of a 'single correct answer'). For myself, all kinds of reactions come to mind about a narrator who *begins* his connection with me by announcing:

> Ever since I lost mine in a road accident when I was eight, I have had my eye on other people's parents.

It is a remarkably *crafted* opening, with the tragedy and the grief of losing your parents cast as an embedded background event to the main point, that this speaker takes a particular and acquisitive interest in other people's parents. In the brief compass of this sentence the speaker has managed to use the first-person pronoun three times – there are three 'I's (and at least two eyes) in this sentence. So, something of an egotist, somewhat self-absorbed. But not defensive about this, not embarrassed to tell us about his inner drives, happy or wretched – and can we tell if he is happy or sad to feel this impulse to try to connect with other's parents? Also not embarrassed to present himself as a little ruthless and predatory and unfeeling – as if he is someone who has long made a coping accommodation with the cruelties and losses and 'unwholenesses' in his life.

ACTIVITY 3

2   In a non-cohesive interpretation of the sentence *I have never seen one fly*, the use of *one* as a determiner meaning roughly 'a single, on-its-own' would come to the fore, so the rogue interpretation of the sentence would be akin to the speaker

saying 'Flies seem never to be on their own'! *One* of course is also used as a nonspecific pronoun, like French *on* and German *man*, but that sense cannot fit this sequence.

3   The *they* of line 21 is not underlined as cohesive since it does not, in fact, link back to any previous phrase also referring to the same group of individuals. It is therefore being used deictically: we have to figure, in terms of our grasp of the situation, that the *they* here refers to human beings in general, although they have not been previously introduced explicitly. Actually the item *they* has been used earlier in the poem – but to denote a quite different group, namely 'Caxtons'. It is one of the most remarkable things about pronouns and how we use them that, when we read line 21, none of us interprets this as saying 'If the ghost cries, caxtons carry it to their lips and soothe it to sleep with sounds.'

4   Briefly, this is 'outsider' language, the language of the dispassionate analytical observer, not that of the empathizing fellow participant. It is a style of language that humans adopt – even when referring to other human beings and their bodies – when they want their thinking to be shaped by objective reason, not emotions. Thus it is often the language of scientists, physicians, anthropologists – and even more 'dispassionate' observers such as Martians.

ACTIVITY 4

The passage reports developments from the experiential perspective of young Ike, who attempts to organize and control his search for the bear and yet is increasingly confused by events – until he 'relinquishes' his own will to control, and accepts his place in the wilderness on its terms, not his. Initially, carefully structured sentences involve a *pre*posed *did* ellipsis construction, cohesively tied to a later verbal phrasing – e.g., *made a cast to cross his back-track*. Indeed this construction is used three times over, the third being the most curious since, arguably, the postposed specification of what Ike 'did last' is never actually stated – its articulation having been preempted by Ike's sighting of 'the crooked print'. The latter is textually interesting too – this first mention of the print, consonant with the *in medias res* emphasis of the whole passage, uses the deictic definite article rather than the introductory indefinite one. But in this passage we are most misled, as Ike himself apparently is, by being given the impression, twice over, that in retracing his steps Ike gets back to *the* tree where he has left his watch and compass. We are misled since the text speaks of Ike returning to *the tree* and *it*, when in fact the references should be to *a (different) tree* and *this one*, and so on.

3

Modality and attitude

Modality has come to mean a variety of different things in different academic and cultural domains. In linguistics it is the cover term for the ways that are available to a speaker within a language for expressing 'opinion or attitude' (Lyons, 1978: 452). In particular, modality denotes the linguistic means available for **qualifying** any claim or commitment you make in language. Qualifying in what ways, exactly? Following systemic linguistics (as set out in Halliday, 1994), I shall focus on four parameters, in particular, in respect of which a speaker's utterances can be qualified: qualifications of probability, obligation, willingness, or usuality. Most of the utterances we make can be qualified in terms of the strength (or weakness) of the probability, or obligation, or willingness, or usuality, with which we stand by them. Take the case of someone speaking about a new person in their life, with whom they are becoming romantically involved. If he says *She certainly is an interesting person* he has included probability modality (underlined); if he adds *I need to think of some really fun activity to invite her to* he is using obligation modality (again, underlined); *I wonder if she'd like to go iceskating?* is willingness modality (here, attributed to the other party, not the speaker); *I rarely meet people I feel this good about* carries usuality modality. Of the four modality parameters I will focus on, perhaps the more interesting are the first two, probability and obligation. I will discuss, in turn, the chief means of expressing modality, beginning with modal verbs.

Expressing modality: modal verbs

Take any bare factual statement, such as these:

> *Billings is in Montana.*

> *Billings is not in Montana.*

In a sense both of these are 'absolute': they are absolutely positive and negative respectively. The speaker is admitting no shadow of doubt into either statement, nor anything of his or her own attitude about these statements. But between the absolutely positive and absolutely negative sentences, we can fashion many kinds of 'in-between' or qualified sentences, which, revealingly, are less than absolute about something being or not being the case. These are the kind of thing I mean by modalized sentences, or 'sentences with modality'. And, as noted above, we modalize sentences chiefly in terms of one or more of the following four parameters:

> probability
> obligatoriness
> willingness
> usuality

Now if we construct modalized sentences about Billings and Montana in terms of these four parameters, some of them will sound distinctly odd, given what we know about Billings.

> **probability**: *Billings might be in Montana.*

> **obligation**: *Billings should be in Montana.*

> **willingness**: *Billings would be in Montana if it were given the choice.*

> **usuality**: *Billings is usually in Montana.*

But notice two things: these sentences are not actually ungrammatical, and their oddness does not simply rest in the sentences themselves but points back to some oddness in their utterer. This is the essence of modality: to be revealing of the speaker's attitudes and judgements. Incidentally, although usuality-modality applied to Billings sounds strange, it is less so with contested cities such as Gdansk/Danzig: *Gdansk is usually in Poland.*

To recap, a statement like *Billings is in Montana* can be qualified by formulations which disclose some of the speaker's less-than-total commitment to the truth of the statement, or which disclose some of the speaker's wishes or attitude concerning the statement and its elements. The most grammatically established way of adding such qualifications, such modality-expressions, is by using certain of the modal auxiliaries:

> *Billings must be in Montana.* (it's certain that)

> *If the garage is empty and the house lights are off, he must be away from home.* (it quasi-logically follows that)

> *The Sonics must win tonight.* (it's crucial, vital that they win [NB, not 'it's certain'])

Here, immediately, is a first complication: a modal verb like *must* has at least two rather different senses: certainty and obligation.

Time Out: what *are* modal verbs?

Modal verbs, also known as modal auxiliaries, are a small set of verbs which can appear just to the left of a 'main' or 'content' verbal word. The list includes *can, could, may, might, must, should, will, would, ought to*, and a very few others. Notice that this list does not include the verbs *have* and *be*, which are virtually the only other verbs that regularly accompany a main verb by appearing to the left of it. In fact, the English verbal construction can be thought of, in a simplified picture, as comprising three parts:

1	2	3
one and only one modal verb (optional)	one *have* form and two *be* forms (all optional)	one main verb (obligatory)

Jill	*may*		*visit Jack.*
Jack	*would*	*have been*	*visited by Jill.*
Jill			*met Jack.*
Joe	*should (never)*	*have been being*	*advised by Sam.*

As the name auxiliary suggests, modal auxiliaries support and modify the main verb, particularly with meanings to do with ability, permission, obligation, and so on.

Other versatile modals include *may, can, should, ought to* and *might*; for example, *should* sometimes conveys obligation – *You really should see a doctor* – and on other occasions conveys probability – *They should have reached their hotel by now.* When confirming for yourself that different meanings are indeed involved, it is tremendously useful to devise paraphrases of the sentences you are examining, and in particular paraphrases which contain modality language of the appropriate kind. Thus, one might paraphrase

> *You really should see a doctor*

with

> *It is (fairly strongly) required that you see a doctor.*
> (= obligation)

The target sentence is not accurately paraphrased as

> *It is certain that you (will) see a doctor.*

By contrast

> *They should have reached their hotel by now*

is satisfactorily paraphrased by

> *It is very probable that they have reached their hotel by now*
> (= probability)

but not by

> *It is strongly required or advised that they have reached their hotel by now.*

The modal verbs mentioned so far also fall into 'scales' of intensity or emphaticness, relative to each other, particularly in relation to probability and obligation. Thus the following series of sentences shows a steady increase in probability modality, from weak possibility to near-certainty:

> *Yeltsin might fall.*
>
> *Yeltsin may fall.*
>
> *Yeltsin will probably fall.*
>
> *Yeltsin must fall.*

THE MEANING OF *WILL*: MODALITY OR FUTURITY (OR BOTH)?

There is one modal verb, *will*, which causes particular difficulties when one is identifying modal signals in a text, since it sometimes expresses probability, other times willingness, and other times again, I shall argue, no modality whatsoever. The next few paragraphs are spent on sorting out these distinctions.

Whenever the auxiliary verb *will* is used in texts, deciding whether or not the verb is genuinely expressive of a modalizing meaning is particularly contentious; grammarians of English are still arguing over the issues involved. Here we will take the view that *will* commonly, but not always, carries one or the other of two modality meanings: probability, as in *That lad will come to a sticky end*, or willingness, as in *Will you have some Yogi tea?* Hence *will* usually means roughly 'it is very probable that' or 'the individual(s) denoted by the clause subject is/are willing to'. On some other occasions, however, neither of these modality meanings is uppermost, and then the verb is an almost 'modality-free' marker of future time reference. When the school principal announces that

> *The silent auction will take place in the gym*

or when an astronomer informs us that

> *At 6.17 GMT on 5 January 1997 there will be a partial lunar eclipse*

there is no sense of the speakers qualifying their statements by adding a 'very probably': we are being told in a virtually unqualified way just where the auction will be held and just when the eclipse will occur. These future events are seemingly non-negotiable: it has been determined or *ordained* that they will come to pass as described. Furthermore, there is very little sense of a particular speaker of these sentences, and that absence is part of the 'unmodalized' nature; they are depersonalized pronouncements. In sharp contrast, where *will* is modality-conveying, as when someone hears the doorbell ring and remarks *That'll be John*, this can hardly be paraphrased as 'It is ordained that John is at the door'. We do have to add the rider that this 'it is ordained that' use of *will* is 'virtually unqualified', however, if only because any description of future events has a kind of provisionality which sets it apart from descriptions of present or past events. Of course descriptions of present or past events can also be 'unreliable', but here the inaccuracies lie with the speaker's words, insofar as they fail to match up with the world that has already passed away; in the case of future events, one could as easily complain, where a future-reference utterance turns out to be inaccurate (because, for example, the silent auction took place in the dining room, not the gym), that the world failed to match the words as that the words failed to match the world. Henceforth I shall refer to these 'virtually unqualified' uses of *will* as 'unmodalized future' uses, to highlight the contrast with the uses of *will* where modality is clearly and deliberately involved. Faced with sentences using the 'unmodalized future' *will*, we are in no way drawn to dwell upon the personality, attitudes or judgement of their speaker.

In formal terms, too, there frequently seems to be a contrast between modalized uses of *will* and what I am calling unmodalized, 'pure future reference' uses of *will*. This is that the latter, unlike the former, typically can be paired with a semantically equivalent and acceptable simple present-tense version of the same proposition, without the *will* auxiliary at all. That is, alongside

Tomorrow he will sign the bill into law

we can have

Tomorrow he signs the bill into law

and alongside

The silent auction will take place in the gym

we can say

The silent auction takes place in the gym.

By contrast, where *will* has a predominantly modalizing meaning, there is not available a simple present-tense version, which is both semantically equivalent and acceptable:

> *That boy will come to a sticky end*
> *?That boy comes to a sticky end*
>
> *The Sonics will win big tonight*
> *?The Sonics win big tonight*
>
> *I'll do the washing-up if you like*
> *?I do the washing-up if you like*

In the case of *That'll be John*, although you can put *That's John* alongside it, it is not a semantically equivalent claim, being much stronger.

The upshot of the foregoing discussion is that a three-way classification of *will* seems most appropriate:

$$will \begin{cases} \text{probability} \\ \text{willingness} \\ \text{unmodalized futurity} \end{cases}$$

Before moving on to review the other main ways of expressing modality, mention may be made of 'weather forecast' uses of *will*, as in

> *Tomorrow will be dry, with temperatures reaching the low seventies*

and Mr Tansley's notorious killjoy remark, at the beginning of Virginia Woolf's *To the Lighthouse*:

> *There'll be no landing at the Lighthouse tomorrow.*

Mr Tansley's remark is related to weather forecasting, not least since the claimed impossibility of a rowing-boat landing at the lighthouse is directly determined by the predicted inclement weather. Although in both cases, logically and epistemically, the speaker is not justified in any absolute prediction of just what the weather will be the next day, still the speaker has cast these sentences as though they were. In the case of weather forecasts this may give unwarranted assurance or reassurance; in the case of Tansley's remark, to the ears of Mrs Ramsey and her son James, the absoluteness is ugly and unsympathetic.

Expressing modality: modal adverbs

The second commonest way of expressing modality is by means of modal adverbs: *probably, possibly, certainly, necessarily, usually, always, obligatorily, definitely, surely*, and so on.

> *Jerry always outwits Tom.*

> *Popeye certainly loves spinach.*

And of course modal auxiliary and adverb can be combined:

> *Billings must surely be in Montana.*

To re-iterate the idea that modality is the formulating of statements, offers, etc. which lie somewhere between an absolute positive or negative, notice that even the 'strong' expression of certainty –

> *I definitely, certainly saw Jim take the money*

– is less absolute than

> *I saw Jim take the money.*

A good way of highlighting how or what modality adds to a sentence is to add it to the kind of sentence where only the absolute or unqualified form seems ordinarily reasonable:

> *Four and three are seven.*

> *H_2O is the chemical formula for water.*

> *I am reading this.*

> *Four and three should be seven.*
> *Possibly, four and three are seven.*

> *H_2O might be the chemical formula for water.*
> *H_2O is usually the chemical formula for water.*

> *I might be reading this.*
> *I ought to be reading this.*

Expressing modality: further means

Beyond modal verbs and adverbs, there are many other ways, roughly parallel, for formulating these same factors of probability, obligation, usuality, and willingness. Some examples of modalized sentences:

> *You must be patient!* (= obligation) (optional rejoinder: *Then you must be Nurse!*)
>
> *I must have left my hat at the café.* (= probability)
>
> *It's usual for the hair to fall out in the spring.* (= usuality)
>
> *I'm sure I paid for this in advance.* (= probability)
>
> *It is required that you submit an LSAT score with your application.* (= obligation)
>
> *Would you give me a hand with this table?* (= willingness)
>
> *That's what you always say.* (= usuality)
>
> *My 15-year-old car needs a new engine.* (= obligation) *But I am reluctant to spend more money on a clunker.* (= willingness)
>
> *Often he worked late in the library.* (= usuality) *He just had to get everything noted and filed away in his brain.* (= obligation) *He just had to have been a really dull roommate.* (= probability – and somewhat dialectal)

METAPHORIZED OR 'ADVANCED' MODALITY

English has yet more ways of encoding these qualifications to do with probability, obligation, usuality, and willingness. Consider, for instance, how we use the verbs *reckon*, *guess*, *believe* and *think*, as in:

> *I don't believe we've met. (= probability)*
>
> *I think it's going to rain. (= probability)*

There are good reasons for saying that, in both of these, the speaker's subjective modality is being expressed. One thing that seems clear is that no ordinary processes of believing or thinking are being reported here, in the way that they are in the following:

> *I don't believe in guardian angels.*
>
> *I think while I'm on the bus.*

Someone who says *I don't believe we've met* is emphatically not reporting a belief they have (as is the case in the guardian angels sentence, which contains no modality qualification). It is worth noting that we leave a good deal to contextual disambiguation when we use the verb *believe (in)*: consider the differences in what we really have in mind, usually, when we say *I don't believe in guardian angels* and *I don't believe in that politician*.

Confirming the suspicion that the first two sentences above carry modality, we can accurately paraphrase them using conventional modal expressions:

> *I don't believe we've met.* = *We surely have not met.*
>
> *I think it's going to rain.* = *It will probably rain, IMHO* [in my humble opinion].

Because there's no genuine process of thinking or believing or guessing, etc., going on in such situations, it is argued that *think, believe*, etc., are being used in a rather metaphorical way: the literal way of saying probably is 'probably', or 'may'; the metaphorical way of saying it is 'I think'.

Thus constructions of the form *I think (that + sentence)* are usually sentences prefaced by probability modality. *I think/guess/reckon*, etc. are clearly *subjective* in the sense that they draw attention to the modality assessment being the speaker's. There are objective counterparts of these, some of which are rather formal:

> *It is thought* . . .
>
> *It seems* . . .
>
> *It is believed* . . .

along with

> *It is certain/likely/possible/essential* (etc.) (*that*).

Poor old Stevens, the emotionally illiterate butler in Kazuo Ishiguro's *The Remains of the Day*, relies particularly heavily on these latter. Indeed, the novel begins: *It seems increasingly likely that I really will undertake the expedition that has been preoccupying my imagination now for some days.* The entire novel can be read as an illumination of the inhumanity at the heart of deferential hierarchy, and the modality-choked language which characterizes Stevens's style is a key element in that illumination. The novel's fuller opening is:

> It seems increasingly likely that I really will undertake the expedition that has been preoccupying my imagination now for some days. An expedition, I should say, which I will undertake alone, in the comfort of Mr Farraday's Ford; an expedition which, as I foresee it, will take me through much of

the finest countryside of England to the West Country, and may keep me away from Darlington Hall for as much as five or six days.

But so far I have mentioned only the most established ways of reformulating modality. More creatively – particularly in spoken English – we can re-cast possibilities and obligations as quite strange-sounding noun phrases:

> *'Van der Graaf's Folly' is a dead cert for the 3:30 at Ascot.*

> *Bill says he's a definite maybe for the reception on Friday.*

Again, the basis for claiming that *is a dead cert* is a reformulated way of expressing modality is the fact that you can accurately paraphrase the given sentence using a more conventional modality expression: *'Van der Graaf's Folly' will certainly win the 3:30 at Ascot.*

All this may seem a little challenging when you set out to identify all the instances of modality marking in a text. But the challenge can be met. What you do have to remember, in the light of the above instances of 'metaphorized' modality, is that, rather than reading modality off the surface of a text, you will often have to uncover modality by *interpreting* that text. That is, instead of simply looking for particular wordings (*may, often, obligatory*, etc.), you have to decide on the *meanings* of utterances, and in particular decide whether some comment on the probability, usuality, obligatoriness, or speaker-willingness is included.

Let us return now to the basic and central idea: There are ways, in the language, for a speaker/writer to express their less-than-absolute commitment to or assessment of a statement, or an offer, or a suggestion, or whatever. And all these qualifications away from an absolute positive or negative sentence disclose the speaker's judgments about:

> the *probability* of the sentence's truth
> the *obligatoriness* of the sentence process actually transpiring
> the *willingness* of the sentence's protagonist to act in the way s/he is depicted acting

or

> the *usuality* of the sentence's protagonist acting in the way s/he is depicted acting.

Anne: *Perhaps John will do the washing up. You ought to John; it's your turn.*
John: *Would you help me, Chris?*
Chris: *But I'm always doing the washing up!*

And all this is done with modal verbs, modal adverbs, and various lexical substitutes for these.

Beyond modality: evaluative devices

In addition to the modality devices listed above, we can look at other means by which the text-speaker's stance or attitude towards the material she relates is revealed. In particular, we can note three kinds of highly evaluative items:

1   evaluative verbs (with first-person texts): *deplore, regret, welcome, concede, deny.* Each of these carries a clear presupposition (an important topic in itself, discussed fully in Chapter 9).

2   evaluative adjectives and adverbs: *regrettably, surprisingly, thankfully*; *deplorable, admirable, incredible,* etc.

3   generic sentences:

> *The first casualty of war is truth.*
>
> *War is diplomacy carried on by other means.*
>
> *War is business carried on by other means.*
>
> *Property is theft.*

In other words, each of the above kinds of language, found in all kinds of discourse, can be a useful pointer to the overt or underlying attitudes and assumptions, indeed the ideological commitments, of the individuals with which they are associated. If a narrator or character says that they *deplore the lack of respect shown to the monarchy and our heritage* you know you are not listening to a republican. If they write *Unfortunately he turned out to be gay* you can suspect homophobia. And when the lawyer in Agathie Christie's story 'Witness for the Prosecution' opines that *Women were the devil when they got their knife into you* one is justified in suspecting him of a general misogyny.

Items in number 2 here are likely to cause most trouble. The question that frequently gets asked, when one is looking for attitude-expressive adjectives in a text, is 'Where does one call a halt?'. The answer is that there is not always a hard-and-fast way of separating out those adjectives in a text which are related to an individual's distinct perspective from the larger set of evaluative adjectives which are simply contributing to descriptions in a more neutral way. You have to apply a rule of thumb, which is: do you judge this adjectival evaluation to be specifically the opinion of the speaker (hence speaker-expressive), or is this adjective a relatively neutral or impartial description of the entity being described? Only the former, of course, are relevant here.

I shall say more about item number 3, generic sentences, shortly. But first I would like you to apply the foregoing account of modality options to an analysis of the following poem.

Activities

ACTIVITY 1

Identify as best you can all those words and structures in the following poem by Adrienne Rich which encode some expression of the speaker's assessment of probability, obligation, usuality or willingness.

Living in Sin

She had thought the studio would keep itself;
no dust upon the furniture of love.
Half heresy, to wish the taps less vocal,
the panes relieved of grime. A plate of pears,
a piano with a Persian shawl, a cat   5
stalking the picturesque amusing mouse
had risen at his urging.
Not that at five each separate stair would writhe
under the milkman's tramp; that morning light
so coldly would delineate the scraps   10
of last night's cheese and three sepulchral bottles;
that on the kitchen shelf among the saucers
a pair of beetle-eyes would fix her own –
envoy from some village in the moldings . . .
Meanwhile, he, with a yawn,   15
sounded a dozen notes upon the keyboard,
declared it out of tune, shrugged at the mirror,
rubbed at his beard, went out for cigarettes;
while she, jeered by the minor demons,
pulled back the sheets and made the bed and found   20
a towel to dust the table-top,
and let the coffee-pot boil over on the stove.
By evening she was back in love again,
though not so wholly but throughout the night
she woke sometimes to feel the daylight coming   25
like a relentless milkman up the stairs.

1   What does the first line's use of the past perfect, *had thought*, imply about whether, in fact, the studio 'kept itself'? What type of modality does the *would* of line 1 express? And what is the persona's inferrable attitude to this state of affairs? Similarly, the poem says it would be 'half heresy' for the woman to wish for silent plumbing and clean windows, but what further inference can we then reasonably make?(§)

2   Let us look again at the sentence which runs from lines 4 to 7 – not strictly a sentence at all, but a series of noun phrases. Imagining ourselves into the position of the woman observing these items in her apartment, what can we speculate as being her likely reactions to the four items mentioned, in turn? And how could we relate the progression of these evaluative reactions to the encompassing evaluative progression that the poem seems to be obliquely reporting?

3   Incidentally, the phrase *half heresy* was noted above: not an everyday phrase, and particularly not an everyday phrase to use in talking about love relationships. But 'heresy' is not an isolated word in the poem: list all the other words in the poem which we might conventionally expect to appear in the same context as 'heresy' (this is a 'lexical cohesion' question, of course – to use the terms of Chapter 2). What are they all doing here?

4   The poem is repeatedly challenging and creative in its use of ellipsis cohesion – perhaps never more so than at the opening of line 8, which runs *Not that at five each separate stair would writhe under the milkman's tramp*. Rewrite this sentence, incorporating material from previous lines that in your judgement has been ellipted here so as to avoid repetition. Try to make your rewritten sentence accord with the seeming sense of Rich's original.(§)

5   The close of the poem says that 'throughout the night/she woke sometimes to feel the daylight coming'. What do you make of this combination of usuality-modality statements?

ACTIVITY 2

By way of practice in identifying words expressive of the four main modality types, look again at the passage of dialogue, between Harriet and Jack in Brookner's *A Closed Eye*, used in an examination of cohesion in the previous chapter (I have removed the marking of cohesive connections which I inserted into the version used in that chapter). List all the phrases which contribute to the expression of modality.

> 'Do you do this all the time?'
>
> 'Not all the time, no. You could stay, you know.'
>
> 'Why should I?'
>
> 'Possibly because you want to. And because I might want you to.'
>
> 'You?' There was no answer. 'I have to leave, you see. You do see, don't you?'
>
> 'I should expect nothing less of you.'
>
> 'Oh, don't be so . . . so rude,' she said angrily.
>
> They both smiled.
>
> 'Goodbye, Jack,' she said, holding out her hand. He kissed her again. There was no doubt now about her response. 'That's better,' he said. 'I loathe soulful women, with consciences.'

MORE ON GENERIC SENTENCES

I have listed generic sentences as the third kind of evaluative device particularly deserving attention, as revealing of speaker attitude. Generic sentences are sentences which assert something to be a general truth, typically timelessly true (i.e., true throughout time). And the 'truth' asserted is predicated not of a specific individual, but of a whole set of things, which is also an open (or potentially open) set of things. That is, it is typically impossible to list all the members of the set indicated by the generic referent:

> *The panda's preferred diet is bamboo shoots.*
>
> *Pandas' preferred diet is bamboo shoots.*
>
> *A panda's preferred diet is bamboo shoots.*

All three of these are generic sentences. Regardless of whether the definite or indefinite article is used, the sense of all three is something like the following:

> *Among the open set of pandas, including those long dead and those yet to be born, it is the case that their preferred diet is bamboo shoots.*

Additionally, grammatically, generic sentences are typically in the simple present tense (the tense usually used for timeless truths). In passing it is perhaps worth noting a direct connection between generic sentences and modality: since all generic sentences are implicitly introduced by the formulation 'It is always the case that . . . ', there is a clear sense in which they occupy the endpoint of the scale of usuality-modality.

Now something that purports to be the truth may be totally false, or nonsense, or vile discrimination. Nevertheless the speaker who utters such a sentence (without irony) is attempting to pass off their assertion as incontestable truth or wisdom, like a proverb or saying – proverbs themselves being, typically, generic sentences. Thus all the following are generic sentences:

> *The English are a nation of shopkeepers.*

> *Scots are awfully careful with their money.*

> *Every Welshman is an unsung Caruso.*

> *The Irish can talk the hind legs off a donkey.*

In each of these cases the speaker is declaring, as a general truth, something about individuals of a certain type – any individual of that type. Each sentence makes a claim about what is always true, or *typically* true (clearly this can be an important distinction), of that set of individuals. So generic sentences range from the scientifically a-social:

> *Hydrogen atoms are lighter than oxygen atoms*

to the stereotypical:

> *Canadians say 'aboat' and 'eh' all the time*

to the sharply partisan:

> *What really upsets Americans about the French is the fact that the latter are the more civilized nation.*

As mentioned above, producing a generic sentence which you intend to be interpreted ironically changes the situation subtly. For in such cases you are parading a proposition which might appear to be the bearer of a great truth, but now you intend the recipient to realize that it embodies a great foolishness or prejudice. Thus, in the emerging context, we assume Jane Austen's narrator is intending irony when they announce, at the opening of *Pride and Prejudice*: 'It is a truth universally acknowledged, that a single man in possession of a good fortune, must be in want of a wife.' Here is a further selection of generic sentences, or longer passages with generic sentences woven into them, for your delectation:

> Slavery is so vile and miserable an Estate of Man, and so directly opposite to the generous Temper and Courage of our Nation; that 'tis hardly to be conceived, that an English-

man, much less a Gentleman, should plead for't. . . . I therefore took [Sir Robert Filmer's *Patriarcha* – a work of political
theory which, in broad terms, defended hierarchy and inher-
ited authority] into my hands with all the expectation, and
read it through with all the attention due to a Treatise, that
made such a noise at its coming abroad, and cannot but
confess my self mightily surprised, that in a Book, which
was to provide Chains for all Mankind, I should find nothing
but a Rope of Sand, useful perhaps to such, whose Skill and
Business it is to raise Dust, and would blind the People, the
better to mislead them, but in truth not of any force to draw
those into Bondage, who have their Eyes open, and so much
Sense about them as to consider, that Chains are but an ill
wearing, how much Care soever hath been taken to file and
polish them.

> John Locke, opening of *The First Treatise of Civil*
> *Government* (1690)

In the movies, the blind moved slowly and never laughed.
Sometimes they were led by seeing-eye dogs.

> Raymond Carver, part of the opening of 'Cathedral'

A good book may have three openings entirely dissimilar and
inter-related only in the prescience of the author, or for that
matter one hundred times as many endings.

> Flann O'Brien, opening of *At Swim-Two-Birds*

'Do many men kill themselves, Daddy?'
'Not very many, Nick.'
'Do many women?'
'Hardly ever.'
'Don't they ever?'
'Oh, yes. They do sometimes.'

> Ernest Hemingway, near close of 'Indian Camp'

Since he belonged, even at the age of six, to that great clan
which cannot keep this feeling separate from that, but must let
future prospects, with their joys and sorrows, cloud what is
actually at hand, since to such people even in earliest childhood any turn in the wheel of sensation has the power to
crystallize and transfix the moment upon which its gloom or
radiance rests, James Ramsay, sitting on the floor cutting out
pictures from the illustrated catalogue of the Army and Navy
Stores, endowed the picture of a refrigerator as his mother

spoke with heavenly bliss.

part of opening of Virginia Woolf's *To the Lighthouse*

But there certainly are not so many men of large fortune in the world, as there are pretty women to deserve them.

Jane Austen, part of opening of *Mansfield Park*

Sun destroys
The interest of what's happening in the shade.

Philip Larkin, 'The Whitsun Weddings'

Love is not love
Which alters when it alteration finds,
Or bends with the remover to remove.

William Shakespeare, sonnet 116

Horses sweat, men perspire, ladies gently glow.

The men that is now is only all palaver and what they can get out of you.

Lily, in James Joyce's 'The Dead'

Now a man who passes a general judgment ventures more than one who merely reports a single fact; and the transition between the two activities confronts the reader with a marked shift of the scope of claimed authority.

R. Fowler, 'The Referential Code and Narrative Authority'
in *Literature as Social Discourse* (1981: 119), discussing
generic sentences

Notice, among the passages above, how generic sentences may be embedded to different degrees and in different ways, in different texts. Thus, in the extract from Locke's *First Treatise of Civil Government*, besides the opening generic declaration ('Slavery is so vile . . . that it is hard to conceive that an Englishman should plead for it'), there are also more embedded generics, which take some effort for the reader to extract and reconstruct., such as: 'A Treatise that makes such [unspecified] a noise at its coming abroad is due much expectation and attention.' And later: 'A Rope of Sand is useful perhaps for the raising of Dust and the blinding of the People, but lacks the power to draw the perceptive into Bondage.' Similarly, the Hemingway extract is interesting, since Hemingway is notoriously sparing in his use of narratorial commentary; nor are his characters usually of the kind prone to reflective generalization. Nevertheless, in the course of this conversation between Nick and his father, some thought-provoking generic understandings are articulated.

But among this selection perhaps the Woolf passage wins the prize for richness and particularity of the embedded generic condition, attributed to the young James Ramsay. Here, in alluding to the existence of a certain *great clan*, and in proceeding via the restrictive relative clause (*which cannot keep this feeling separate from that, but must . . .*, etc.) to describe the clan *in terms not confined to a particular time or place*, the generic sense is established. The latter point is crucial for the achievement of genericness. Thus if the passage had asserted that James Ramsay belonged to that great clan who wanted Zambinella to win the Monaco Grand Prix next week, then the spatio-temporal delimitation of that clan cancels any suggestion of genericness. But in the Woolf text the genericness is readily apparent, and can be recapitulated thus: 'There exists a large number of people who cannot keep this feeling separate from that, but must let future prospects, with their joys and sorrows, cloud what is actually at hand, since to them even in earliest childhood any turn in the wheel of sensation has the power to crystallize and transfix the moment upon which its gloom or radiance rests.'

Finally, consider the following sentence:

> Always some piece of news, some wrangle or excitement, once you get inside [the Home for Mentally Handicapped Adults].
> Alice Munro, 'Circle of Prayer'

This sentence, I would suggest, constitutes a 'limited generic' instance. It is generic insofar as it implicates that it is always the case that whenever a person steps inside the Home for the Mentally Handicapped, they will encounter some news or excitement or other. The limitedness, of course, has to do with the severely proscribed domain within which news and excitement are always encountered: they always occur only within the mentioned Home. This severely limits the genericness: it makes the statement relevant only to the few, including the character Trudy (from whose viewpoint the sentence comes), who ever get inside the Home. But do such restrictions cancel the genericness? Consider the following:

> When a man is tired of London, he is tired of life; for there is in London all that life can afford.
> from James Boswell's *Life of Johnson*

This is generic too, surely, although it is arguably restricted in reference to the London of Johnson's time, in the eighteenth century – rather different from the London of today. The fact that London still exists today makes it a particularly debatable point whether Johnson's verdict is timelessly valid, that is, applies to the London of all eras. In a sense then the Johnson generic sentence is intermediate between the quite limited generic sentence about the Home, and standard 'unlimitedly' generic sentences.

It will probably already be clear to you why generic sentences pack such a punch, wherever they show up. They purport to be incontrovertible and foundational orientations, like specifications of horizontal plane and vertical plane, 'true' north, due west, sea level, and so on: without such given and known foundations, one could hardly purposefully voyage anywhere. Generic sentences are more like presuppositions than assertions (see the discussion of this distinction in Chapter 9): they purport to be the background facts – perhaps deeply insightful, perhaps utterly obvious – which can go unchallenged. In discoursing on any complex topic, there will be more than enough issues concerning which we can have doubts and questions: generic sentences appear to lighten the burden somewhat by bracketing off certain propositions as beyond doubt, beyond question, and concluded. *We hold these truths to be self-evident*, famously begins the United States Declaration of Independence, before proceeding to list certain generic facts that it regards as unquestionable, such as the following:

> All men are endowed by their Creator with certain unalienable rights.

Generic sentences are more consensus-assuming than consensus-forming; they serve as the grounds upon which consensus or persuasion can be effected with regard to more specific policies and opinions.

In relation to narratives, generic sentences can be thought of as trans-narrative. Whatever the particular narrative (whatever the occasion on which one encounters a Scot, or a Canadian, or an atom of hydrogen) this fact or attribute will invariably hold. Thus generic sentences are evaluations which would claim to be *potentially* insertable – with greater or lesser relevance – in absolutely any narrative one might manage to construct. A 'robust' generic sentence – *Cold-blooded murder is always wrong* – might not always be terribly relevant to a given narrative but, so the reasoning would run, it should never be *false* relative to *any* narrative: by definition we should expect it to be *true*, in all narratives. By virtue of this universal applicability, generic sentences can be regarded as both a pan-narrative item and an anti-narrative device. To misuse Dickens, in relation to narrative, generic sentences are the best of sentences and the worst of sentences. They are the very opposite of those descriptions, treatable as singular, which help render unique the stories in which they appear. And someone who thought and wrote only in generic sentences would never be able to produce a narrative. Instead such a speaker would deliver a flow of information ranging from encyclopedic wisdom, insight, objective fact, and generalization, to opinion, stereotyping, and prejudice, all jostling in a timeless present with no clear sense of a before and an after, let alone a consequentially related before and after.

However, as noted, the suggestion that generic sentences are 'universally true', unquestionable, and neutral is only half the picture; that is what they purport to be rather than what they invariably are. We have seen how generic sentences can also be highly partial and particular and questionable – and all the more dangerous because their format makes them look like unquestionable universals. When Isabel Archer thinks 'It is the essence of any marriage to be open to criticism' and 'One's cousin always pretends to hate one's husband', in Henry James's *Portrait of a Lady*, these disturbing generalizations do nothing so much as point to the fallibilities and blind spots of Isabel herself. At a more general level, the proverbs and well-worn precepts of a culture are its generic sentences, and we may expect noticeably distinct cultures to live by (or claim to live by) somewhat contrasting sets of such generic sentences. If such proverbs and generic sentences are the 'known and established truths' of the given society, then they will also be the background in relation to which a society will tell the stories it tells. That is, in the simplest situation (i.e., setting aside, for now, the stories of ironists, the disaffected and the rebellious, the discontented), a society's 'mainstream' generic truths and proverbs will be confirmed and exemplified by the particular stories the culture tells itself. I think this is clear enough if we relate the Rocky and Rambo film narratives of the 1980s to certain mainstream generic sentences, such as that 'the American (male) individual, when he fully and fearlessly believes in himself and commits himself, can overcome any adversity'.

Activities

ACTIVITY 3

Read over the following poem by Anne Stevenson, and comment briefly on the contribution that the several probability-modality expressions and the single generic sentence make to the ambivalent or tentative tone of the whole. What do you imagine might be the 'context of utterance' out of which this poem might have emerged? Who is the 'she' of this poem?

The Marriage

They will fit, she thinks,
but only if her backbone
cuts exactly into his rib cage,
and only if his knees
dock exactly under her knees
and all four
agree on a common angle.

All would be well
if only
they could face each other.

Even as it is
there are compensations
for having to meet
nose to neck
chest to scapula
groin to rump
when they sleep.

They look, at least,
as if they were going
in the same direction.

ACTIVITY 4

Read over the following speech a couple of times. It was William Faulkner's address upon receiving the Nobel Prize for Literature, in Stockholm, December 1950.

> I feel that this award was not made to me as a man, but to my work – a life's work in the agony and sweat of the human spirit, not for glory and least of all for profit, but to create out of the materials of the human spirit something which did not exist before. So this award is only mine in trust. It will not be difficult to find a dedication for the money part of it commensurate with the purpose and significance of its origin. But I would like to do the same with the acclaim too, by using this moment as a pinnacle from which I might be listened to by the young men and women already dedicated to the same anguish and travail, among whom is already that one who will some day stand here where I am standing.
>
> Our tragedy today is a general and universal fear so long sustained by now that we can even bear it. There are no longer

problems of the spirit. There is only the question: When will I be blown up? Because of this, the young man or woman writing today has forgotten the problems of the human heart in conflict with itself which alone can make good writing because only that is worth writing about, worth the agony and the sweat.

He must learn them again. He must teach himself that the basest of all things is to be afraid; and, teaching himself that, forget it forever, leaving no room in his workshop for anything but the old verities and truths of the heart, the old universal truths lacking which any story is ephemeral and doomed–love and honor and pity and pride and compassion and sacrifice. Until he does so, he labors under a curse. He writes not of love but of lust, of defeats in which nobody loses anything of value, of victories without hope and, worst of all, without pity or compassion. His griefs grieve on no universal bones, leaving no scars. He writes not of the heart but of the glands.

Until he relearns these things, he will write as though he stood among and watched the end of man. I decline to accept the end of man. It is easy enough to say that man is immortal simply because he will endure: that when the last ding-dong of doom has clanged and faded from the last worthless rock hanging tideless in the last red and dying evening, that even then there will still be one more sound: that of his puny inexhaustible voice, still talking. I refuse to accept this. I believe that man will not merely endure: he will prevail. He is immortal, not because he alone among creatures has an inexhaustible voice, but because he has a soul, a spirit capable of compassion and sacrifice and endurance. The poet's, the writer's, duty is to write about these things. It is his privilege to help man endure by lifting his heart, by reminding him of the courage and honor and hope and pride and compassion and pity and sacrifice which have been the glory of his past. The poet's voice need not merely be the record of man, it can be one of the props, the pillars to help him endure and prevail.

1 There are very many modality and evaluation features in the speech. Which do you regard as the most characteristic?

2 Why might there be quite so much modality and evaluation in just this text? In what ways do you think the particular occasion might 'call for' this kind of language? Do you see any differences in the *strength* of the modality and evalution utterances Faulkner uses to express his own convictions, and the

strength of such utterances he uses to express any insistence that he be listened to?

3   There are many uses of *will* as a probability marker in the speech. But what about the sentence 'When will I be blown up'? Why does the *will* in that sentence seem to convey a non-modal, 'definite future' meaning? Can you think up some similar sentences to support this interpretation?(§)

4   Would you agree that, although declarations like *man will not merely endure: he will prevail* are also very confident predictions about the future, nevertheless they are not 'non-modal, definite future' uses of *will*? How does the way Faulkner introduces this declaration support this interpretation? Faulkner *could* have written that 'man not merely endures, he prevails'; what different effect would that formulation have created?

5   Are there any generic sentences in Faulkner's speech which you find it particularly hard to agree with? If so, why?

6   Look again at the long sentence which begins 'It is easy enough to say . . . '. Read that sentence aloud. Do you agree that, on a purely literal and mechanical level, that sentence 'is easy enough to say'? If it isn't, is this some kind of unwitting joke, on Faulkner's part? How does he end the sentence: what is the sentence's theme? In light of the latter, can we reassess the whole sentence as a quite complex matching of form to argument? (Form-to-meaning matchings are often termed 'iconic' in literary analysis.) In short, is this sentence awfully clumsy, or awfully clever?

ACTIVITY 5

Answer the following question with three different one-word replies, which respectively express probability, usuality and willingness:

Do you eat tofu?(§)

ACTIVITY 6

Discuss the kinds of modality exploited in the following Catch-22:

1   Yossarian wants to get out of the army.

2   But in order to get out of the army, you must be mentally ill.

3 Anyone who declares they want to get out of the army, as Yossarian has done, must be sane.

4 So Yossarian must be sane and therefore may not leave the army.

ACTIVITY 7

Examine the following passage, from Michael Frayn's novel *A Landing on the Sun*, for what it does with modality, and what it has to say about it. Dr Serafin is an Oxford philosophy don, who has been appointed, in 1974, to chair a tiny civil service commission of inquiry (in fact, the commission comprises just herself and her civil servant 'minder', Summerchild). The commission has been assigned the task of examining the notion 'the quality of life'. Here Serafin is beginning to explore the questions involved. Comment, particularly, on the ways in which particular kinds of modality are portrayed – quite amusingly – as characteristic of a particular cast of mind and temperament.

SERAFIN: To recapitulate: 'the quality of life' is some property which is in one way or another promoted or enhanced by washing-machines. Now, I take 'washing-machines' in this context to be a synecdoche . . . for domestic machinery in general.

SUMMERCHILD: I imagine it is. But . . . it's not a phrase I've had occasion to use all that much.

SERAFIN: But you have used it? You've read it, for instance?

SUMMERCHILD: I suppose so. In minutes and reports, and so forth.

SERAFIN: You've never written it?

SUMMERCHILD: Oh, very possibly.

SERAFIN: Also in minutes and reports?

SUMMERCHILD: I imagine it was.

SERAFIN: Which you regard as being different from using it in private conversation?

SUMMERCHILD: I suspect I do.

SERAFIN: I find your repeated appeal to what you suspect you think and what you imagine you did deeply suggestive. We tend to assume, I think, in normal usage, that I have to suspect what you are thinking, and to imagine or conjecture what you mean by an expression, but that you have some direct and privileged access to your intentions which enables you to know what you mean. But you find it quite natural to resort to conjecture yourself to establish what you think and what you mean. However, that is by the way. I am taking for granted that if you used the term, even in minutes and reports, you must have meant something by it. Yes?

From Michael Frayn, *A Landing on the Sun*
(New York: Viking, 1992), p. 81

ACTIVITY 8

One late-eighteenth-century commentator makes the following generic pronouncement:

> A human being in perfection ought always to preserve a calm and peaceful mind, and never to allow passion or a transitory desire to disturb his tranquillity. I do not think that the pursuit of knowledge is an exception to this rule. If the study to which you apply yourself has a tendency to weaken your affections, and to destroy your taste for those simple pleasures in which no alloy can possibly mix, then that study is certainly unlawful, that is to say, not befitting the human mind.

Do you agree? Give examples in support of or against the view stated here. What kind of individual do you imagine made this pronouncement? (You might begin with speculations about their nationality, gender, age, ethnicity, religion, level of education, level of affluence, and possible emotional and temperamental disposition.)(§)

ACTIVITY 9

Finally, and – like the previous extract – more for the joy of the thing than for its application to an exercise, think about how much modality contributes to the effectiveness of the following passage, which is taken from Barry Targan's short story, 'Dominion'. Morton Poverman is the ageing Jewish owner of a women's clothing store, beaten down by the struggle to survive and prosper, and previously the victim of a business partner who absconded, leaving him with substantial debts to work off. Now, Morton's chief source of pride, his gifted but suggestible son Robert, has taken up with a fundamentalist Christian sect, The Society of the Holy Word. Under its influence, Robert is not merely turning away from his parents, but is also threatening to pass up a brilliant career at college and beyond (culminating, in his father's imagination, in appointment to the Supreme Court!), in favour of declaring for the Lord, Bible school, and so on. At this point in the story, Morton begins a 'rescue' attempt, by paying a visit to the downtown store of The Society of the Holy Word.

After reading through the extract a couple of times, make a note of all the words and phrases that contribute to the modalized representation of what's going on. Comment on the kind of picture that these help give of both Morton Poverman and George Fetler.

> 'Yes? Can I help you?' the tall man asked. He was very clean, scrubbed so that he was pink and white . . . .
>
> 'Just looking,' Poverman said.
>
> [. . .]
>
> He turned and walked back to the pink and white man.
>
> 'I'm Morton Poverman,' he said, and put out his hand.
>
> 'I'm George Fetler,' the pink and white man said, and took the hand.
>
> 'I've got a son, Robert Poverman. He comes here.'
>
> 'Oh yes. Robert. A wonderful boy. Brilliant. Absolutely brilliant. I'm very pleased to meet you. You must be very proud of such a son.'
>
> But Poverman did not have time for this playing. Even now, four blocks away in his own store, United Parcel trucks would be arriving with goods he must pay for and he had not yet made the deposit in the bank that would cover them, and Francine Feynman (now working full time) would be on two customers at once (or worse, none), and the phone would ring with the call from Philadelphia about the slightly faded orlon sweaters. And what had he come here for, this man's opinions?
>
> 'Yes,' Poverman said. 'Proud.' But he did not know what to say, nor what to do. What he *wanted* to do was dump five gallons of gasoline over everything – the books, the newspapers, the green pamphlets – and put a match to it. But there were too many other empty store fronts downtown for that to matter. So he was stuck.
>
> George Fetler said, 'You're probably here because you're worried about Robert.'
>
> 'Yes. That's right. Exactly.' Poverman beat down the small loop of gratitude.
>
> 'Robert's such a thoughtful fellow. He's quite uncertain about college now, about his future. I suppose you and Mrs

Poverman must be concerned.'

'Yes,' Poverman said again, eagerly, even before he could stop himself. Oh this guy was smooth. He was a salesman, all right, as soft as Poverman was hard.

'You're probably upset with the Society of the Holy Word, too.'

Poverman clamped his lips but nodded.

'You must think that we've probably poisoned your son's mind.'

Poverman nodded again. What else?

'Let's sit down, Mr Poverman, and let me tell you about us. Briefly. You're probably anxious to get back to your business.'

Oh good, good. Oh terrific. All his life Morton Poverman wished he could have been so smooth with customers – buying, selling, complaints, but with him it had always been a frontal attack. A joke, a little screaming or a quick retreat into a deal for twenty percent off. But never like this, quiet, slick as oil, full of probabilities, the ways so easily greased. Yes yes yes where do I sign?

Commentaries

ACTIVITY 1

1   In terms of modality, the *would* in *the studio would keep itself* expresses probability, here a defeated probability or expectation. *She had thought the studio would keep itself* strongly implies that, contrary to that expectation, the studio has not 'kept itself'. We can further infer that either it has become untidy and dirty, or it has not done so only because someone (possibly the 'She') has made efforts to keep it otherwise – efforts she is ambivalent about having to make: isn't true love supposed to be effortless?

What 'tells' us that her expectation, that the studio would keep itself, has probably been defeated? It is partly conveyed by the past perfect auxiliary *had* (cf., *I had hoped for a quite evening in front of the telly, but now I have to go out* etc.). It is also partly due to the simple sense of the proposition that the studio might keep itself: from real-world knowledge we know that this is no more possible than dinner plates that wash themselves, and so on. But, to allude to a topic fully discussed in Chapter 9, it should be noted that this is not a case of genuine presupposition: *She had thought it would stay clean* does not presuppose 'It would not stay clean'. This is because of the nature of the verb *think*. The verb *know* would have worked differently: *She had known the studio would get dirty* does presuppose 'The studio got dirty' – as does the negated counterpart, *She had not known that the studio would get dirty*. Everything to do with presupposition will be made clear in Chapter 9. In general, we can infer that the woman here regrets the extent to which, she has found, she does not live in a state of natural or spontaneous cleanliness. Similarly, lovers are supposed to be 'true believers', are not supposed to complain – or indeed notice – such material trivia as plumbing noises and grubby windows, any more than a devout believer is supposed to become distracted by the priest's jarring vowels or stains on the altar cloth. Of course, by the time you have become this aware of your own mixed feelings, of commitment and qualification, you have certainly entered the world of doubt, shame, guilt, and divided loyalties. Isn't this exactly what sin is, under one of its literal or metaphorical guises?

4   There at least two possible expansions:

(i)   She had not thought that at five each separate stair would writhe under the milkman's tramp.

(ii)   (She thought?) (it was) half heresy to wish that at five each separate stair would not writhe under the milkman's tramp.

The second of these would be my own tentative, ellipsis-removing 'gloss' of lines 8–9. But what is surely beyond doubt is that, if Rich has ellipted in the complex ways I have assumed, then she has done so in ways not permitted in the standard patternings of English. Relatedly, I would defy any *speaker* of the poem to deliver lines 8 and 9 orally in such a way as to make the sense (as reconstructed above) clear. I don't believe it can be done! In other words, the *hearer/listener*, with only partial guidance from the writer/speaker, has to do some of the processing work effectively unaided.

ACTIVITY 4

3   The 'definiteness' of the *will* in 'When will I be blown up?'
    seems to be rooted in the fact that this is a '*When*'-clause in the
    first place. Whenever we ask genuine (non-rhetorical) ques-
    tions which contain a statement, we are assuming that the
    contained statement is itself true. In this case, the question
    amounts to saying *I know I'm going to be blown up at some point
    in time: can you tell me when precisely that time is?* Other When-
    constructions carry the same kind of 'definite background':
    When did you meet Bill? (I know you met Bill at some time;
    when was that exactly?); *I bought this sweater when I was in
    Galway* (I have been to Galway). The linguistic phenomenon
    at work here is presupposition, explained in full in Chapter 9.

ACTIVITY 5

Certainly! Frequently! Gladly!

ACTIVITY 8

The words quoted are those of Victor Frankenstein, in Chapter 4 of
Mary Shelley's *Frankenstein*, just before he creates the monster. In the
narrative relayed to us, it is already apparent that he is possessed by a
Nietzschean scientistic will to power; and before too long it is evident
how creating the monster brings in train the destruction of all Frankenstein's connections of love and friendship. So we can certainly read
unwitting irony in these lines. Immediately following the sentences
quoted, Frankenstein adds:

> If this rule were always observed; if no man allowed any
> pursuit whatsoever to interfere with the tranquillity of his
> domestic affections, Greece had not been enslaved; Casesa
> would have spared his country; America would have been
> discovered more gradually; and the empires of Mexico and
> Peru had not been destroyed.

4

Processes and participants

How many different processes are going on in the world – or in the world articulated by the language one is using? Looked at one way, you might say there's a near infinity of different processes, and you could begin a list simply by noting all the different verbs recorded in a dictionary of the language. Every different verb, we might argue, describes one of the myriad different processes which recurrently happens in our human world.

And yet, are all those different verbs reporting fundamentally distinct and different processes? Or can we make some bold generalizations, grouping the multitudes of different activities into just a few, fundamental and contrasting kinds? Consider these three processes: *riding a bike, walking along a path*, and *being an undergraduate*. Aren't the first two similar to each other, versions of physical activity, in a way which radically contrasts with the status-description involved in the third? This chapter is all about the grouping and generalization of English's innumerable verbally expressed activities into a small set of basic kinds of process. Later we will argue that it is because these basic kinds of process are distinct, few in number, and robustly contrasting with each other, that study of how they are used in discourses – or avoided in discourses – can be so revealing.

Which verbally expressed activities should we group together, then, and which activities should we hold apart? Let us begin with the process of *drink(ing)*: surely this is not radically distinct from *imbibing, taking in, quaffing, guzzling, consuming, downing* and so on? And going further in the way of categorizing, why not acknowledge a commonality between *drinking, eating, smoking*, and so on, all of which remain radically distinct, in meaning and grammar, from a process such as *realizing*? (They differ in grammer in various ways: we can say *I drink (eat/smoke) when I'm nervous* but hardly? *I realize when I'm nervous*; and we can say *I realize that you're nervous* but hardly *I drink (eat/smoke) that you're nervous.*)

On the one hand, then, a language can be viewed as recording the multitude of distinct processes or activities going on in the world, when that language is looked at particular by particular. On the other hand we can also look at a language in its totality, as grouping those innumerable activities together as instances of remarkably few, fundamentally distinct, processes. Those few kinds of process are most sharply distinct from each other if attention is paid to their different semantic and grammatical tendencies. In this chapter, I shall try to explain the idea that English can be thought of as categorizing the world into four most fundamental processes:

doings
thinkings
sayings
characterizings

You might like to pause at this point and think of as many activities or verbs as you can, and decide whether each of these can be seen as a kind of doing, or thinking, or saying, or characterizing, when considered at a most general level.

The basis of this rudimentary semantic categorization is the conviction that, at root, any verbally expressed activity you care to think of amounts to a version of just one of those four most 'foundational' kinds of activity. Now this four-way classification would be particularly arbitrary and controversial were it not for the fact that the four semantic kinds seem to correlate with various syntactic contrasts among verbs in the different classes. To give one simple example, compare how we report typical present-time activities of doing versus present-time activities of thinking. Notice the different verb forms, the -*ing* ending versus the non-progressive ending (that is, non-*ing* ending), in the replies to the following questions:

A: *What's your task?*
B: *I'm removing the innards and coating the outside with olive oil.*

A: *What's your opinion?*
B: *I don't understand why anyone would vote for him.*

The first B says *I'm removing*, etc. (not *I remove*), in describing a current physical engagement, but the second B says *I don't understand* (not *I'm not understanding*) when reporting the mental engagement. More will be said about these differences below. In addition, in characterizing these 'ways of expressing' – which we shall call the different semantic processes and participants expressed in English clauses – we are also asserting something about English language-culture, namely that it tends to see and represent the world along the lines made available by these established syntactic-semantic templates.

It can be argued that there are just four most prominent kinds of process expressed in the vast majority of English clauses:

> processes of **doing** (physical activity)
> processes of **mental activity** (sensing, thinking, etc.)
> processes of **communicating** (saying, telling, reporting,)
> processes of **characterizing** (describing X – or an x – as a y, or as y-like)

Our more formal labels for these four most important kinds of semantic process are, in order:

> **material** processes
> **mental** processes
> **verbal** processes
> **relational** processes

Two other, rarer and less significant processes will also be briefly noted below: they are **behavioural** processes and **existential** processes.

When we examine the major kinds of process represented in English clauses – material, mental, and so on – we are also immediately involved in identifying the types of 'participant roles' that such a process commonly involves. 'Participant roles' (hereafter shortened to 'participants' – as in the chapter title – for convenience) are also sometimes referred to as 'roles', or 'thematic relations'. I will review the full list of types of participant shortly, when saying more about the process types; but you will begin to get the idea of them if you agree that material process clauses (that is, processes of physical activity) always involve a participant entity that is *acted upon* in some way (here, that role is called the medium), and that all mental processes involve a participant who performs some kind of mental processing (here, the role is termed the senser).

Because each type of process has several participant roles associated with it, and because these roles are somewhat different from one process to the next, the full list of participant roles is a little longer (it amounts to about a dozen main types) than the simple four kinds of process. Just who or what fills the participant roles directly involved with particular kinds of process is highly significant.

Finally, so that we have covered all the major semantic dimensions of the typical English clause, mention should be made of a third element, in addition to the process and participants involved: there may be one or more 'background' phrases to do with time, place, manner and so on, that is, 'adverbial' contextualizations of the process. These are called circumstances, and a little more will be said about them later.

Time Out: what is a transitive (or an intransitive) clause?

A **transitive** clause is a clause containing an object. Most commonly the object is a noun phrase that appears right after the verb; and it is defining of objects that they can be 'turned into' subjects if you reformulate an active sentence as a passive one. Thus:

Bill tickled Mary

is a transtive clause since it contains an object noun phrase, *Mary*, and if we passivize the sentence, true to form, this becomes the sentence's subject:

Mary was tickled by Bill.

Intransitive clauses are those describing an activity which does not 'go across' from the subject to an object. They are not two-party activities but one-party ones (or, 'clauses of object-less activity'). Hence there is no object in an intransitive clause, nor even the grammatical possibility of one. Verbs like *laugh, object, complain, groan, walk, sigh, sprint*, and many more, are the kinds that are commonly used in intransitive clauses. And in

Mary objected loudly when Bill tickled her

the main verb *object* has no object, and relatedly passivization is impossible:

*When Bill tickled her was loudly objected to by Mary

Do not be misled into thinking that all clauses are either transitive of intransitive: a third major type, called **intensive** clauses (which always express a relational process), should be noted. Intensive clauses – *I was the captain; They were unhelpful* – involve no activity at all, but simply a state:

transitive:	activity	+ object
intransitive:	activity	no object
intensive:	no activity	(no object)

To recap, every English clause, semantically, involves a particular process, one or more associated participants, and optionally one or more circumstances. The following are note-form characterizations of each of the major process types, and of the participant types associated with them, in order. The account is heavily indebted to Halliday (1994), to which the reader is directed for a more detailed description.

Material processes (clauses of action, concrete or abstract)

- Something physical and observable is done or happens, and you 'probe' a material process clause by asking 'What did [the subject] do?' or 'What happened?'

  e.g. *The penguin felt the edge of the diving board*
  ⇒ 'What did the penguin do?'
- Every participant is a 'thing' (an entity or process, but not a fact or proposition)
- a material process will invariably have a medium participant, an entity to which something happens or is done. As far as grammar is concerned, the medium will be the subject if the clause is intransitive – *Mary roared with laughter* – but it will be the direct object if the clause is transitive – *Bill nudged Mary in the ribs.*

- Participant roles (underlined), with example sentences:

Medium

> *Mary ate the tofu.*
>
> *Bill groaned.*
>
> *The eggs cooked in a minute.*

Effected medium (rare subtype, where the medium comes into existence in the course of the process)

> *Kim painted a beautiful landscape.*
>
> *Jules made ratatouille for Jim.*

Agent (rarer, in this system, than you might expect: an agent is a human intentional actor who acts upon a given medium; hence, when analysing sentences, you should always identify the process's medium first, before looking for any agent)

> *Mary ate the tofu.*
>
> *Kim painted a beautiful landscape.*

Beneficiary (often preceded – or 'precedable' – by *for*)

> *Jules made ratatouille for <u>Jim</u>.*
>
> *Mary bought <u>me</u> that TV.*

Recipient (often preceded by *to*)

> *The store delivered to <u>me</u> the TV Mary bought.*

Instrument (often preceded by *with*)

> *Mary ate the tofu with <u>a knife and fork</u>.*
>
> *With <u>this ring</u>, I thee wed.*
>
> *Surfaces are bleached <u>with a mild solution of sulphuric acid</u>.*

Force (often preceded by *by*)

> *The forest was scarred by <u>acid rain</u>.*
>
> <u>*The summer sun*</u> *had bleached his hair.*
>
> *By nightfall, everyone had been told by the police that the road was blocked by <u>an avalanche</u>.*
> [In that last example, only *an avalanche* is a Force; *the police* is sayer of a verbal process, and *By nightfall* is a temporal circumstance – on these, see below.]

To re-cap, in material process clauses, in addition to the obligatory medium participant, which is the 'done-to' participant, there may be a 'do-er' represented. There are three kinds of 'do-er' participant that appear in transitive clauses: a conscious human agent, or an inanimate instrument wielded by an implied or declared human agent, or an inanimate natural force acting wholly outside the control of human beings. (A fourth kind of 'do-er' role, a human medium-actor in an intransitive clause, will be explained further below.)

Some more analysed examples ('mat. pro.' stands for 'material process'):

> medium   mat. pro.
> *The tree   fell down.*

> agent   mat. pro.   medium
> *Mary   chopped down   the tree.*

> force   mat. pro.   medium
> *The storm   flattened   the tree.*

| instrument | mat. pro. | medium |
| The chainsaw | demolished | the tree. |

| agent | mat. pro. | medium | instrument |
| Mary | demolished | the tree | with her chainsaw. |

Mental processes: clauses of thinking, internal feeling and perceiving (perception, reaction, cognition)

- Mental processes always have (at least) one human or human-like participant, the 'do-er' of the mental process.
- The target of the mental process may well be, instead of a 'thing', a fact/proposition: thus, besides *Pam likes the painting*, we can equally have *Pam considered what Al had suggested.*
- The present tense normally used is the simple present (whereas in present-time *material* processes it is present progressive): *Pam likes that painting* [not '*is liking*'] *and so she is buying it* [not '*buys*'].
- Unlike material processes, some mental processes have counterparts with participants reversed:

    I like it ⇔ *it pleases me*

    She is buying it ⇔ ?

- Unlike material processes, mental processes cannot be 'probed' by a 'What did x do?' question.

    What did Pam do? She bought the painting. (material process)

    What did Pam do? * *She liked the painting.*

- Participant roles:
    senser: the individual (usually human) who does the perceiving, realizing, or similar.
    phenomenon: that which is perceived, realized, or similar, by the senser.

| senser | ment. pro. | phenomenon |
| I | can't stand | Martin Amis novels. |

| phenomenon | circ. | ment. pro. | phenomenon |
| Time's Arrow | really | upset | me. |

| senser | ment. pro. | phenomenon |
| Are we | supposed | to regard Otto/Todd as culpable or not? |

senser   ment. pro.   phenomenon
Do   you   recall   what 'unverdorben' means?

senser ment. pro. phenomenon   circ.
I   heard   Amis interviewed on the radio   the other day.

Relational processes: clauses of being (having the condition or status of)

- Syntactically, relational processes are typically of the form, *NP be AdjP*; *NP be NP*: that is, they are intensive clauses (clauses using *be* as the main verb, or one of a small set of verbs that are semantically close to *be*: *seem, become, appear, get, sound, look*). Refer to the time-out panel above, where intensive clauses are contrasted with transitive ones. Note that many times the verbs here (*sound, look,* etc.) have other uses, in mental or material processes; but when they are used almost interchangeably with *be* then they are being used in relational clauses:

    Bill was/sounded/looked weird.

  Compare

    Bill sounded the gong (material).

    Bill looked at the menu (mental).

- Relational process clauses basically do one of two things: they either attribute some quality or status to an entity (*John is sexy, John is a dweeb*) or identify an entity as having a particular and defining role or standing (*John is the sexiest man in the office*). Thus relational process clauses are either attributive or identificatory. A further means of distinguishing these two types is that the latter can be 'reversed' (thus, *The sexiest man in the office is John*) while the former, outside poetry, cannot (**Sexy is John, *A dweeb is John*).

- Note that other verbs, besides *be, seem,* etc., sometimes function in relational processes; e.g. *amount to* (as in *The prize amounted to some three thousand pounds*) and *have* (as in *Maria has blonde hair*). A useful test for the 'relational' status of a particular clause where a verb like *get* or *amount to* is used is to try substituting an appropriate form of the verb *be*:

    Maria has blonde hair ⇔ Maria is blonde.

- Participant roles:
  Carrier and **attribute**, in the nonreversible descriptions:

> *John   is   sexy.*
> *Mary   is   a chartered accountant.*
> carrier   rel. pro.   attribute

Identified and **identifier**, in the reversible identifications:

> *John   is   the sexiest man in the office.*
> *Mary   is   chair of the accounts committee.*
> identified rel. pro. identifier

- Examples of relational processes:

  > *The sea is calm tonight.*

  > *Tonight, tonight, won't be just any night.*

  > *The night is the earth's resting time.*

  > *The time is out of joint.*

  > *This joint is really jumping.*

  > *Jumping the horse was my favourite gym activity.*

(Most of the above are carrier + rel.pro. + attribute. Pick out the two which are identified + rel. pro. + identifier.)

Behavioural processes: clauses of involuntary human reaction

- Processes of physiological and psychological behaviour, in which a (typically human) animate participant behaves in a certain way but does so neither intentionally nor accidentally, but more via a reflex or instinctively: *breathing, smiling, coughing, dreaming, choking* (on a chicken bone), *gagging, fainting, blinking* or *ducking* (when an object is flying towards your head), *flinching, crying, laughing, listening*, etc. The sole participant, the behaver, is typically a conscious being acting unconsciously (hence, behaving). Behavioural processes are intermediate between mental and material processes, but closer to the latter.
- When in the present tense, these are usually progressive:

  > *Doctor, my child is throwing up every 10 minutes.*

  > *OK, bring her straight in.*

As a result, if the progressive is *not* used, the activity may sound less involuntary, more wilful, and not a behavioural process but a material one:

Doctor, my child throws up every 10 minutes.

That must get tiresome.

- Participant roles:
  Behaver, the do-er of the process, is the only role.

Verbal processes: clauses of communicating (implicit message) to (implicit addressee)

- Processes of communicating – expressing, reporting, saying, telling etc. Typically, a human sayer, but could also be a watch, a notice, a computer screen . . .

  Joy said she would be late.

  Mrs Thompson told the class to form a circle.

  The screen says 'Out of Memory'.

  The little red man says 'Don't Walk'.

- Participant roles:
  Sayer, a **said**, and an **addressee**

sayer	verbal pro.	addressee	said
Mrs Thompson	*told*	*the class*	*to form a circle.*

Existential processes: clauses of existing

- Clauses introduced by *There*, which represent that someone or something exists or has happened:

  There are three crows sitting on the telephone wire.

  There has been an accident.

  There's no one there.

  There were hosts of golden daffodils all around.

- Sometimes existential sentences occur with *there* deleted:

  All around were hosts of golden daffodils.

  No one's there.

- Participant roles:
  Existent only

	existential pro.	existent
There	*has been*	*an accident.*

Those, then, are the major process- and participant-types in the English clause. As mentioned, these are frequently accompanied by a third element, circumstantial items. A detailed commentary on these is not necessary here. Suffice it to say that, in form, they are often prepositional phrases, or adverbial phrases, or adverbial clauses. They carry information which is usually nonessential structurally or grammatically, but which is semantically very significant – information to do with the time, place, manner, cause, etc. of the stated process.

Activities

ACTIVITY 1

Identify any mediums, agents, instruments or forces you can find in the following material process clauses:

1   He washed his feet.

   He burned his corns with acid.

   The corns were caused by tight shoes.

2   Jack and Jill went up the hill / to fetch a pail of water;

   Jack fell down / and broke his crown / and Jill came tumbling after.

   Up Jack got / and home did trot / as fast as he could caper;

   He went to bed / to mend his head with vinegar and brown paper. (§)

3   Identify the various main- and subordinate-clause processes and participants in the following two passages. Note that the circumstances have been underlined in the first extract (you may decide what *kind* of circumstance each is).

   (a)

Musée des Beaux Arts

<u>About suffering</u> they were <u>never</u> wrong,

The Old Masters: <u>how well</u> they understood

Its human position; how it takes place

While someone else is eating or opening a window or just
   walking <u>dully along</u>;

How, when the aged are <u>reverently</u>, <u>passionately</u> waiting

For the miraculous birth, there <u>always</u> must be

Children who did not <u>specially</u> want it to happen, skating

On a pond at the edge of the wood:

They <u>never</u> forgot

That even the dreadful martyrdom must run its course

<u>Anyhow in a corner, some untidy spot</u>

Where the dogs go on with their doggy life and the torturer's
   horse

Scratches its innocent behind <u>on a tree</u>.(§)

(b)

It worries me how silent everything is. I don't like it.

— You needn't be scared. If there was anything out there we'd
hear it coming.

I know. I believe you. But the quiet puzzles me all the same.

Listen. Can you feel that throbbing? It hurts my ears.

In analysing the two passages above into processes and participants you
will have come across one of the permanent difficulties with the system:
how to deal with subordinate clauses such as *While someone else is eating
or opening a window or just walking dully along*. For at one level this entire
sequence is simply a circumstantial addition to the main clause process,
[Suffering] takes place. At the same time the circumstantial itself contains three processes, material ones, expressed by finite verbs, and it
would seem to be terribly incomplete for our analysis not to register that
— particularly since these material processes each involve just one
human participant, and are three glimpses of non-interactive human
activity. There is no single solution to this procedural difficulty. But as a
general rule of thumb I would advise that you classify all the processes
and participants in a text, whether main-clause or subordinate. If you
judge it appropriate to distinguish between main-clause processes and
subordinate ones, then that is a more detailed analysis that may on
occasion be justified.

The labelling of material process clauses proposed here, in terms of mediums and agents, contrasts with a different labelling system, in terms of actors and goals, which you may find used in many other introductory coursebooks. These are not mere notational variants, however ('agent' and 'medium' are not merely alternative labels directly replacing 'actor' and 'goal' respectively). In the actor–goal system, *John* in *John laughed hysterically* would be actor; in the system used here *John* is explicitly not agentive, but medium. There's something to be said for each labelling: *John* is active to some degree, in the given sentence, in a way which the label medium hardly reflects; on the other hand he is not agentive in the sense of acting directly upon any other participant.

For our text-analysing purposes, and in view of the way it seems insufficient to call *John* in *John laughed hysterically* merely medium (as if there is no substantial contrast with the participant role of *John* – also medium – in *Bill pushed John over*), it seems worthwhile to make a proper distinction between two subtypes of human medium:

1   Human mediums which are grammatical subject in intransitive clauses, apparently acting intentionally (like *John* in *John laughed hysterically* and *John jumped from the divingboard*).

2   All other cases: human mediums, whether grammatical subject or object, evidently acting in a way not purposefully intended by them (like *John* in both *John fell from the ledge* and *Bill pushed John off the ledge*).

The reason for making such a distinction is that we may want to contrast the degree of 'mediumness' and subjection which is true of *John* in the second and third sentences below with that in the first, even though *John* in each case is the medium:

John laughed hysterically. (medium type 1)

Bill shook John hysterically. (medium type 2)

John was shaken hysterically. (medium type 2)

In short, in some intransitive material process verbs, such as *laugh*, *jump*, etc., the animate medium filling the subject position is a rather more active, intending, and dynamic medium than either the medium in transitive clauses, or the medium in intransitive clauses who is assumed to be undergoing the process unintentionally. We shall call the first of these mediums, the 'jumping' medium, an initiating medium, while the second type, the 'pushed' medium, may be called a target medium, that being the status of *John* in the second and third sentences immediately above. And since an abbreviated labelling is sometimes useful, a simple emendation distinguishing a medium-initiator from a medium-target can be adopted:

> Medium-i: medium, and volitional human initiator of the process.
>
> Medium-t: medium, and the human target of the process.

Notice that the sublabelling (i vs. t) focuses on kinds of human interactant; but it does not fully distinguish human and nonhuman participants, which might be felt to be a major contrast. But just such a distinction can be established if we retain the bare label medium, alongside medium-i and medium-t, and if we apply the bare label to nonhuman participants and the sublabelled ones to human participants. Mediums would be thus of three kinds:

> Medium: nonhuman medium
>
> Medium-i: human medium, and volitional initiator of the process.
>
> Medium-t: human medium, and the target of the process.

process	participants	circumstances
material	medium (-i, -t) agent force instrument recipient beneficiary	temporal locative directional manner causal conditional concessive etc.
mental	senser phenomenon	
relational	carrier + attribute identified + identifier	
behavioural	behaver	
verbal	sayer said addressee	
existential	existent	

Our labelling can now display a contrast between *John fell down* and *The tree fell down* (the former has a medium-t, the latter a medium) and between *Bill kicked John* and *Bill kicked the tree* (in each pair John is the medium-t while the tree is simply the medium). And of course the John of *John dived to the floor* is importantly distinguished from all the above, being the medium-i.

Below, in summary tabular form, is a listing of all the kinds of process and associated participants that we have identified.

Powerful vs. powerless in material processes

We have now identified five major types of participant-role in material process clauses (seven, if we subdivide medium into medium, medium-i and medium-t). We can now rank these in terms of the degree of active, powerful, controlling engagement that the role implicitly ascribes to the individual filling it. The ranking is as follows, going from the material process participant that is most active and in control to that participant that is most acted upon, controlled, and objectified:

Agent
Force   } kinds of do-er
Instrument
Medium-initiator

Beneficiary or recipient
Medium-target   } kinds of done-to individual
Medium

One can even attempt to draw up a scale ranking all the kinds of participant roles, in all the kinds of process (material, mental, etc.) in a single hierarchy running from most dynamic or effectual to least (cf. Hasan, 1985: 45–6), but this becomes rather problematic. It is difficult to establish a general ranking or comparison of agents, sayers, and sensers, for example; nevertheless, it is reasonable to call the sayer, senser, and behaver the 'do-er' participant of their respective processes.

Focusing on the seven-point scaling of roles in material process clauses, we can further group the entities – as in the figure above – into a set of four roles which are do-er roles, and those roles in which something is done for or given to an individual (but that individual is not him- or herself directly acted upon) or – most passive – something is directly done to the individual. Evidently an agent is 'most powerful' and a medium-t is 'least powerful', among specifically human participants. All of this classifying becomes useful when we look closely at particular pieces of language, and the representation of particular individuals in those discourses which involve them. Most starkly, if we find that a certain human individual is repeatedly cast, in a narrative or conversation, as medium-t, and rarely as agent, we can argue that he or she is thereby being represented as subjected and disempowered. In fact the scheme is predictive in both directions: it predicts that powerful individuals will be relatively often cast as agent, relatively rarely as medium-t; and it predicts that anyone often cast as medium-t and rarely as agent is being represented as (and assumed to be) powerless. And the scheme implicitly argues that, for example, if you want to represent a particular group as actually independent and agentive, then you need to ensure that you depict them, discoursally, with an appropriate ratio of dynamic participant roles.

But just as interesting are those texts where, for example, forces or instruments are repeatedly cast in the 'do-er' role (typically, grammatical subject of the clause). On a basis which may be as much cultural as natural, we humans seem to have strong expectations that, by and large, and particularly where human interventions are pervasive, the 'do-ers' in texts will be human agents. Or, more carefully, perhaps we should say that English language-culture tends to promote that habitual line of thinking (which, in a more extended discussion, might be related to longstanding western conceptions of rationality, technology, and scientific objectivism). As a result any recurrent use of forces, especially, in the 'do-er' role (particularly when the force is not merely a convenient established metaphor, as in *The salt on the streets has eaten away the body of my car*) is a kind of foregrounding, usually worth closer consideration: the teller may be denying that any human has an agentive role in the events depicted, or may be attempting to conceal or disregard implicit human participation.

Activities

ACTIVITY 2

Here is the final stanza of Larkin's 'The Whitsun Weddings', a poem mentioned earlier in this book (see Chapter 1, Activity 1, part 12). On a Saturday afternoon, travelling by train to London, the speaker has found that at each station more newlyweds going away on their honeymoons have boarded the train. The speaker is struck by the way that all these travellers, including himself, have become accidental witnesses to a major change in the lives of so many people; these diverse travellers have seen 'a dozen marriages [get] under way'. The final stanza, in which the initial deictic *There* refers to London, runs:

There we were aimed. And as we raced across
  Bright knots of rail
Past standing Pullmans, walls of blackened moss
Came close, and it was nearly done, this frail
Travelling coincidence; and what it held
Stood ready to be loosed with all the power
That being changed can give.
We slowed again,
And as the tightened brakes took hold, there swelled
A sense of falling, like an arrow-shower
Sent out of sight, somewhere becoming rain.

1 Analyse the stanza in terms of processes and participants.
Would you agree that, even on the basis of a cursory inspection, the processes in this final stanza are more complex and
varied than those in earlier ones?

2 Are there any clauses in which humans are agents?

3 Are there any clauses in which humans are medium-initiators?

4 In short, are humans cast here at all as genuine do-ers of what
is done, of what happens? If not, why not? What is the
implication about the position of the speaker, and these newly
married couples, in relation to the momentous transition being
effected?

5 If we rephrase the powerful but powerfully abstract lines 4 and
5 of the extract, we might say that the speaker asserts: 'That
which the frail travelling coincidence held stood ready to be
loosed with all the power that being changed can give.' What
does this mean? How can this complex claim be paraphrased?
Why the verb *stood*, and what is it precisely that 'stands' and is
'ready to be loosed'? Where, in this commentary, are the
specific characters (the speaker, the newlyweds) formerly
introduced into the poem? Indeed, where is the train itself?
Is it entirely clear, for example, what is being referred to by
the phrase *this frail travelling coincidence*? It would seem to be
something rather more complex and intangible than the mere
train or the train-journey, although these are the occasion out
of which the description emerges.

ACTIVITY 3

Now I would like you to use process-and-participant analysis in a
comparative context. Below are two contrasting passages, taken from

the opening and the middle, respectively, of a near-contemporary novel: J. M. Coetzee's *Life & Times of Michael K*. The *K* of passage 2 is the *Michael K* of passage 1, but by the time of passage 2 Michael is living, alone, on an abandoned farm out in the country, hiding from guerrillas and security forces. The specific analytical tasks I would like you to do are given after the passages.

PASSAGE 1

The first thing the midwife noticed about Michael K when she helped him out of his mother into the world was that he had a hare lip. The lip curled like a snail's foot, the left nostril gaped. Obscuring the child for a moment from its mother, she prodded open the tiny bud of a mouth and was thankful to find the palate whole.

To the mother she said: 'You should be happy, they bring luck to the household.' But from the first Anna K did not like the mouth that would not close and the living pink flesh it bared to her. She shivered to think of what had been growing in her all these months. The child could not suck from the breast and cried with hunger. She tried a bottle; when it could not suck from the bottle she fed it with a teaspoon, fretting with impatience when it coughed and spluttered and cried. 'It will close up as he grows older,' the midwife promised. However, the lip did not close, or did not close enough, nor did the nose come straight.

She took the child with her to work and continued to take it when it was no longer a baby. Because their smiles and whispers hurt her, she kept it away from other children. Year after year Michael K sat on a blanket watching his mother polish other people's floors, learning to be quiet.

PASSAGE 2

Among the seeds he had sown had been a melon seed. Now two pale green melons were growing on the far side of the field. It seemed to him that he loved these two, which he thought of as two sisters, even more than the pumpkins, which he thought of as a bank of brothers. Under the melons he placed pads of grass so that their skins should not bruise.

Then came the evening when the first pumpkin was ripe enough to cut. It had grown earlier and faster than the others, in the very centre of the field; K had marked it out as the first fruit, the firstborn. The shell was soft, the knife sank in without a struggle. The flesh, though still rimmed with green, was a deep orange. On the wire grid he had made he laid strips of pumpkin over a bed of coals that glowed brighter and brighter as the dark came on. The fragrance of the burning flesh rose into the sky. Speaking the words he had been taught, directing them no longer upward but to the earth on which he knelt, he prayed: 'For what we are about to receive make us truly thankful.' With two wire skewers he turned the strips, and in mid-act felt his heart suddenly flow over with thankfulness. It was exactly as they had described it, like a gush of warm water. Now it is completed, he said to himself. All that remains is to live here quietly for the rest of my life, eating the food that my own labour has made the earth to yield.

1   Label all the processes and participants in each passage, indicating via square brackets any 'embedded' processes (i.e. processes which appear in clauses subordinate to some matrix clause and process).

2   Comment on which participant role(s) Michael K commonly fills in passage 1, and which roles he rarely fills there.

3   Comment on which participant role(s) Michael K commonly fills in passage 2.

4   How has Michael K changed, from passage 1 to passage 2, judging by the transitivity presentation of him in the later scene? (§)

As you become more familiar with the process-and-participant descriptive system, I hope that you will begin to see the range of ways in which it can potentially be used in textual analysis. Stylisticians frequently invoke transitivity analysis when looking at situations where one person (or a group) controls another. But it might be worth considering just how infrequent and atypical such a pattern is or should be. I would suggest that experiential structures with the sequence agent–material process–medium–t, where both participants are human, may be somewhat exceptional, and not at all the norm of many kinds of discourse. A text in which one individual is in a position frequently to fill the agentive role, with another individual as medium, in a nonmetaphorical process, is arguably a situation of exceptional power or exceptional intimacy (the canonical exemplar processes being, perhaps, hitting and kissing, respectively). There may be an overlooked parallel here, with those situations in which the 'intimate' second-person pronoun (*thou, tu, Du,* etc.) is or was used. In the broadest terms, the pronouns *tu, Du,* etc., are only used either mutually by intimates (e.g., lovers) or nonsymmetrically, by an assumed superior to an inferior (but not the reverse). It may be that something parallel applies to the agent–material process–medium–t structure: that it is frequent only in descriptions of the interaction either of intimates or of the very powerful acting upon the powerless. But only detailed study of actual language use can support or disprove this speculation.

I have suggested, above, that mediums be 'subcategorized' into three distinct classes, process-initiating human mediums (*Mary,* in *Mary painted well*) and target-denoting ones (*The spy* in *The spy was broken in three days*), and nonhuman mediums (*The plate* in *The plate broke in two*). Animate subject NPs in intransitive material process clauses will typically be medium-i, i.e., typically denote a medium participant who is also the initiator rather than the target of the process denoted: *Mary painted well, Jim laughed, The women strolled along the beach.*

However, there are a few verbs which, in context, allow for either a medium-i or medium-t interpretation of the intransitive animate subject, depending on the understood situation and the participant's controlling agency:

> *The clown flew through the air, when released from the enormous catapult.*

> *She flew through the air, skilfully steering the glider.*

The most useful probe procedure in such cases is to ask youself whether the given sentence more appropriately answers the question 'What did [the subject] *do?*' – in which case that human subject is a medium-i or 'What *happened* to [the Subject]?' – in which case that human subject is a medium-t. (For more on this topic, see Lyons, 1978: 356.)

BODY PARTS AS AGENT METONYMS

Despite the subcategories which have already been introduced, the analytical system described in this chapter remains quite broad-grained and one invariably encounters, often quite frequently, textual examples which do not fit comfortably the 'grid' of categories set up so far. This is perhaps most noticeable with material process clauses. What, for example, is one to do with sentences like the following:

1   *He returned to the surface of the lakse. His lungs expelled the air forcefully.*

2   *His hand brushed her cheek tenderly.*

Specifically, how should *His lungs* in 1 and *His hand* in 2 be classified? Since *the air* and *her cheek* are the medium in each case, one is inclined to apply one of the other participant labels; but body-parts like lungs and hands are quite unlike typical forces (which are usually natural causes), and are somewhat unlike typical instruments, in being integral non-detachable parts of an intending human participant. Did the individual in sentence 2 *use* his hand in the way one might use a key to open a door or a fist to pound a table? (What, you might ask, is the difference between a hand and a fist? Arguably hands are intrinsic and permanent body-parts in a way that fists are not: you *make a fist* before you punch something, but you cannot ?*make a hand*. But these are deep semantic waters!) Much depends on the degree to which you regard the male participant in 1 and 2 as expelling air or brushing the cheek *intentionally*: to the extent that these are intentional, they seem material rather than behavioural, and to some degree agentive. And yet, very clearly, *His lungs* and *His hand* do not look like our typical intentional human agent; they denote parts of a human being, rather than the intending individual as a whole. The solution I propose is that such cases be annotated as 'agent metonyms', on the grounds that, while in themselves they appear quite instrument-like, at the same time they 'stand in' for an inferrable agent, being a very *part* of that agent, in a way that classic instruments (keys, calculators) do not. 'Agent metonyms' imply a participating agent, without explicitly specifying him, her, or them; usually that implied agent is easily retrieved from adjacent discourse. When agent metonyms are extensively used in a passage, the motivations may be various; often an effect of detachment or alienation, between an individual and their physical faculties, is conveyed. Or a sense is created of the 'diminished responsibility' of someone for how their own body is acting: a memorable example of this is Conrad's depiction of Winnie Verloc's revenge killing of her husband in *The Secret Agent*. In that remarkable passage, indeed, not only Mrs Verloc's physical faculties, but even genuine instruments such as the murder weapon, repeatedly take over the 'doer' role, and Mrs Verloc as a culpable agent is scarcely mentioned (see the discussion of this passage in Kennedy, 1982).

Process-and-participant reconfigurations

We saw, in Chapter 3, that modality in English is sometimes expressed by rather indirect or unexpected means, in which metaphorical phrases may be used in place of the conventional modal verbs and adverbs: phrases like *a sure-fire thing*, to express strong probability, for example. A directly related tendency is apparent with respect to processes and participants. In particular, you will find many cases in which you may feel that while *superficially* you are being presented with one kind of process (a relational one, for example), *underlyingly* another kind of process (e.g. a material one) is implied. In effect, such clauses can be labelled twice over, in terms of both their surface and their underlying sense. Here are a couple of examples of this. Suppose your sentence for analysis reads

> *That new Suede CD really blew me away.*

Superficially, this is a material process with accompanying medium-t and force; but underlyingly you could well argue that this is simply a figurative way of expressing what is really a mental process, with the album as phenomenon, not force. Also very common is the case involving a participant which, being a nominalization, itself entails a backgrounded process:

> *Western prevarication was a disgrace.*

The carrier in this relational process is not merely a nominal entity, as a basic carrier would be, but also logically a material process (answering the question 'What happened?': *The West prevaricated*).

Time out: what is a nominalization?

A large set of basic nouns are 'things', stable or inactive. But some nouns or noun phrases, which look like stable 'things' or 'facts' simply by virtue of being noun phrases (and not verbs), directly entail an activity or verbal procedure. In a hidden way, they are clause-size activities re-packaged as isolated stable things; this process of turning a clause-size process into a noun-phrase-size thing is called nominalization. Take the phrase *global pollution*: this is a nominalization which bundles up, into the background, the clausal activity it entails: *Someone/something pollutes the globe*. Similarly, with *hirings* (as in *Seasonal hirings are at an all-time low*): *hirings* entails the clause *X hires/has hired Y*. Nominalizations are often an invaluable means of packing dense information into text, but they are also notoriously ideologically charged – e.g. when, during the war in Vietnam, the US government referred to their bombing activities as *pacification*.

A third example of process reconfiguration is the following, taken from Halliday (1994: 344):

> *The guests' supper was followed by a gentle swim.*

What is basically a relational process (one activity was after another) is recast as if it were a material one, of *following*: clearly dinner wasn't followed by a swim in the way that the thieves' getaway car might be followed by the police. But in order for us to see this 'double' analysis of the sentence, we have to share the view that there is a more 'basic' meaning of *follow* and a more idiomatic or figurative one. Similarly, with *blow* as used in the first example: do you agree that *blow* is primarily a material process and that only in secondary circumstances does it mean 'astound and inspire'? Doubts and difficulties about whether particular sentences merit a double analysis usually stem from differing judgements about the meaning and metaphoricality of the verbs involved; and those differences of opinion are perfectly legitimate.

The foregoing is an inevitably simplified and abbreviated outline of the process-and-participant grammar of English. When you turn to actual texts you are sure to find difficult sentences where it is hard to decide quite what process and what participants are involved, and whether some are missing or not. Two useful rules of thumb:

1   Always try out paraphrase sentences to help you see which kind of process is underlyingly involved.

2   Set greater store by the underlying analysis.

Activities

ACTIVITY 4

Here is a sample annotation of the processes and participants *in the finite clauses only*, of a passage from Nadine Gordimer's novel *The Conservationist*. The passage describes conditions in a South African township, around 1970. After reviewing this labelling, comment on any tendencies you notice in the way particular processes or participant roles are used in the description of the township people, and on what cumulative effect these create.

medium   mat.   mat.
Thousands of pieces of paper take to the air and are plastered

circ.   force   mat.
against the location fence when the August winds come. The

medium
assortment of covering worn by the children and old people

mat.   circ.
who scavenge the rubbish dump is moulded against their

mat.   circ.   carrier rel.
bodies or bloated away from them. Sometimes the wind is

attribute
strong enough to cart-wheel sheets of board and send boxes

medium mat.   circ.
slamming over and over until they slither across the road and

mat.   medium   mat.   circ.
meet the obstacle of the fence, or are flattened like the bodies

of cats or dogs under the wheels of the traffic. The newspaper,

*carrier   *rel   *attribute
ash, bones and smashed bottles come from the location; the

*carrier   *rel.   *Attribute
boxes and board and straw come from the factories and

warehouses not far across the veld where many of the location

medium mat.   agent   mat.
people work. People waiting at the roadside for buses cover

medium   instrument
their mouths with woollen scarves against the red dust;

[mat. med instr.]   agent
so   do   the women who sit at their pitches selling

carrier
oranges or yellow mealies roasting on braziers. The scavengers

rel. attribute   carr. rel. attrib.
are patient–leisurely or feeble, it's difficult, in passing, to judge

carrier   [Agent
– and their bare feet and legs and the hands with which they

mat.   medium] *rel. attribute   circ.   medium
pick over the dirt are coated grey with ash. Two of the older

mat.   circ.   medium
children from the farm go to school in the location. They

mat.   circ.   [med. mat.]   circ.
could return as they come, across the veld and through the

[agent mat.   medium   circ.]
gap cut in the fence by gangs who bring stolen goods in that

agent   mat.   medium   circ.
way, but they lengthen the long walk home by going to have a

    medium agent   mat.   circ.   senser mental
look at what people are seeking, on the dump. They do not

    phen. [phen. senser mental]   senser mental phen.
know what it is they would hope to find; they learn   that

[identifed [med.   agent mat.] rel. identifier [phenom.   senser
what experienced ones seek   is   whatever they

    mental]]   senser   mental   phenom.
happen to find. They have seen an ash-covered forefinger the
size of their own dipping into a sardine-tin under whose

                           circ. [medium   mat.]
curled-back top some oil still shone. When the oil was licked

   exist.   existent
up there was still the key to be unravelled from the tin. There

   exist.   existent
have been odd shoes, casts of bunions and misshapen toes in

                            carrier
sweat and dirt and worn leather; a broken hat. The old tyres

rel. attribute   circ.   [agent   mat. medium]
are hardest to get because people make sandals out of them.

   circ.   [medium   mat.
From hoardings along the railway line, which also runs

                                 ]medium
through the industries, providing sidings, black men with

                      mat.   circ.
strong muscles and big grins look down, brushing their
teeth, drinking canned beer or putting money in a savings

           sayer   verbal
bank. Industries and factories announce themselves – gas

  (said?)
welding, artistic garden pots, luxury posture-corrective

    [carr. rel.   attrib]
mattresses, THIS IS THE HOME OF FIAT.

Notes: bear in mind that this is just one possible analysis of the finite
clauses of the passage and that, given the complexity of the writing,
there are likely to be points where you may disagree with my analysis.
For example, I have asterisked the analysis, as a relational process, of
The newspapers . . . come from the location: I regard the *come from* here
as a variant of *are from* (compare *These oranges come from Florida* =
These oranges are Floridian), and have set aside the 'active' material
process sense that usually associates with *come*. The analytical decision
might have been different if the text had read *The newspapers came
from the location*. Note also that analyses within square brackets are
those of subordinate clauses. Perhaps the most complex of these here,

which is not well displayed in the linear labelling above, is that of the half-sentence: *they learn that what experienced ones seek is whatever they happen to find*. I treat this as a projecting mental process (they learn + phenom.), where the phenomenon 'learnt' is a relational clause, 'that X is Y', and where the particular X is itself a material process and the Y is a mental one:

Senser	ment.	phenomenon
they	*learn*	*that what experienced ones seek is whatever they happen to find.*
		[identified rel. identifier]
		medium agent mat. phenom. senser mental

Undoubtedly, with this sentence and with several others, variant analyses are possible.

ACTIVITY 5

In the following poem, which kind of transitivity processes are relatively prominent? Why so?

Dover Beach

The sea is calm tonight.
The tide is full, the moon lies fair
Upon the straits – on the French coast the light
Gleams and is gone; the cliffs of England stand,
Glimmering and vast, out in the tranquil bay.
Come to the window, sweet is the night air!
Only, from the long line of spray
Where the sea meets the moon-blanched land,
Listen! you hear the grating roar
Of pebbles which the waves draw back, and fling,
At their return, up the high strand,
Begin, and cease, and then again begin,
With tremulous cadence slow, and bring
The eternal note of sadness in.

Sophocles long ago
Heard it on the Aegean, and it brought
Into his mind the turbid ebb and flow
Of human misery; we
Find also in the sound a thought,
Hearing it by this distant northern sea.

The Sea of Faith
Was once, too, at the full, and round earth's shore

Lay like the folds of a bright girdle furled.
But now I only hear
Its melancholy, long, withdrawing roar,
Retreating, to the breath
Of the night wind, down the vast edges drear
And naked shingles of the world.

Ah, love, let us be true
To one another! for the world, which seems
To lie before us like a land of dreams,
So various, so beautiful, so new,
Hath really neither joy, nor love, nor light,
Nor certitude, nor peace, nor help for pain;
And we are here as on a darkling plain
Swept with confused alarms of struggle and flight,
Where ignorant armies clash by night.

Matthew Arnold, *c.*1851

ACTIVITY 6

Identify and label all the processes and participants (in the transivity terms we have reviewed) used in the final two stanzas of Lowell's draft poem 'Inspiration', and the poem this turned into, 'Skunk Hour' (these are supplied in Activity 3 of Chapter 1, pp. 16–17). Try to be as systematic and methodical as possible, listing all the instances of material processes, mental processes, etc., and also listing who or what is what kind of participant in those processes. And in particular I would like you to consider whether any significant differences – in the content, tone or message – between the draft version and the final poem, are highlighted by this analysis. How many two-participant material processes (i.e., with both a medium and an agent) do you find in each version? Do the processes and participants, or the way of presenting particular participants, change, from the draft to the final poem? How, with what effects? (NB: read each of these poems in full; but analyse here just their final two stanzas.)

ACTIVITY 7

Let us close with a sublime Shakespearean sonnet, on the oldest tragic theme, 'time conquers all'. If you agree that this is indeed the sonnet's theme – at least until the final couplet – you might think about what simple paraphrases this gives rise to: *time consumes life and beauty*; *time is a destroyer*; *time is ruthless*; *humankind is mortal*; and so on. In short, simple material and relational process clauses, with time as agent or carrier, humankind as medium or entailed within the medium, or as carrier. Now look closely at the variety and ingenuity of process-types and participant roles that Shakespeare actually creates, for time, human beauty, and decay, in the sonnet. Comment on the diversity you find, and particularly comment on the processes and participants you find in the 'resolving' final couplet.

Sonnet 65

Since brass, nor stone, nor earth, nor boundless sea
But sad mortality o'er-sways their power,
How with this rage shall beauty hold a plea,
Whose action is no stronger than a flower?
O how shall summer's honey breath hold out
Against the wreckful siege of batt'ring days,
When rocks impregnable are not so stout,
Nor gates of steel so strong, but Time decays?
O fearful meditation! where, alack,
Shall Time's best jewel from Time's chest lie hid?
Or what strong hand can hold his swift foot back?
Or who his spoil of beauty can forbid?
O, none, unless this miracle have might,
That in black ink my love may still shine bright.

(1609)

Incidentally, the topics covered in earlier chapters should be beginning to be useful, in combination with those covered in this chapter. For instance, Shakespeare's sonnets are extraordinarily rich in their exploitation of kinds of cohesion, particularly ellipsis cohesion. 'Understood' phrases are widely ellipted. Thus when the poem asks:

O how shall summer's honey breath hold out
Against the wreckful siege of batt'ring days,
When rocks impregnable are not so stout,
Nor gates of steel so strong, but Time decays?

one thing the speaker categorically is *not* saying is that 'Time decays'. Rather the speaker says that Time decays even impregnable rocks and gates of steel, and the speaker says this without supplying a reference cohesion second mention of those impregnables (e.g. *them*).

Commentaries

ACTIVITY 1

2 *Jack and Jill went up the hill/ to fetch a pail of water;*
mediums   mat. circ.   circ.[containing mat.+medium]

Jack   fell down/ and broke his crown/ and Jill came tumbling after.
medium mat. circ. (agent) mat. medium   medium mat.   circ. circ.

Up Jack got/ and home did trot/ as fast as he could caper;
circ. medium mat.   circ. mat.   circ.[containing med.+material pro.]

He   went to bed/ to mend his head with vinegar and brown paper.
medium mat. circ. circ.[containing mat.+medium+circ.]

3 (a) Most of the process and participant labelling here is
relatively straightforward, but the case of the torturer's horse
that *scratches its innocent behind on a tree* might seem problematic. The horse is no conscious human participant, so hardly
merits classification as an agent, even if there is something
almost human about its casual scratching. Since *its behind* is
the indispensable medium of the process, the system draws us
to classify *the torturer's horse* as a second medium. This is not
an unreasonable solution; you will find that material processes
do occasionally involve two distinct mediums.

ACTIVITY 3

4 The Michael K of passage 1, on the basis of a process analysis
as well as by other means, is a profoundly powerless and
dehumanized individual. Sentences repeatedly cast him as
powerless medium-t in material processes, and in addition
allude not to him, as a whole person, but to various of his
body parts (*the pink flesh, the lip, the nose*). Occasionally, like
other babies, he is behaver in behavioural process clauses: *The
child could not suck from the breast and cried with hunger.* By
means of its construction, the opening sentence treats
Michael's birth as less significant than his hare lip, and treats
the experience of Michael and his mother as less significant
than 'what the midwife noticed'. Perhaps the nadir of dehu-
manization is reached in the clause which reports that
Michael's mother *kept it* [sic] *away from other children.* Michael
never interacts as agent with other people. Only one clause
represents him as a senser of a mental process, but this turns

out to be a cruel perversion of true childhood development: he sits, *learning to be quiet*.

In vivid contrast, Michael K emerges as a full human being, independent and self-controlling, in passage 2. Not only does he occupy centre-stage in a world extensively peopled by his thoughts, his mental processing; furthermore, these thoughts advance to the metaphorical, as when he thinks of the melons and pumpkins as sisters and brothers. He is repeatedly agent in material process clauses, material processes involving plans and purposes rather than extempore reaction: *Under the melons he placed pads of grass so that their skins should not bruise.* (Where passage 1 had dehumanized Michael to the status of a vegetable, Michael's contribution to passage 2 elevates the vegetables to the status of humans.) No matter that no other human beings are present, in this passage Michael also speaks (is sayer of verbal processes). The scene clearly has an especially charged nature in several respects; it is a pastoral communion service with several echoes of Christ's passion which could have seemed tasteless in a different setting (the gush of warm water, the acknowledgement of release. *Now it is completed*). Part of the heightened stylistic quality is achieved by the text's transitions from narrative to indirect discourse to free indirect discourse (*it was exactly as they had desribed it, like a gush of warm water*) to the direct discourse of the final sentence. (These kinds of speech- and thought-rendering are explained at length in Chapter 5.)

5

Recording speech and thought

When you tell a simple narrative, you tell an addressee about some significant event or change that, typically, has been experienced by some character. In literary narratives, the writer usually tells of multiple events affecting several related characters. The simplest way of doing this is by reporting basic events, in the third or first person, and in the simple past or present tense. This we might call 'basic narration', and is more fully discussed in Chapter 6. But even in oral narratives of personal experience, people go to some trouble to make their narratives more interesting, more evaluated, and more 'tellable'. Flat, chronicle-like telling is displaced by various ways of showing, performing, or acting out of the story. We make the characters speak or think 'in their own words'.

Imagine you are telling a friend about how, yesterday lunchtime when you were walking down the street, a young man in sharp office-worker's suit came up to you and asked you if you were interested in halving your heating bills and helping protect the ozone layer at the same time. How do you relate your reaction to this enquiry, in the story you're telling your friend? Here are some options:

1 *I said I wasn't interested and walked on.*

2 *I wasn't interested, and walked on.*

3 *I shrugged and walked on.*

4 *I didn't say anything but I was thinking to myself 'What a bore!'*

5 *I said 'Sure, but not right now.'*

6 *And I'm like 'Puh-leaze'.*

7 *And I'm like* [makes waving away gesture].

8 [You roll your eyes upwards, and take a deep breath.]

These eight alternative 'responses' are not, in the telling of the story, entirely equivalent, of course; but I'd say they are all possible. And, roughly, they range from least engaged, most told, most reported, to most engaged, most shown, most performed. And in highly performed versions, like number 8, you seem temporarily to stop being the narrator, and become the character – something which is not at all true of numbers 1–3.

This is all by way of preamble to considering the specific issue of narrative dramatization, and of how narrative showing can seem to take over from narrative telling, in the displaying of characters' speech and thought.

The basic options in the displaying of a given character's words or thoughts are exemplified by the following two sentences:

9   *She said, 'I'm sorry I can't stop right now.'*

10   *She wondered why those types always picked out her to ask.*

Notice, first, that each of these sentences comprises a matrix clause (*She said, She wondered*) and a dependent clause. Here we shall call the matrix clause the framing clause, for the obvious reason that it supplies a frame, telling you who it is who is doing the speaking or thinking; relatedly the 'framer' of the framing clause is always the narrator: it is the narrator, not any character, who in number 9 tells you that a certain *She* performed an act of saying. In all the following sentences, the framing clause is the narrator's, directly. It is the 'ownership' of the dependent clause, in each case, which is more variable and interesting.

The dependent clause in both of the above (numbers 9 and 10) is recording, in some form, the character's speech or thought. The dependent clause in 9 is of course direct speech, since it purports to be a direct and verbatim copy of precisely what the individual actually said. By convention, everything between the speech marks 'belongs to' the specified speaker, directly. In 10, the dependent clause is one of indirect thought; it purports to be a reliable report of what the individual thought, though it is not a verbatim copy – which is why it is called indirect. Specifically, no one would be likely to think to themselves this actual sequence of words:

Why those types always picked out her to ask?

What the speaker might have thought to themselves would be something like this:

Why do these types always pick out me to ask?

As a result, a third format, in addition to direct speech and indirect thought, emerges as an option in narratives. It is direct thought:

11   *She wondered to herself, 'Why do those types always pick out me to ask?'*

Structurally, direct thought is identical to direct speech, the only difference being that one reports 'heard words' while the other reports 'internal words'. (NB: from now on I will sometimes abbreviate direct thought as DT, indirect thought as IT, etc.).

Several grammatical features of the dependent clause in 10 highlight its difference from a direct version; the differences are easier to see when we put the two clauses together:

< DT >
She wondered, 'Why do these types always pick out me to ask?'.

< IT >
She wondered why those types always picked out her to ask.

The major differences are as follows:

i   IT has tense shifted to match the tense of the surrounding narrative; DT stays in the 'original' present tense.

ii   IT questions lack the subj–aux inversion of the 'original' question.

iii   IT shifts any deictic items from the direct thinker's orientation to that of the framing narrator (here, *me* ⇒ *her*, *these types* ⇒ *those types*).

iv   Although it doesn't show up in the example above, various 'colourful' expressions and interjections of a character, which are acceptable in direct thought, cannot very naturally carry over into an IT version, e.g. *Hell!*:

She wondered, 'Why do these types always pick out me to ask? Hell!'. (DT)

? She wondered why those types always picked out her to ask, Hell. (IT)

Given the above contrasts between IT and DT, which seem to favour DT as more versatile, dramatic, etc., one might wonder why one would ever use IT. But then I just did, in the last sentence. Pay attention! (direct speech). Given the above contrasts between IT and DT, which seem to favour DT as more versatile, dramatic, etc., one might wonder 'Why does anyone ever use anything other than DT?' But DT, as in the immediately preceding sentence, can often seem *too* dramatic. In lots of situations a narrator may prefer not to foreground a character's every word, by rendering it in direct form.

For one thing, DS or DT rendering tends to imply narratorial respect for a character, and that, as teller, you don't mind your readers getting 'close' to the character in this way, by encountering their direct words or thoughts. And, on another tack, for a writer to produce direct speech or thought is fraught with difficulties: imagine you had to write a page reporting, through indirect speech, what Bill said to Hillary at breakfast this morning; now imagine you had to write a page reporting what he said in direct speech. The latter, I think, might be much harder to get right, and easy to get wrong: *Pass thuh honeh, honeh.*

So far, as forms for recording characters' words or thoughts, we have surveyed DS, IT and DT. An obvious fourth option, then, is IS, indirect speech. Sentence 12 below is the IS version of sentence 9, which is DS:

9   She said, 'I'm sorry I can't stop right now.'

12   She said she was sorry but that she couldn't stop right then.

As you can see, all the items listed under roman numerals i–iv above, highlighting the differences between DT and IT, also distinguish DS from IS. And what that entails is that in very many respects DS and DT are very similar – certainly grammatically – while IS and IT are also alike. You will therefore often find these pairs 'collapsed' into the simple binary contrast of direct discourse and indirect discourse:

direct discourse   vs.   indirect discourse

| |

direct speech   indirect speech
direct thought   indirect thought

Now we have four common discourse-representing categories (DS, IS, DT and IT); just two pairs more to go!

Question: what is the difference between the direct discourse sentences in 9 and 11, and sentences 13 and 14?

9   She said, 'I'm sorry I can't stop right now.'

11   She wondered to herself, 'Why do those types always pick out me to ask?'

13   I'm sorry I can't stop right now.

14   Why do those types always pick out me to ask?

Answer: not a great deal, except that the quotation marks are absent in the latter versions and, much more importantly, the framing clause (*She said/She wondered to herself*) is gone. Sentences such as 13 and 14 are kinds of direct speech and thought, respectively, but in being 'free' of a narrator's framing clause they are specifically free direct speech and free direct thought sentences.

Imagine how sentence 14, the FDT version, might continue:

> Why do those types always pick out me to ask? Must think I'm some sort of soft touch. Idiots! Must see if that Enya album is in at Tower Records before I go to the bank. Cross quickly, any cops about? They're always around when you don't need them. Ticketing for jaywalking while Rome burns; pathetic! Whoops, are you gonna stop, mister? . . . thanks . . . everyone in a hurry . . . stop and smell the . . . what? roses? . . . concrete more like, coffee sure . . .

By the end of the passage above, what we are reading is something that has every appearance of being the verbatim 'mental flow' of the character from whom it comes; this style has long been termed stream-of-consciousness (also known as 'interior monologue'). Thus we can see that stream-of-consciousness is at the 'loose' end of free direct thought; it is FDT with various sentence-grammar conventions relaxed or absent. And it is because free direct thought can so easily modulate into stream-of-consciousness that it merits recognition as a significantly different kind of reporting from framed direct thought (a parallel significant difference separates FDS from DS).

We now have six distinct categories of speech- or thought-representation:

FDT	DT	IT
FDS	DS	IS

Given the features being combined here (+/− free; direct vs. indirect; and thought vs speech), it is clear that just two styles remain to be noted, two styles whose emergence is, as it were, guaranteed in advance. These are two styles of speech- and thought-representation which did, indeed, emerge many hundreds of years later than some of the other forms and, in some ways, are much the most interesting:

FDT	DT	IT	**FIT**
FDS	DS	IS	**FIS**

Alongside FDT, DT and IT there is the intriguing hybrid known as FIT, free indirect thought; and alongside the speech options, there is FIS or free indirect speech. (Just as the other speech and thought pairs are sometimes collapsed, so too can this one be, into the category of FID, free indirect discourse.)

Some of the features of FID are similarly predictable, given its composition: it has some of the features of indirect speech or thought, but is 'free of' the framing clause of IS or IT. But if that were all that was involved, then since sentences 10 and 12, repeated here, are IT and IS, sentences 15 and 16 would be free indirect speech and free indirect thought:

10 She wondered why those types always picked out her to ask. IT

12 She said she was sorry but that she couldn't stop right then. IS

15 Why those types always picked out her to ask. ?FIT

16 She was sorry but that she couldn't stop right then. ?FIS

But sentences 15 and 16 clearly do not work: there is something wrong with both of them. Evidently, FID is a little more interesting than merely being ID with the framing clause lopped off. (Similarly, you might argue, stream-of-consciousness is rather more interesting than just DT with the framing clause lopped off.) How would you 'correct' sentences 15 and 16 in order to make them viable? Pencil in your own emendations now, before reading on.

I'm hoping that your amended versions of 15 and 16 might look like these:

15′ Why did those types always pick out her to ask?

16′ She was sorry but she couldn't stop right then.

In the amended version of 15, the *do* auxiliary has been introduced, along with subject–verb inversion and the addition of the final question mark – all features of direct discourse. In the amended version of 16, the only change is the removal of the clause-introducer *that* (a stark feature of indirect discourse, never used to introduce direct discourse utterances). In summary, the changes have made the sentences rather more direct-seeming than they would otherwise have been, more directly expressive of the speaking or thinking character. We have seen, summarized under roman numerals i–iv, what makes for directness as against indirectness in discourse-representation. In view of the comments under numeral iii, one can amend sentence 16 one step further towards the character's perspective, thus:

16″ She was sorry but she couldn't stop right now.

15′, 16′, and 16″ are all FID sentences (whether each one is spoken or merely thought, i.e. whether each is FIS or FIT, is secondary at this point, and can only really be decided in context). We shall treat 16″ as more canonically FID than 16′. A canonical, 'best exemplar' FID sentence contains an uncanny blend of direct discourse and indirect discourse features. Here, for ease of reference, I summarize those criteria of DD–ID contrast listed earlier:

i ID tense matches the surrounding narrative's tense; DD stays in the 'original' present tense.

ii ID questions lack the subj-aux inversion of the 'original' question.

iii ID shifts any deictic items from the direct speaker's or thinker's orientation to that of the framing narrator.

iv Various 'colourful' and 'characterful' expressions, acceptable in direct discourse, cannot very naturally carry over into an ID version.

How are these criteria present or absent, when we look at an FID sentence such as 16″, or the others that I supply below?

16″ *She was sorry but she couldn't stop right now.*

17 *Damn! The line was still busy! What on earth did they find to gas about for so long?*

18 *Surely his little mnouchkine would remember to bring them tonight.*

19 [Narrative sentence: *She grabbed the phone and frantically punched in Wally's number.*] *Could he come over straight away? Something bloody awful had happened.*

20 *And Old Ben too, Old Ben too; they would give him his paw back even, certainly they would give him his paw back.*

It seems that FID is like ID as far as i is concerned (i.e. tense is shifted); like DD as far as ii is concerned (i.e., direct question word-order); and like DD as far as iv is concerned. And there's a split-decision on iii: the addresser and addressee are denoted by third-person pronouns (*she, he*) if that's how they are denoted in the rest of the narrative (= indirect or narratorial orientation); but, in canonical FID, all other deictic forms reflect the addresser's own position (that is, they imply a direct or characterological orientation).

As noted, items under iv in FID are character-expressive just as they are in DD. But we can see from examples 17–19 that more kinds of 'character-expressivity' need to be listed under iv. In particular, we should add here expressions of modality, interjections, expletives, distinctive dialectalisms and colloquialisms, and emotive language.

By way of review, here are eight versions of roughly the same sentence, cast in the forms of speech and thought representation we have identified:

She said: 'I won't now, regardless of what you say.' (DS)

> She thought: 'I won't now, regardless of what you say.' (DT)
>
> I won't now, regardless of what you say. (FDS)
>
> I won't now, regardless of what you say. (FDT)
>
> She wouldn't now, regardless of what they said. (FIS)
>
> She wouldn't now, regardless of what they said. (FIT)
>
> She said (that) she wouldn't then, regardless of what they said. (IS)
>
> She thought (that) she wouldn't then, regardless of what they said. (IT)

These examples make clear the extent to which particular speech and thought forms are similar: outside of specific contextual circumstances, there is little difference between, e.g., FDS and FDT. Thus the eight versions reduce to four discoursal ones: DD, FDD, FID, and ID.

Now compare the ID versions above (the last two of the eight) with sentences such as these:

> She then decided she wouldn't, no matter what they said.
>
> She resolved not to, whatever the circumstances.
>
> She set her mind entirely against it.

If what the participant had actually thought or said was *I won't now, regardless of what you say*, then these last three renderings are more remote from that original, more indirect, than indirect discourse. There are scant traces of the character's voice in these versions, and the voice is fully narratorial. So these are a type of narrative sentence, but with the proviso that they narrate – in the narrator's words – the character's speaking or thinking. Certainly they are one move away from direct observation of events of the kind that so-called 'pure narrative' sentences relate, such as the following: *She laboured down the stairs, holding firmly to the banister.* As a result some analysts find it useful to specify a transitional category between indirect discourse representation and narration of visible physical actions (e.g. Leech and Short, 1981), a category of narrative reports of discoursal acts, NRDA; clearly the latter can be subdivided into NRTA and NRSA, depending on whether the narrative summary is of a character's thoughts or speech, respectively.

This brings us to one final crucial point. We have to remember to set all the foregoing options, for representing a character's words, beside the other dominant textual mode, plain or pure narrative (which I will abbreviate as PN). A typical literary narrative involves a subtle weaving of PN, DS, IS, DT, FIT, NRTA, etc. If we set aside the distinction between speech and thought, thus focusing on choices at the level of *discourse*, and if we treat NRDA as a sub-branch of narrative, then we can identify four major narrational modes:

```
        ID

PN    FID    DD
```

This is a very tentative attempt to represent, spatially, the relative nearness or distance of each mode from its partner modes: farthest apart, most sharply distinct, are pure narrative and direct discourse; intermediate between these two are indirect discourse and free indirect discourse, with the proviso that FID is closer to *both* pure narrative *and* direct discourse than ID is. Thus, again, FID has a special status. Because although FID does indeed display a mixture of features taken from both DD and ID, it is rarely in practice confused with these (DD will commonly be quite different in tense and pronouns, ID will always have the framing clause). What FID does get confused with is PN, pure narrative. For example, in some contexts, assuming a particular kind of intrusive, pushy narrator (the kind that snaps 'Pay attention!' at the reader), sentence 17' could be read as PN rather than FID:

17'   The line was still busy! What on earth did they find to gas about for so long?

That is, 17' could be read as expressing the narrator's viewpoint and (sincere?) question, rather than the character's. And if this uncertainty recurs many times through a narrative, readers can form very different interpretations of the 'same' character and narrator, depending on whether they treat such 'ambiguous' sentences as revealing the character's mind or the narrator's.

The question then arises, how can we distinguish or tease apart pure narrative from free indirect discourse? The broad test is that of seeing whether it 'sounds right' to treat the sentence you are inspecting as coming from the narrator to you, or as essentially, and despite the third-person pronouns (and, usually, past tense) as coming from a character to him- or herself or to another character. Let us see this at work in an extended passage. The text below is taken from Brian Moore's novel, *The Temptation of Eileen Hughes*, set in Ulster in the 1980s. In this passage, Eileen's aged mother is introduced.

When she had finished doing her face, Agnes Hughes went downstairs, taking a good hold on the banister as she went. Pain is normal, it's a warning, and it's not necessarily something for you to be alarmed about, the doctor had said. And the other doctor, the specialist at the Royal Victoria Hospital in Belfast, had told her she should try as far as possible to lead a normal life. That was what she was trying to do. And maybe next spring, if she kept on improving, she would finally get to Toronto. She went down carefully and along the back hall to the kitchen. The kitchen looked out on a narrow back yard, with a ten-foot-high brick wall around it. She had put geraniums in pots to cheer up the yard, but the trouble was the sun had to fight its way in there. Twenty-three years she had lived in this house and could count the days you didn't have to switch the light on in the kitchen. She switched it on now as she went in. The kitchen clock said ten to eight. Eileen would probably ring early. Anyway, no need to worry about hurrying to the phone. Eileen knew it took her a minute to get there. She had thought of her daughter a lot these past days, thought of her away there in London. London and New York and Paris were the places Eileen dreamed about, and now she was in London with the McAuleys, who would show her the best of everything and make her fall in love with it altogether. She was lucky, wasn't she? But, on reflection, Agnes Hughes did not think her daughter was lucky. All this holiday would do would be to make her pine to go to London and live there. Which she can't do with me around her neck. She's not lucky, Eileen, she never was lucky. She was born at the wrong time. Ever since she was old enough to go out and play, there's been no playing in the streets here in Lismore. Nothing but British Army patrols and searches and bombs and shootings and burn-outs. And, going on these fifteen years, nobody goes out at night. Children used to be able to go off after teatime to play with their friends in one another's houses, and girls used to go off to dances, you never worried so long as they weren't home too late, so long as some boy didn't have them off up a lane. It's not boys the people worry about now: I wish it were. It's bombs and bullets. And the people don't see each other the way they used to: the old life is gone forever, everybody stays at home, stuck up to the telly, you never go over to your neighbour's, is it any wonder there's more drink and tranquillizers than ever?

Our interest is in distinguishing, where this is appropriate, between pure narrative text and free indirect discourse text. And I have suggested that this is best done by assessing the 'attributability' of the general wording (setting personal pronouns and tense on one side temporarily) to a character rather than a narrator. Let us review the passage's opening sentence. This runs:

> When she had finished doing her face, Agnes Hughes went downstairs, taking a good hold on the banister as she went.

Now the question is whether we see this as 'coming' from a narrator or (allowing for tense and pronoun adjustments) from the character, Agnes Hughes. Is this plausibly interpreted as the following:

> (I, the narrator, am telling you, the reader, that) When she had finished doing her face, Agnes Hughes went downstairs, taking a good hold on the banister as she went. = PN

Or is it more plausibly interpreted as telling us that:

> (I, Agnes Hughes, am telling myself that) When I have finished doing my face, I go downstairs, taking a good hold on the banister as I go. = FID

Clearly there's no question: even bending the rules to convert the phrase *Agnes Hughes* to *I* in the latter version, this version still looks and sounds bizarre: people just don't produce running commentaries on their routine physical actions in this way. The opening is clearly narrative (PN). But now consider the sentence just five lines further on, by which point the text is turning to Agnes's possible future plans, if she stays well:

> And maybe next spring, if she kept on improving, she would finally get to Toronto.

Using the same interpretation test again, is this underlyingly:

> (I, the narrator, am telling you, the reader, that) (And) maybe next spring, if she kept on improving, she would finally get to Toronto.

Or is it underlyingly:

> (I, Agnes Hughes, am telling myself that) (And) maybe next spring, if I keep on improving, I will finally get to Toronto.

Who is hoping here, character or narrator? Whose *maybe* is this – the narrator's or the character's? The character's, I'd say. Therefore the sentence is free indirect discourse.

Activities

ACTIVITY 1

Work through the rest of the Agnes Hughes passage, deciding who speaks, who thinks (character or narrator, and if character, directly or indirectly) each successive clause and sentence. On that basis you should be able to label each successive textual chunk. To simplify matters slightly, you might wish to use just the discoursal labels initially – DD, ID, FDD and FID – together, of course, with PN and NRDA.

Having charted the various shifts in the passage, from one narrational mode to another, can you begin to answer the question why Brian Moore might have adopted the modes, and the shifts in mode, that you find? Are the choices well motivated, in terms of the topic or the character they present? Why not have the entire passage in pure narrative, or direct discourse? Comment on this issue of the 'fit' between narrative modes and characterization. (§)

Why study speech- and thought-modes?

The question may by now have arisen in your minds, 'Why devote so much time and detailed attention to these distinctions between PN, FIT, DS, and so on?'. The best answer to this should emerge from the activities that follow. If you find that keeping in mind the categories I have mentioned is useful, when you attempt close analysis of the way authors modulate from narration to 'internal' character-reflection, then focusing on those categories is worthwhile. Looking at the grammar of these speech and thought modes, as we are doing here, is part and parcel of the broader effort to recognize and understand **the grammar of effect and affect**. How does a narrator ironize a character's views: FID is often an effective vehicle. How does a narrator indicate that a character's precise words are not of great importance: by using IS or NRSA. How does a narrator sometimes suggest that a character's (important) **spoken words** are either particularly admirable or particularly distasteful? By relaying them in direct speech, giving the impression that the character is an independent individual, speaking on their own behalf in fully their own terms. How does a narrator sometimes suggest that a character's **articulated thoughts** are particularly worthy of attention? By reporting them as fully as a chronicling observer usually can, namely in indirect thought. By contrast, if a narrator reports a character by means of direct thought, this can be interpreted as an enormous presumption – the presumption that I, the narrator, can 'see inside the heads of' my characters, and can render their thoughts in the first person. Thus indirect thought is a kind of 'norm' for reporting characters' thoughts (see Leech and Short, 1981, for more on this notion), while, by extension, *free* indirect thought is often an attractive alternative to IT, dispensing with the formality of *she thought that* clauses, creating the 'character-alignedness' of the character's dialect and orientational words, while not crossing that notional boundary of plausibility and 'respect for characterological independence' that seems involved in moving from third-person narration to direct thought – a kind of invasive excess.

So the short answer to the question 'Why study the modes of speech and thought presentation?' is that, as addressees, we should always be thinking about who it is that is speaking to us, particularly in those situations where one speaker, a reporter, is merely a channel for some other individual's words. Or seems to be merely a channel. Politicians and political analysts these days are acutely sensitive to the differences between 'what the minister said' and what someone else 'said they said'; lawyers and jurists have always held 'hearsay evidence' in low regard. So a host of issues to do with misquoting, misrepresentation, impersonation, and downright fabrication tie in with study, in narratives of all kinds, of the continuum from PN to FDS. Politicians are ever grappling with the paradox of producing a quotable quote or 'soundbite' on the one hand, and of not committing themselves to some claim that will come to haunt them, on the other. George Bush, in the run-up to his election as president in 1988, famously fell foul of this trap, using a formulation which vividly acknowledged that here was the directest of direct speech: 'Read my lips: No new taxes', he informed a roaring Republican Convention, only to have his own words endlessly quoted back at him over the next four years, as he signed a number of tax rises into law.

But all that is on the 'legalistic' side of speech- and thought-presentation, where issues of narrator- and character-reliability are involved. There is, as I hope you can see, another side to the use of direct and free indirect representation, which concerns liveliness of narration. For there is, arguably, nothing so conducive to the projection of a narrative as the vivid experience of real people as the use of direct and free indirect discourse. A text rich in these modes is one in which we sense that real people are speaking out, in their own words, and disclosing their thoughts in their own words. Instead of a detached and summarized telling of what happened, we witness an involved and elaborated showing of what happened – and in fact that phrase 'what happened' ceases to be entirely fitting as a result: when the showing is sufficiently direct and displayed, through the pages of the text, we feel we are witnessing 'what is happening' rather than merely 'what happened'.

Activities

ACTIVITY 2

The extract that follows is from very near the opening of Jane Austen's *Mansfield Park*. The preceding text has related the varying fortunes in life and marriage of the three Ward sisters. Most comfortably situated is Miss Maria, who, having married Sir Thomas Bertram, is now mistress of Mansfield Park – 'an handsome house and large income'; the elder sister subsequently 'found herself obliged to be attached to the Rev. Mr Norris' [discuss Austen's use of modality there!], a friend of Sir Thomas, who bestows upon him the living of Mansfield. But the third sister, Miss Frances, makes an 'untoward choice' of husband, a lieutenant of marines. As Mrs Price, her material circumstances steadily deteriorate, in lowly Portsmouth; and, fuelled by an intemperate correspondence, there is a falling-out with her sisters and her influential brother-in-law. But now, overwhelmed by debts and children, Fanny has written a reconciliatory letter to her sister, Lady Bertram.

After you have read through the passage carefully, work through it again, identifying those places where pure narrative modulates into narrative reports of speech acts, indirect speech, direct speech, or free indirect speech. Comment on any differences you notice between the text's use of quotation marks and our conventions today.

> She addressed Lady Bertram in a letter which spoke so much contrition and despondence, such a superfluity of children, and such a want of almost every thing else, as could not but dispose them all to a reconciliation. She was preparing for her ninth lying-in, and after bewailing the circumstance, and imploring their countenance as sponsors to the expected child, she could not conceal how important she felt they might be to the future maintenance of the eight already in being. Her eldest son was a boy of ten years old, a fine spirited fellow who longed to be out in the world; but what could she do? Was there any chance of his being hereafter useful to Sir Thomas

in the concerns of his West Indian property? No situation would be beneath him – or what did Sir Thomas think of Woolwich?[1] or how could a boy be sent out to the East?

The letter was not unproductive. It re-established peace and kindness. Sir Thomas sent friendly advice and professions, Lady Bertram dispatched money and baby-linen, and Mrs Norris wrote the letters.

Such were its immediate effects, and within a twelvemonth a more important advantage to Mrs Price resulted from it. Mrs Norris was often observing to the others, that she could not get her poor sister and her family out of her head, and that much as they had all done for her, she seemed to be wanting to do more: and at length she could not but own it to be her wish, that poor Mrs Price should be relieved from the charge and expense of one child entirely out of her great number. 'What if they were among them to undertake the care of her eldest daughter, a girl now nine years old, of an age to require more attention than her mother could possibly give? The trouble and expense of it to them, would be nothing compared with the benevolence of the action.' Lady Bertram agreed with her instantly. 'I think we cannot do better,' said she, 'let us send for the child.'

Sir Thomas could not give so instantaneous and unqualified a consent. He debated and hesitated; – it was a serious charge; – a girl so brought up must be adequately provided for, or there would be cruelty instead of kindness in taking her from her family. He thought of his own four children – of his two sons – of cousins in love, &c.; – but no sooner had he deliberately begun to state his objections, than Mrs Norris interrupted him with a reply to them all whether stated or not.

[1] A military academy; gaining admission to it no doubt required funds and influence.

If you have access to the full text of *Mansfield Park*, you might take this opportunity to look closely at the modality used in the opening paragraphs. What kinds of modality are commonest, for example, in the speeches of Mrs Norris; and how do these compare or contrast with those of Sir Thomas and/or Lady Bertram? You could annotate, also, the patterns of naming of the main characters (at least, of Sir Thomas and the three sisters), in the opening chapter, making a tally of how often each is designated by (a) a proper name, and which, precisely; (b) a pronoun; and (c) a definite description – and again, what kind of definite description. Do these ways of naming shift as the chapter proceeds? What kind of evaluation, and comparative status, do these namings begin to suggest of the respective characters?

ACTIVITY 3

The passage that follows comes from the final pages of Raymond Carver's short story, 'Cathedral'. Robert, who is blind, has asked the narrator-figure to describe the medieval cathedrals that he and his host (the narrator) have been watching on television; but it transpires that the narrator lacks the vocabulary or the articulacy to do this. But then Robert 'has an idea' about how cathedrals can be described to him. Take the direct speech portions of the passage below, and convert them to either indirect speech or free indirect speech, rephrasing or rewriting as necessary.

Which works better, IS or FIS? Which involves more rewriting? Why might neither of these modes work as well, in this particular context, as the direct speech which Carver opted for?

> It was then that the blind man cleared his throat. He brought something up. He took a handkerchief from his back pocket. Then he said, 'I get it, bub. It's okay. It happens. Don't worry about it,' he said. 'Hey, listen to me. Will you do me a favor? I got an idea. Why don't you find us some heavy paper? And a pen. We'll do something. We'll draw one together. Get us a pen and some heavy paper. Go on, bub, get the stuff,' he said.
>
> [. . .]
>
> 'All right,' he said. 'All right, let's do her.'
> He found my hand, the hand with the pen. He closed his hand over my hand. 'Go ahead, bub, draw,' he said. 'Draw. You'll see. I'll follow along with you. It'll be okay. Just begin now like I'm telling you. You'll see. Draw,' the blind man said.
> So I began. First I drew a box that looked like a house. It could have been the house I lived in. Then I put a roof on it. At either end of the roof, I drew spires. Crazy.
> 'Swell,' he said. 'Terrific. You're doing fine,' he said. 'Never thought anything like this could happen in your lifetime, did you, bub? Well, it's a strange life, we all know that. Go on now. Keep it up.'
> I put in windows with arches. I drew flying buttresses. I hung great doors. I couldn't stop. The TV station went off the air. I put down the pen and closed and opened my fingers. The blind man felt around over the paper. He moved the tips of his fingers over the paper, all over what I had drawn, and he nodded.
> 'Doing fine,' the blind man said.

ACTIVITY 4

This extract is from Saul Bellow's novel, *Herzog* (pp. 38–9). Moses Herzog is going through a mid-life crisis, re-examining everything. The passage begins at a point where Herzog, intent on escape from the stressful intensity of New York City, is taking a cab to Grand Central station, where he will take a train to the rural peace of New England. Read the passage carefully, so that you don't lose track of the way it contains remembered journeys *within* the present cab journey to Grand Central station.

The cab was held up by trucks in the garment district. The electric machines thundered in the lofts and the whole street quivered. It sounded as though cloth were being torn, not sewn. The street was plunged, drowned in these waves of thunder. Through it a Negro pushed a wagon of ladies' coats. He had a beautiful beard and blew a gilt toy trumpet.(5) You couldn't hear him.

Then the traffic opened and the cab rattled in low gear and jerked into second. 'For Christ sake, let's make time,' the driver said. They made a sweeping turn into Park Avenue and Herzog clutched the broken window handle. It wouldn't open.(10) But if it opened dust would pour in. They were demolishing and raising buildings. The Avenue was filled with concrete-mixing trucks, smells of wet sand and powdery grey cement. Crashing, stamping pile-driving below, and, higher, structural steel, interminably and hungrily going up into the cooler, more delicate blue. Orange beams hung from the cranes like straws.(15) But down in the street where the buses were spurting the poisonous exhaust of cheap fuel, and the cars were crammed together, it was stifling, grinding, the racket of machinery and the desperately purposeful crowds – horrible! He had to get out to the seashore where he could breathe. He ought to have booked a flight. But he had had enough of planes last winter, especially on the Polish airline. The machines were old.(20) He took off from Warsaw airport in the front seat of a two-engine LOT plane, bracing his feet on the bulkhead before him and holding his hat. There were no seat belts. The wings were dented, the cowls scorched. There were mail pouches and crates sliding behind. They flew through angry spinning snow clouds over white Polish forests, fields, pits, factories, rivers dogging their banks, in, out, in, and a terrain of white and brown diagrams.(25)

Anyway, a holiday should begin with a train ride, as it had when he was a kid in Montreal. The whole family took the street-car to the Grand Trunk Station with a basket (frail, splintering wood) of pears, overripe, a bargain bought by Jonah Herzog at the Rachel Street Market, the fruit spotty, ready for wasps, just about to decay, but marvellously fragrant. And inside the train on the worn green bristle of the seats, Father Herzog sat peeling the fruit with his Russian pearl-handled knife. He peeled and twirled and cut with European efficiency. Meanwhile, the locomotive cried and the iron-studded cars began to move.(30) Sun and girders divided the soot geometrically. By the factory walls the grimy weeds grew. A smell of malt came from the breweries.

The train crossed the St Lawrence. Moses pressed the pedal and through the stained funnel of the toilet he saw the river frothing.(35) Then he stood at the window. The water shone and curved on great slabs of rock, spinning into foam at the Lachine Rapids, where it sucked and rumbled. On the other shore was Caughnawaga, where the Indians lived in shacks raised on stilts. Then came the burnt summer fields. The windows were open.(40) The echo of the train came back from the straw like a voice through a beard. The engine sowed cinders and soot over the fiery flowers and the hairy knobs of weed.

But that was forty years behind him. Now the train was ribbed for speed, a segmented tube of brilliant steel. There were no pears, no Willie, no Shura, no Helen, no Mother.(45) Leaving the cab, he thought how his mother would moisten her handkerchief at her mouth and rub his face clean. He had no business to recall this, he knew, and turned towards Grand Central in his straw hat. He was of the mature generation now, and life was his to do something with, if he could. But he had not forgotten the odour of his mother's saliva on the hand-kerchief that summer morning in the squat hollow Canadian station, the black iron and the sublime brass. All children have cheeks and all mothers spittle to wipe them tenderly.(50) These things either matter or they do not matter. It depends upon the universe, what it is. These acute memories are probably symptoms of disorder. To him, perpetual thought of death was a sin. Drive your cart and your plough over the bones of the dead.(55)

1   Identify the points at which you feel the text shifts from pure narrative to free indirect discourse. Comment on any com-plexities you find; for example, would it be fair to say that the kind of language used *at the beginning* of Herzog's FID pas-

sages tends to be 'more FID' than the language in which those FID passages continue? (§)

2   How many generic sentences can you find in this passage? Where do they cluster? Whose judgements are they? (§)

ACTIVITY 5

This passage is from early in John Updike's *Rabbit is Rich*, the third in Updike's tetralogy about the life and times of one Harry 'Rabbit' (his teeth) Angstrom, an irascible white blue-collar American now in middle-age. *Rabbit is Rich* takes Harry through the 1970s; and at this point in the novel Rabbit is driving home from work.

Some car with double headlights, a yellow LeMans with that big vertical bar in the middle of the grille, is riding his tail so close he eases over behind a parked car and lets the bastard by: a young blonde with a tipped-up tiny profile is driving, how often that seems to be the case these days, some pushy road-hog you hate turns out to have a little girl at the wheel, who must be somebody's daughter and from the lackadaisical glassy look on her face has no idea of being rude, just wants to get there. When Rabbit first began to drive the road was full of old fogeys going too slow and now it seems nothing but kids in a hell of a hurry, pushing. Let 'em by, is his motto. Maybe they'll kill themselves on a telephone pole in the next mile. He hopes so.

His route takes him up into the area of the stately Brewer High School, called the Castle, built in 1933, the year of his birth is how he remembers. They wouldn't build it now, no faith in education, indeed they say with zero growth approaching there aren't enough students to fill the schools now, they are closing a lot of the elementary schools down. Up this high the city builders had run out of seasons and went to tree names. Locust Boulevard east of the Castle is lined with houses with lawns all around, though the strips between are narrow and dark and rhododendrons die for lack of sun. The better-off live up here, the bone surgeons and legal eagles and middle management of the plants that never had the wit to go south or have come in since. When Locust begins to curve through the municipal park its name changes in Cityview Drive, though with all the trees that have grown up in time there isn't much view left, Brewer can be seen all spread out really only from the Pinnacle Hotel, now a site of vandalism and terror where once there had been dancing and necking.

Something about spics they don't like to see white kids making out, they surround the car and smash the windshield with rocks and slit the clothes off the girl while roughing up the boy. What a world to grow up in, especially for a girl. He and Ruth walked up to the pinnacle once or twice. The railroad tie steps probably rotted now. She took off her shoes because the high heels dug into the gravel between the railroad ties, he remembers her city-pale feet lifting ahead of him under his eyes, naked for him as it seemed. People satisfied with less then. In the park a World War II tank, made into a monument, points its guns at tennis courts where the nets, even the ones made of playground fencing, keep getting ripped away. The strength these kids use, just to destroy. Was he that way at that age? You want to make a mark. The world seems indestructible and won't let you out. Let 'em by.

The modulations between narrative and free indirect discourse in this passage are made a little more complicated by the fact that the narrative itself is, as in many recent novels, in the present tense. Using examples from the opening paragraph, comment on how the text seems to 'slip' from PN to FID, or vice versa, under the influence of particular single words, which are arguably expressive of the character's mindset, or of the narratorial position, respectively.

ACTIVITY 6

The following extract is derived from Alice Munro's story, 'Circle of Prayer', a brilliantly crafted portrait of the relationship between Trudy and her teenage daughter, Robin. Many issues are involved, but the narrative is 'triggered' by the fact that Robin has infuriated Trudy by lightly placing a family keepsake, a jade necklace, in the coffin of a school acquaintance – a girl she scarcely knew – who has been killed tragically in a car crash. The following conversation, between Trudy and her husband Dan, with a brief interruption from their daughter Robin, occurs at a point where their marriage is on the point of collapse, a collapse hastened by Dan's relationship with a younger woman called Genevieve.

1   As a means of examining closely the varying effects of direct and free indirect reporting, convert all the underlined text in the passage: convert the DS turns of talk into FIS, and those in FIS below into DS. Non-underlined text is chiefly narrative, and can be left unchanged. Note that the first underlined material here in, direct speech, comes from Dan (so his 'I' pronouns will convert to *he*), while the free indirect speech

remarks chiefly come from Trudy. Remember to add or delete speech marks as appropriate, and bear in mind that some of the 'translation' work will involve some rephrasing. For instance, direct commands cannot easily be expressed in FIS, while they are quite natural in DS; thus, for example, the rather awkward *Robin should go back to bed!* (FIS) converts into the more natural-sounding *Robin, go back to bed!*.

Not for years had he had so much to say about how he loved her. 'I love your skinny bones, your curly hair, your roughening skin, your way of coming into a room with a stride that shakes the windows, your jokes, your clowning, your tough talk. I love your mind and your soul. I always will. But the part of my life that was bound up with yours is over.'
That was just talk, that was talking like an idiot! Trudy said. Robin should go back to bed! For Robin in her skimpy nightgown was standing at the top of the steps.
She could hear them yelling and screaming, Robin said.
They weren't yelling and screaming, Trudy said. They were trying to talking about something private.
What?
She had told her, it was something private.
When Robin sulked off to bed, Dan said he thought they should tell her. It was better for kids to know. Genevieve didn't have any secrets from her kids. Josie was only five, and she had come into the bedroom one afternoon –
Then Trudy did start yelling and screaming. She clawed through a cushion cover. He should stop telling her about his sweet fucking Genevieve and her sweet fucking bedroom and her asshole kids – he should shut up, and not tell her anymore! He was just a big dribbling mouth without any brains. She didn't care what he did, if he just shut up! (§)

2 Convert the following FIS passage into direct speech. The 'speaker' here is Trudy, addressing Robin, and the two *she*'s in the first sentence are Trudy and Robin, respectively.

All she wanted was to know why she had done it. Had she just done it for show? Like her father – for show? It wasn't the necklace so much. But it had been a beautiful thing – she loved jet beads. It had been the only thing they both had of her grandmother's. It had been her right, but she had no right to have taken her by surprise like that. She deserved an explanation. She had always loved jet beads. Why?

3 Now construct a narrative report of a discourse act version of this same material, reducing the paragraph by about half.

4 Comment on the different impact and advantages or disadvantages of the three formats.

ACTIVITY 7

The next passage is from Toni Morrison's *Beloved* (p. 17), the story of Sethe, a Negro woman who has lived through terrible times in pre-Emancipation America. In this scene, which also makes passing reference to her daughter Denver, she is comforted by her old friend, Paul D, someone she has known since the days when they both laboured on the 'Sweet Home' estate. The allusion to 'her chokecherry tree' is to the tree-like network of scars on Sethe's back, put there by the beatings she suffered at the hands of white slaveowners in her early years.

> The fat white circles of dough lined the pan in rows. Once more Sethe touched a wet forefinger to the stove. She opened the door and slid the pan of biscuits in. As she raised up from the heat she felt Paul D behind her and his hands under breasts. She straightened up and knew, but could not feel, that his cheek was pressing into the branches of her chokecherry tree.
>
> Not even trying, he had become the kind of man who could walk into a house and make the women cry. Because with him, in his presence, they could. There was something blessed in his manner. Women saw him and wanted to weep – to tell him that their chest hurt and their knees did too. Strong women and wise saw him and told him things they only told each other: that way past the Change of Life, desire in them had suddenly become enormous, greedy, more savage than when they were fifteen, and that it embarrassed them and made them sad; that secretly they longed to die – to be quit of it – that sleep was more precious to them than any waking day. Young girls sidled up to him to confess or describe how well-dressed the visitations were that had followed them straight from their dreams. Therefore, although he did not understand why this was so, he was not surprised when Denver dripped tears into the stovefire. Nor, fifteen minutes later, after telling him about her stolen milk, her mother wept as well. Behind her, bending down, his body an arc of kindness, he held her breasts in the palms of his hands. He rubbed his cheek on her back and learned that way her sorrow, the roots of it; its wide trunk and intricate branches. Raising his fingers to the hooks

of her dress, he knew without seeing them or hearing any sigh that the tears were coming fast. And when the top of her dress was around her hips and he saw the sculpture her back had become, like the decorative work of an ironsmith too passionate for display, he could think but not say, 'Aw, Lord, girl.' And he would tolerate no peace until he had touched every ridge and leaf of it with his mouth, none of which Sethe could feel because her back skin had been dead for years. What she knew was that the responsibility for her breasts, at last, was in somebody else's hands.

Would there be a little space, she wondered, a little time, some way to hold off eventfulness, to push busyness into the corners of the room and just stand there a minute or two, naked from shoulder blade to waist, relieved of the weight of her breasts, smelling the stolen milk again and the pleasure of baking bread? Maybe this one time she could stop dead still in the middle of a cooking meal – not even leave the stove and feel the hurt her back ought to. Trust things and remember things because the last of the Sweet Home men was there to catch her if she sank?

Comment on the way the text moves from simple narrative – *The fat white circles of dough lined the pan in rows* – to relaying Paul D's thoughts, to Sethe's free indirect rhetorical hopes and questions at the close. Would you agree that, at many points in this passage, the descriptions and phrasings used run the risk of being taken wrongly by the reader? Comment on the *riskiness* (and its concomitant, the *courage*) of the author's chosen presentation here.

ACTIVITY 8

What follows is journalist Robert Crampton's profile of the highly successful British scriptwriter, Jimmy McGovern, published in *The Times* in March 1995. Like the literary texts presented earlier, it uses interesting sequences of direct and indirect reporting of McGovern's speech. Identify some of the passages of PN, DS, IS, FIS and NRSA in the text. As noted earlier, choice of one mode of speech-presentation rather than another often seems to contribute to the reader's impression that the narrator is highly sympathetic (at one extreme) or sharply antipathetic (at the other extreme) towards that reported individual. What tenor of relationship would you say is projected, by the mode choices here, between Crampton and McGovern?

SCOUSE GRIT: JIMMY MCGOVERN
by Robert Crampton, 11 March 1995

Jimmy McGovern wrote *Cracker*, the biggest – and best – television drama hit of the last two years: 13 and a half million viewers, lots of awards for McGovern and the lead actor, Robbie Coltrane. Jimmy McGovern wrote *Hearts and Minds*, which has just concluded on Channel 4.

Hearts and Minds was, unusually, advertised on the strength of its writer's name. Jimmy McGovern is writing two other television dramas and a third series of *Cracker* for broadcast later this year, early next. And now Jimmy McGovern has written *Priest*, which will open in British cinemas this Friday. Jimmy McGovern starts to look like a power in the screen-writing land. Jimmy McGovern starts to look like the flavour of the Nineties so far.

What flavour is that then? Well, his credentials say he is gritty northern social realist soapbox flavour, very strong, extra topping, big side order of chips on shoulder, hold any more subtle ingredients. And, superficially, his subject matter says that too. If you hadn't seen McGovern's work, but you knew that it was all set up north and dealt, as the phrase has it, in the harsh realities of inner city life, and that it all carried the signature headbutt of north-west drama, then you might be well on the way to concluding that this man has more to do with the Seventies than the Nineties.

You would be wrong. *Hearts and Minds*, for instance, set in a school, was all set to be classic blame-the-Tories television. But: 'It's too bloody easy to blame the government. Teachers are quite well-paid actually.' McGovern did not ignore the economic realities of the dole queue, but neither did he ignore individual human beings: behaving badly, behaving decently in a mess not all of their making, but not all of some system's making either. Times change, good writers change with them and McGovern is about as spot-on contemporary as they come, which is why he and his work, and what his work represents, are so interesting.

But first, those credentials. Let's go back to 1949, and examine them. Jimmy McGovern is born, the fifth of what will be the nine children of a working-class Catholic couple in a two up, two down in Liverpool. His dad works 'in a bakehouse'. Jimmy is bright at school – 'we were all bright, really' – can write well, but he can't, or won't, talk. Up until he is eight or nine, he makes only noises, comprehensible solely to his older brother Joey. 'I had a lot of time to meself as a kid. There were so many people in the family to watch, I'd just watch people. If me parents had had a row, I was aware. You know as a child you are, you feel for these things. And I'd watch for those moments.' So, he is bright and sensitive and a bit unhappy. For a writer, the best possible start.

He passes the 11 plus, goes to a grammar school run by Jesuits, still has a bad stammer. 'They had a Mass attendance register and you had to say "9 o'clock mass and holy communion", I couldn't say "nine". I'd go "N-n-n-n-n-n-". I used to do this (he bangs his hand against his hip) to be able to speak and the other kids would all imitate that in the playground. But I was strong, fit. Small but strong. So I would stick up for meself. But I wouldn't hurt anybody, I could always put myself in their position.' He is closer to his mother than his father. 'Up until I was 21 I wanted to kill him. I'm sure we all do.' No we don't. 'Well, you know, he was me dad. You're young, your body's changing, you're frustrated, and there's this male figure . . .' So, he is bright, sensitive, a bit unhappy, persecuted, aggressive and he has a problem with his dad. So much the better.

Jimmy is good at English, enjoys it, wants to be a journalist, doesn't lack the confidence, but rather the knowledge, 'I just didn't know how to go about it,' and besides, he hates school, hates the priests, feels a bit isolated as one of the few poor boys there – 'They didn't understand the problems that poverty brings.' So he leaves at 16 and – this was the Sixties – goes from one job to another as he pleases, a 'Bolshie bastard, I'd insult someone and walk out.' So, he is all of the above, and he is unfulfilled, resentful and he doesn't much like other forms of authority either.

He turns up, aged 21, working in a hotel in the Lake District. There, he meets Eileen. They marry and, back in Liverpool, have three children, bang bang bang, and then Jimmy – 'I've never worn a condom in my life' – has a vasectomy at 23. 'The wife came for me in the clinic eight months pregnant pushing two children, the nurses must have been howling with laughter.' The couple live in a tower block, then get a mortgage off the council and buy a little house.

McGovern goes to Anfield. He watches *Z-Cars*, 'set in Huyton, yeah, we were all into that', and Coronation Street, 'It was good then, Ken Barlow was radical.' He is a car worker, a chemical worker, a bus conductor, he runs pretty much the whole gamut of unglamorous, semi-skilled, working-class male jobs. He's in the union, but he's not especially active. So, now he is all of the above, but he is also bored, badly paid, going nowhere. And suddenly we are up to the mid-Seventies, and the jobs aren't coming so easily anymore. So what does he do? He trains to be a teacher, of course.

No, that's not fair. What happened was this. He still harboured the ambition to write, he has written 'a few short stories, poems, lousy poems' but he has started going to writers' workshops. There, he was coaxed back into education, he rediscovered a love of books, he trained and, brimful of idealism, he became an English teacher in an inner city comprehensive. Those readers who watched *Hearts and Minds*, which was about a former car worker who becomes an English teacher in an inner city comprehensive, wants to change the world and finds he can't, will know the next bit: McGovern captured neither hearts nor minds, or not enough to make it worthwhile. His idealism dried up. Was teaching as bad — pupils cynical, staff decayed — as he depicted it on screen? 'It was worse, a lot worse.'

[. . .]

Unsurprisingly, McGovern persisted with his writing. He was 30 and running out of time, but he was beginning to get a bit of work staged in local theatres and then Alan Bleasdale, another Liverpudlian writer with a beard who used to be a teacher, just a few years older than McGovern but already successful with *Boys from the Blackstuff*, did him a favour. 'I'd just got a play on and I'd fallen out with them all in the theatre,' says McGovern. 'Bleasdale took me to a pub, we had a few pints and he told me the facts of life.' What were they? 'He said: "Keep that (mouth) shut and these (ears) open. You're far too young and inexperienced to be mouthing off. These people are good, these people can teach you things." Stuff like that.'

McGovern took at least half the advice, kept his ears open, and found that his route back out lay down *Brookside* close. He joined the Channel 4 soap as a regular writer in 1983, in the days when the channel was still embarrassingly and self-consciously hot on its politics. He wrote mainly for the Grants, a working-class Catholic family, and he discovered, and it must have been a sweet discovery, that his background became an advantage. He says that, yes, he 'exhaustively played the class card to get my ideas incorporated into the storyline'. How so? 'I just argued that my ideas were somehow more real and more valid because I knew the working class.' Shameless, no? 'Oh yeah. But we're talking about a commission for a few thousand quid, you know what I mean?' McGovern stayed with *Brookside* for six years.

Brookside was good to him. The money was good. The discipline of turning out scripts quickly was good. The culture and tone – set by Phil Redmond, another working class Liverpudlian – suited him. And he began to change, began to mature as a dramatist, away from Seventies agitprop towards the impressive psychological complexity of *Cracker* and *Priest*. It was a slow process. He says he looks back at his *Brooksides* now (he wrote about 80 episodes) and thinks they suffered because the characters were mouthpieces for him and what he had to say then wasn't that interesting. 'I had me Belgrano speech, about a lot of young men dying in the south Atlantic to cheer us up and re-elect Thatcher, and I kept putting it in and they kept taking it out, and eventually Bobby Grant did make that speech, but . . . you learn your characters have to have free will.'

Commentaries

ACTIVITY 1

Sentence 1, as indicated, is PN – with arguably a 'trace' of Agnes's own speech (hence, a trace here of FID) in the phrase *a good hold*. Although it lacks speech marks, *Pain is normal . . . and its not necessarily something for you to be alarmed about* is clearly, at first glance, direct speech, as the following framing clause indicates: *the doctor had said*. But the example is a little more complex than this. Why, for instance, does the text run *the doctor had said* and not simply *the doctor said*? Because this is not a 'current' conversation, simultaneous with Agnes's going downstairs; it is a recalling of an earlier conversation, and the recall is performed by Agnes, not the narrator. It is a matter of 'I, Agnes Hughes, recall to myself that the doctor said . . .' and not 'I, the narrator, tell you, the reader'. Hence the sentence is actually FIT, with recalled DS embedded within it. And FIT, also, is the next sentence, about 'the other doctor'; but this time it is indirect speech which is embedded within it: *she should try . . . to lead a normal life.* The ease with which author and reader, in these lines, accept the switch from referring to Agnes as *you* to referring to her as *she* is worth a study in itself. With *That was what she was trying to do* we get a very clear FIT 'reply' to the doctors' recalled words, which are evidently going through Agnes's mind. Similarly, the speculation about going to Toronto is Agnes's hope, and not the narrator 'playing games with the reader'. Certainly that could be the case in a different kind of fiction: there, narrative sentences beginning 'Maybe' could be 'postmodern' indeterminacies, on the part of the narrator, as to how their characters will fare in the future; but not here.

When we now reach *She went down carefully*, etc., we are firmly back in the domain of pure narrative. The sentence records observations that any detached witness, without benefit of powers to read others' thoughts, could make; in addition, it makes little sense to treat the sentence as specifically Agnes's thoughts: *?I go down carefully and along the back hall*, she thought to herself. The text remains in pure narrative until – in my judgement – some point around the clause *the trouble was the sun had to fight its way in there* and the following inversion. For now the colloquialisms, and the Irish English turns of phrase (you *could count the days*, etc.), and the character-oriented deixis (*in this house*) confirm that these sentences are Agnes's thoughts, indirectly rendered and free of a framing clause (FIT). The following sentences, similarly, alternate fairly pure PN (the FIT trace is the word *now*) – *She switched . . . said ten to eight* – with FIT – *Eileen would probably ring . . . hurrying to the phone.* The FIT question *She was lucky, wasn't she?* is answered by a sentence sufficiently indirect to be best labelled a NRTA: *But, on reflection, Agnes Hughes did not think her daughter was lucky.* This is followed by a return to FIT, with *All this holiday would do would be to make her pine to go to London and live there.* But now, very interestingly, Agnes's line of thought does not continue as before, in the past tense and third-person, but instead switches to the present tense and first person, i.e., direct thought:

Which she can't do with me around her neck.

There is a very practical advantage in such a switch, as can be seen if we consider what the FIT continuation would have looked like:

Which she couldn't do with her around her neck.

She/her pronouns referring to two different women are likely to create distracting confusions. Moore avoids this by switching to DT. But the switch is immensely appropriate to the character too. For without *telling* us in so many words, Moore is *showing* us how isolated and lonely Agnes is, like so many old people: for lack of a companion – *everybody stays at home . . . you never go over to your neighbour's* – Agnes must talk to herself, running on in a flow of questions and answers and voiced anxieties, many cast in the grammatically incomplete sentences so natural in speech. And, emerging from FIT, it is equally natural that these direct thought sentences should similarly stand free of a framing 'She thought to herself:' clause: they are free direct thought sentences. The entire passage is a brilliant use of thought-representation as a means of character-depiction.

ACTIVITY 4

1 My awkwardly expressed question on the *Herzog* passage was intended to lead you to reflect on the narrative – and even seemingly 'pure narrative' – qualities of some of Herzog's FID-triggered flashbacks. But let us first note some of the more significant PN-FID transitions.

Arguably the entire first paragraph is purely narrative, although its final sentence could be interpreted either way: either the neutral observing narrator reports 'you couldn't hear him', or perhaps this is specifically Herzog's FID judgement. Sentence 7 is resolutely narrative, 8 contains direct speech, 9 is back to PN, 10 is transitional, ambiguous between PN and FID, while 11 is, in my view, essentially FID: it is Herzog, not the detached narrator, who speculates that 'if the window opened dust would pour in' – strictly, the narratorial tense selection would be: 'But if it had opened dust would have poured in.' Having recognized sentence 11 as FID, you might look again at the content of sentence 10 and its reference-cohesive link with sentence 9. By the standards of strict grammar, the *it* of 10 would be assumed to denote *the broken window handle* of 9; but 10 can hardly be intended to tell us that *the broken window handle wouldn't open*. What wouldn't open is the window, not the handle, and effectively a slightly improper referential-interpretive shortcut has been performed between sentences 9 and 10: improper by the standards of detached narration, but quite characteristic of the manoeuvres of free indirect discourse, with its mirroring of the little mental jumps of characters' ruminations. The following lines, down to *horrible!*, are ambiguous between narration and FID, and nothing significant hinges on which way you label it: the world depicted is the streetworld of the city, perceptible by a narrator, Herzog, and the cabdriver too. But one is inclined to ascribe the sharply negative evaluations to Herzog himself, especially that *horrible!*, so arguably it is all FID. Incontrovertibly FID is sentence 17, and those that follow: all these judgements about what Moses *had to do* and *ought to have done* are his own, to himself, not pontifications *about* Moses from the narrator.

But now 'licensed' as it were by the switch to FID, to a disclosing of Herzog's own reflections, the text continues with a lengthy recollection of a recent flight in Poland. It is Herzog, not the narrator, who recalls that earlier grim and scary flight. So we can read all the sentences down to 25, and indeed on through the 'deeper' flashback to his Canadian childhood, down to and including sentence 45, as framed by an implicit 'he recalled (to himself)' clause, i.e., as FID. At the same time these lengthy FID passages are not fleeting recollections, but extended narrative ones, vivid, evaluated, and poetical – 'acute memories' as Moses later notes in sentence 53. In their very narrativity, these FID memories are in large part indistinguishable from pure narrative. Only hints of tone, the heightened quality of the language, and such things as the childhood-echoic alliterative innocence of sentences such as *By the factory walls the grimy weeds grew*, point to the suggestible Moses rather than an objective narrator as their source.

2 The generic sentences cluster at the close of the passage, and they can all be attributed to Moses, even if they are relatively uncontroversial (*All children have cheeks and all mothers spittle to wipe them tenderly*) or entirely redundant (*These things either matter or they do not matter*). Some generics are veiled (*Whether these things matter or not depends upon the universe*), or qualified (*To him, perpetual thought was a sin*), or veiled and qualified (*These acute memories are probably symptoms of disorder*). Perhaps the most indirect generic is the final sentence; it is cast as a directive, in imperative grammatical mood, but the sense is 'Each succeeding generation must drive its cart and plough over the bones of past generations.' Clearly, there's no small irony that, in trying to articulate how he must shake off all these thoughts of the dead and gone, Herzog should use a figurative apothegm that makes further reference to the dead.

ACTIVITY 6

Your converted text is unlikely to be identical to the version that follows, since there are several small points where variant renderings are possible. But it should read something like the following:

Not for years had he had so much to say about how he loved her. He loved her skinny bones, her curly hair, her roughening skin, her way of coming into a room with a stride that shook the windows, her jokes, her clowning, her tough talk. He loved her mind and her soul. He always would. But the part of his life that was bound up with hers was over.

'That's just talk, that's talking like an idiot!' Trudy said. 'Robin, go back to bed!' For Robin in her skimpy nightgown was standing at the top of the steps.

'I can hear you yelling and screaming,' Robin said.

'We aren't yelling and screaming,' Trudy said. 'We are trying to talking about something private.'

'What?'

'I told you, it's something private.'

When Robin sulked off to bed, Dan said 'I think we should tell her. It's better for kids to know. Genevieve doesn't have any secrets from her kids. Josie's only five, and she came into the bedroom one afternoon –'

Then Trudy did start yelling and screaming. She clawed through a cushion cover. 'You stop telling me about your sweet fucking Genevieve and her sweet fucking bedroom and her asshole kids – you shut up, and don't tell me anymore! You're just a big dribbling mouth without any brains. I don't care what you do, just shut up!'

This in fact is the actual text from Alice Munro's story, while the earlier version is a fabrication. You might like to track down 'Circle of Prayer', and, having read the full story, reflect further on why this version is preferable to the fabricated one.

6

Narrative structure

Nearly everyone has a strong sense of what is a narrative and what is not a narrative, but failsafe definitions are hard to come by. In order to cut to the chase (a wonderfully narrative-oriented American idiom), so as to devote more space to analyses rather than theory, I shall now offer a sharply summarized 'story' about narrative and about one kind of canonical narrative structure.

A narrative, I shall assume, is at minimum a text (or text-like artistic production) in which the reader or addressee perceives a significant change. In a narrative, something happens, such that we sense a 'before' and an 'after': one state of affairs is displaced by a different state of affairs, and this latter state is, ideally, not merely temporally but causally related to the former state.

It is possible to look at the Mona Lisa or Michelangelo's David or the Taj Mahal for hours and perceive no change; whatever we witness does not include a sense of the object or its parts having changed or become different. What goes for the Mona Lisa applies, too, to our experience of innumerable other objects in the world – and our inspections of descriptions of those objects. This, at base, is why a commonplace distinction among kinds of writing is the sharp separation of description (telling the way things are) from narrative (telling what has happened). By the way, notice that my initial sentence about the 'non-narrative' status of the Mona Lisa, the Taj Mahal, etc. is prefaced by the protective modality expression, 'It is possible to'. The modality device is not merely a defensive escape clause. We do need to allow for, for example, those visitors to the Taj Mahal who, quietly watching the monument as the day fades into a glorious sunset, persuasively report that, for them, the Taj did change and was a narrative. Many would argue that such a sense of change, and movement, often happens in their apperception of seemingly static art objects. So be it. In all such cases, by the definition above, we find more instances of narrative.

As indicated in passing, above, narrative is distinguishable from description (a telling of the way things are). It is also distinguishable from much expository writing and expression of opinion, which are often explanations of the way things are, or an argument for the way you believe things should be.

If the audience's perception that something has happened, some change has occurred, is the essential logical requirement of narrative, then we should immediately add to this what might be called an essential social requirement: the something that has happened needs to be interesting to the audience, and interestingly told.

So a narrative is a text in which something humanly interesting has happened, or a significant change in the situation has occurred.

I now want to jump abruptly to a very specific set of findings, of the American sociolinguist William Labov. In the early 1970s, on the basis of analyses of the oral stories of young African American men in New York, Labov suggested that a fully formed or proficient oral narrative of personal experience (that is, a story you tell about something that happened to you – as contrasted with a narrative of vicarious experience) would have most if not all of the following six elements. Here I list those six elements, in their most commonly cited order, and to the right of each of them I formulate the question or questions which each element seems designed to answer:

1 An abstract	What, in a nutshell, happened? Often, a one-sentence summary of what transpired. (Or, how can you whet my appetite for this story?)
2 An orientation	Who was involved? When and where was this? (Sentences describing the participants, the time and place of events, but not the events themselves.)
3 Complicating action	So what happened first? Then what happened? (Sentences in which the all-important and ordered events of the narrative are reported.)
4 Evaluation	How have you added to the basic story, to highlight how it is interesting or relevant to your addressee or to you, the teller? (*Either* comments, expressing reactions to the events being reported; these are what Labov calls 'external evaluation'. *Or* material which can be regarded as additions to

bare complicating action sentences, material which supplies a 'background' or texture of ongoing activities, reasons, negated events, and dramatizing or emphasizing language, so as to enrich the context of the basic reported event. See 'More on evaluation', below, for fuller explanation.)

5 A resolution

The narrative's answer to the question, 'So what finally happened?' We recipients crave such 'closure', but not all narratives have a clear resolution: it is quite possible for a narrative to report a 'problem' without providing a solution.

6 A coda

Answers the question, 'How does the story relate to us, here and now?' Or it supplies a moral or lesson learned by the protagonist or teller. Often an indication of some way in which the teller, now, is 'still' connected to some person or aspect of the past events which have just been related. Codas are 'bridges' back to the teller-addressee present.

Not all of these six elements are equally crucial. You can probably see that, if my own definition above is to stand, then element 3, some complicating action, is the absolutely required element. This typically pairs with element 5, the resolution. On the other hand, 2 and 4 are somewhat naturally paired too, while 1 and 6 are often, both in literal positioning and figuratively, the most peripheral and nonessential elements.

At the heart of a typical narrative, then, two somewhat contrasting demands need to be met: one is the structural demand for a sequentially related set of events expressing a change from one state to a different one, and the other is the functional demand that this reported change of state and its implications should be interesting, instructive, entertaining, or worth the telling. The structural demand is met by the complicating action and resolution material (narrative event clauses), while the functional demand is met by the evaluative material – and these demands or expectations are ones that both teller and addressee are oriented to. Action and evaluation are intriguingly different animals. Although we have to have action (as defined above) for a text to count as a narrative, it is often not what draws us to narratives: frequently, we do not read or listen to narratives for the events themselves, but for how those events went off, and why, and in what circumstances, and with what attendant accidentals. In other words, we attend to narratives for their evaluation, not their complicating action – despite the fact that the latter is always required and the former is seemingly optional. There is an analogy with a similar paradox in relation to sentence structure, where adjectival and, especially, adverbial material is often the more valuable information relayed, being the more specific information, while the content of the main verb may be relatively banal and predictable – and yet a main verb is structurally required, while 'A' material (adverbial or adjectival) is structurally optional. It is because evaluation has this special status, most optional *and* most important, that its description, as below, is somewhat more elaborated than that of the other five narrative elements.

More on evaluation

As indicated above, the evaluation parts of a narrative, which are not so much a single block as a variety of embellishments scattered through the text, can be subdivided into 'external' and 'internal' ones, depending on whether they are outside or within complicating action sentences. Typical external evaluation sentences are *This is an incredible story*; *This'll make you laugh*; *I thought to myself 'What am I going to do?'*; *She told me I should never have done that*; *It still gives me the creeps when I think about it*; and so on. Not a part of the sequence of events themselves, such remarks are a commentary revealing how some participant in the story *felt* about the unfolding events they were part of – or revealing how some participant feels about those past events now.

More subtle, perhaps, are 'internal' evaluative materials, woven into complicating action sentences. Labov subdivides these into four kinds:

1 Intensifying evaluations which contribute vividness via gestures, repetitions, emphases, or dramatic sounds – all kinds of 'performing' of the narrative:

Elvis thundered down the street, *bddoingg*.

2 Comparator evaluations, sketching in alternative narrative developments which are not actually followed up in the

present narrative, especially using negative, modal and hypothetical sentences:

Elvis *didn't repair any windows*, he just kept breaking them.

3   Correlative evaluations, reporting secondary activities which are contemporaneous with particular events:

While Mr Lacey watered his flowers, Elvis thundered down the street, *bouncing his basketball on any available surface.*

4   Explicative evaluations, which give the background reasons and causes for narrative events.

Elvis made a huge nuisance of himself, *largely because he hated being so big.*

In the simpler oral narratives, and in fables and fairytales, the six elements listed tend to occur, if they do occur, in the order given earlier: abstract, orientation, complicating action, evaluation, resolution, and coda. But it is better to think of this sequencing as the 'default' or simplest format. Almost any pair of these elements can be reordered, and in the more sophisticated narratives they often are.

And that is the point of focusing on Labov's narrative schema: it is quite possible, while allowing for the differences that the different situations create, to apply this six-part 'grammar' of narratives to all sorts of narratives, beyond the simple oral ones of personal experience which were Labov's data set. In particular, short stories, narrative poems, and even novels, can be seen to build upon and exploit these six basic categories of narrative content. When we look at these more sophisticated narratives, however, we find all sorts of rich departures from the ordinary ways of and places for realizing evaluation, orientation, and so on. A sophisticated fiction may well not tell you, virtually at the outset, the precise *Who? When? Where?*, etc. of the story. Nor will evaluative commentary be restricted and separated out in a sharply demarcated section just before the resolution. And there may not be an orthodox resolution – to say nothing of the absence of a coda or moral! But if we are right in saying that – in our culture at least – something like the six-part schema is foundational for narratives, so that each of these six elements is normally 'expectable', then it is important to see a story which, say, has only complicating action and a coda, as not simply a wholly different kind of text, not a narrative at all, but rather as one kind of narrative, one which – *inter alia* – lacks four of the expectable parts. This issue is crucial for the whole analytical enterprise.

Activities

ACTIVITY 1

By way of practice using this approach to narratives, in which we break them up into their component parts, I have devised the following exercise which should enable you to 'build up' a narrative from its most essential element, the complicating action, so as to include all five other accompanying elements. I provide sample elements for all the steps specified below, but I would like you to provide distinctly different sentences of your own. As you can see, my narrative is about car problems; so I would urge you to make the topic for your narrative something radically different from this.

CONSTRUCTING A NARRATIVE

1   Halfway down a blank sheet of paper, write a one-clause narrative – i.e., a sentence in which some change of state applies to one or more entities. This should be the barest of bare narratives, the equivalent of a Labovian complicating action component. It can be first or third person.

e.g. *My car began running raggedly and taking more oil.*

2   Rewrite this one-clause narrative as two sentences, one of which, as before, reports a complicating action, while the new sentence reports a resolution. Again, try to have little or no evaluation, orientation, etc.

e.g. My car began running raggedly and taking more oil. *So I sold it.*

3   Your two sentences (above) will have mentioned one or more protagonists. Now write, fairly high up on the draft page, two sentences introducing those participants (e.g., saying who they are, what their background is, etc.), and describing where and/or when it was that the events reported in 2 happened. This is your rudimentary orientation section. Now look over your two event sentences – they may need slight rephrasing, particularly concerning the naming of participants; but only make those adjustments which are strictly necessary to make the added sentences fit the earlier ones.

e.g. *I once had a ten-year-old Honda Accord, which I bought new. It was metallic blue, with a little rust.* It began running raggedly and using more oil. So I sold it.

4   Between your two 'narrative proper' sentences (from 2 above), now insert two further sentences. The purpose of these sentences will be to add background and interest to the previously formulated narrative sentences; that is, these new sentences will not add new events, nor will they advance the narrative action; in Labov's system they are called 'external evaluative' material. One sentence should be a description of the physical or gestural evaluative reaction of one of the protagonists involved in the narrative, describing not what they did, but how they reacted to what was going on – how their behaviour was a kind of commentary on what was happening. The other sentence should be a 'wholly' external evaluative comment, from you as present writer to your imagined current reader, about some part or all of the story you're telling. So this comment interrupts the storytelling to communicate how you still, today, feel about the events of the story you're telling. This comment isn't remotely part of the story, though it does add to the way you are telling it.

e.g. I once had a ten-year-old Honda Accord, which I bought new. It was metallic blue, with a little rust. It began running raggedly and using more oil. *I remember this bothering me, as if it were an old relative whose health was failing. Isn't it funny how you can get attached to a car?* So I sold it.

5   Add two more sentences to your complicating action section: sentences reporting, in bare form, some events or development leading up to the resolution. Adjust your orientation section if necessary.

e.g. I once had a ten-year-old Honda Accord, which I bought new. It was metallic blue, with a little rust. It began running raggedly and using more oil. I remember this bothering me, as if it were an old relative whose health was failing. Isn't it funny how you can get attached to a car? *So I put a 'for sale' ad in the newspaper and had dozens of phone-calls. A few serious punters came over to check out the car carefully.* Finally I sold it.

6   You should now have at least three bare complicating action sentences, and one resolution sentence. To the first complicating action clause add at least one piece of correlative internal-evaluative material; to the second add an explicative; to the third add at least two comparators; and to the resolution add at least one intensifier. Refer back to pp. 139–40 for examples.

I once had a ten-year-old Honda Accord, which I bought new. It was metallic blue, with a little rust. *While I was using it to commute to Coventry this winter*, it began running raggedly and using more oil. I remember this bothering me, as if it were an old relative whose health was failing. Isn't it funny how you can get attached to a car? So I put a 'for sale' ad in the newspaper, *since this seemed the best way to get a fair price for the car*, and had dozens of phone-calls. *Many of them didn't go further than that*, but a few serious punters came over to check out the car carefully and at great length, *as if it were a Rolls-Royce*. Finally I sold it *'pat', just like that*, in five minutes to a young dealer.

7   Conclude your story with a one-sentence coda in present tense (optionally, perfective aspect: have seen, etc.), and including a usuality modality element (one of the following words, to do with time-relation: *ever, never, always, rarely, usually, since then, now, these days*).

e.g. *Now I'm on the look-out for a two- or three-year-old Mondeo hatchback.*

8   Preface your story with a one-sentence abstract of your own choice.

e.g. *I finally got rid of my trusty old Honda.*

Here then, to recap, is the fully constructed story:

I FINALLY GOT RID OF MY TRUSTY OLD HONDA

I once had a ten-year-old Honda Accord, which I bought new. It was metallic blue, with a little rust. While I was using it to commute to Coventry this winter, it began running raggedly and using more oil. I remember this bothering me, as if it were an old relative whose health was failing. Isn't it funny how you can get attached to a car? So I put a 'for sale' ad in the newspaper, since this seemed the best way to get a fair price for the car, and had dozens of phone-calls. Many of them didn't go further than that, but a few serious punters came over to check out the car carefully and at great length, as if it were a Rolls-Royce. Finally I sold it 'pat', just like that, in five minutes to a young dealer. Now I'm on the look-out for a two- or three-year-old Mondeo hatchback.

And here now is another narrative 'answer,' produced in response to directions 1–8 above:

A PHILOSOPHER-PRINCE RELUCTANTLY ENACTS
REVENGE

In Denmark long ago, there was a king called Hamlet and his queen, Gertrude, and their philosophical son, Hamlet. King Hamlet also had a scheming brother, Claudius.

Claudius murdered his brother, apparently by poisoning him as he lay sleeping, and married Gertrude, even while by ordinary standards she should have been still mourning the death of her husband.

The dead king's ghost, a compelling and unquiet spirit lurking in the shadows of the castle, visited young Hamlet privately. He told young Hamlet of the murder and told him he must not fail to avenge his father.

Young Hamlet was devastated; he became manic and obsessive. The way he turned in on himself is really amazing.

Young Hamlet then finally killed his uncle, in the midst of such an orgy of pretend swordplay and real swordplay, switched goblets of wine which turn out to be poisoned, everyone killing and then getting killed, that you're left appalled.

The story will always be powerfully affecting precisely because the final bloodletting and revenge feels so haphazard and not predestined.

ACTIVITY 2

I'd like you to now 'dismantle' this Hamlet story, along the lines of the earlier directions:

1′ First, remove from the story all the material which you judge to have been added in steps 6, 7, and 8, that is:

(a) At least one piece of correlative internal-evaluative material added to the first complicating action clause; an explicative added to the second complicating action clause; at least two comparators added to the third; and one intensifier added to the resolution.

(b) A one-sentence coda, concluding the story, in present tense and including a usuality modality element.

(c) The prefacing of the story by a one-sentence abstract.

2′ Now remove what must have been added in step 5, namely two additional sentences in the complicating action secton, which report events or development leading up to the resolution. Adjust the orientation section if necessary.

3′ Undo step 4: from between the two 'narrative proper' sentences, remove the two external evaluative sentences. As specified earlier, these excised sentences should be (i) a description of the physical or gestural evaluative reaction of one of the protagonists involved in the narrative, and (ii) a wholly external evaluative comment about some or all of the story being told.

4′ Undo step 3: remove the rudimentary two-sentence orientation section.

5′ Finally, undo step 2: remove the resolution sentence.

You should be left with the barest of narratives, a one-sentence complicating action. To see if your final sentence is the same as the one I started with, and to compare also your intermediate dismantlings with my intermediate assemblies, refer to the proposed solution given in the Commentary on Activity 2 at the end of this chapter. (§)

ACTIVITY 3

Here is a very simple-looking narrative, an eight-line poem by Philip Larkin:

Take One Home for the Kiddies

On shallow straw, in shadeless glass,
Huddled by empty bowls, they sleep:
No dark, no dam, no earth, no grass –
Mam, get us one of them to keep.

Living toys are something novel,
But it soon wears off somehow.
Fetch the shoebox, fetch the shovel –
Mam, we're playing funerals now.

1 Analyse the narrative implicit in these lines into Labov's six elements. (§)

2 Would you agree that the crucial complicating action (and resolution) stages are rather indirectly conveyed? Which important events in the narrative are not explicitly narrated?

3 Does this narrative have a proper abstract or a proper coda? Does it, on the other hand, contain a generic sentence (see Chapter 4) which could conceivably *serve as* a kind of coda? (§)

The Big Nose

ouns a pon a time

ther was a big Nose.

Now lets get on to the

ril story. ther was

a skelatn thet lost

his Nose, 'wer is me my

Nose' a van piae

fand the big Nose

and tok took it to

it's carsll he was

abaot to have it

for dinir. 'Narsty him me

he gobld to him self

he lost the Nose. 'wer

did it go the skelatn

fand ita gen and thae livd

haply evr arfd

ACTIVITY 4

I reproduce opposite a narrative, 'The Big Nose', devised and written by a six-year-old. Using the Labovian narrative scheme as a template, comment on what you would regard as the most interesting features of this story. What, perhaps, does the child's remark 'Now let's get on with the real story', and its particular location, tell us about her own tacit classification of her story opening? Focusing on the complicating action events, what can we say about the connection between one event and the next, in sequence; specifically, are there causal connections between any of the events in this sequence, or simply chronological ones, and what difference does it make? (§)

ACTIVITY 5

For this activity you need to be(come) familiar with a text – a masterpiece – not actually supplied here: James Joyce's story 'The Dead', the final story in his *Dubliners* collection. The following questions (which touch on other issues in addition to narrative structure) attempt to focus on just some of the countless stylistic subtleties of the story. The page references are to the 1992 Penguin paperback edition of *Dubliners*, introduced by Terence Brown, in which 'The Dead' appears on pages 175–225. To provide a rough location of lines of text on the printed page, I use a 'decimal' system. Thus if I refer to p. 176.5, this means 'five-tenths of the way down page 176'.

1   Review the second paragraph of the story:

> It was always a great affair . . . never once had it
> fallen flat . . . For years and years it had gone off in
> splendid style as long as anyone could remember . . .

What is the cumulative effect of these repetitive usuality statements? (Review the discussion of 'usuality' in Chapter 3, if you need to.) What tone do these phrases help create?

2   On p. 176.5 whose *Of course* is this (*Of course they had good reason to be fussy on such a night*)?

3   On pp. 176–8 what does a lily signify; what things are lilies associated with?

4   Comment on Lily's 'bitter' answer to Gabriel (p. 178.1).

5   Read over the upper half of p. 179. What modality dominates the latter half, especially, of Gabriel's introspection, as he waits outside the drawing-room? In the context, what does this indicate about Gabriel?

6   On p. 189, with respect to Gabriel's altercation with Miss Ivors, what can be said about the typical parts or 'moves' in each of his replies? That is, how are his replies structured? For instance, how, typically, does he begin those replies? What might be the reasons for, and effects of, this way of beginning his replies?

7   On pp. 190 and 192 we meet Mrs Malins. Although her actual speech is never recorded directly, what she says is reported indirectly (*She answered* ·. . . *she spoke of* . . ., etc.). List two or three of the words which are most frequent in her indirectly reported speech on these two pages, and comment on what they suggest about her.

8   What part does sexism play in this story? Note, *inter alia*, Gabriel's thoughts on p. 191, line 3 (*Of course the girl or woman, or whatever she was* . . .); and Aunt Kate's 'scandal-giving' criticisms on p. 195.

9   Thinking along the lines suggested in the discussion of lexical cohesion in Chapter 2, comment on the language used to describe the laden dinner table on p. 197.
     Note at least three 'fields' or contexts from which numerous words are taken and used in this descriptive *tour de force*. Do you find any of these clusterings of word-choice surprising?

10   On p. 201.5, what might we infer (since nothing is explicitly stated) from being told that Freddy ate celery with his pudding, and that he would be going down to Mount Melleray in a week or so?

11   Review p. 203.5 ff. Underline the generic sentences in Gabriel's speech. Do you see any unintended ironies in Gabriel's remarks? Identify specific instances.

12   Analyse the 'Johnny' story (pp. 208–9) into Labov's six elements.

13   On p. 215.6, what might be said to be the effect of Gabriel's prediction of the near future? Why might we classify it as evaluation of the comparator type? Compare Gabriel's prediction about future events with what actually happens at p. 218.3. Is the scene at p. 218.3 sad, hilarious, or disturbing?

14   Analyse the Michael Furey story, haltingly told by Gretta across pages 220–3, into the six Labovian elements.

15   Focusing now on the final section of the story, from p. 223.5 to the end, identify any prominent modality features in Gabriel's final paragraphs of reverie.

16 Do you regard Gabriel's final reverie as coda, or resolution, or do you have some other explanation?

17 You will recognize that many lines in the final two pages of the story are free indirect thought from Gabriel, or are ambiguous between pure narrative, indirect thought, and free indirect thought. Are there any stretches of text where you feel it is particularly uncertain who is formulating the thought (Gabriel or the narrator), and where it seems to matter who we deem responsible? For example, consider pp. 224–5.1: *His own identity was fading out into a grey impalpable world . . .* Ordinarily, we might assume this would be too excessively self-conscious and Romantic a remark to be attributed to the character, as FIT (?*Gabriel thought to himself, my own identity is fading out . . .*). And yet do we want to attribute it to the narrator talking directly to us (*I tell you, reader, that Gabriel's own identity was fading out . . .*), the same narrator who immediately afterwards will tell us that a few light taps upon the pane made Gabriel turn to the window?

18 In the next chapter we will focus directly on word-choice, and the way that most localized or specific choices a writer can make, choices at single 'slots' in the textual chain of words, can be crucial and determining of literary effect and the status of a text *as* literature. But since we are here admiring Joyce's 'The Dead' I can't resist mentioning one such remarkable word-choice in the story's final paragraph. Without consulting the story-text again, consider the sentence below, which comes from that final reverie-infused paragraph, about the snow, death, and Gabriel's swooning soul:

> *It* [the snow] *was falling on every part of the dark central plain, on the treeless hills, falling softly upon the Bog of Allen and, farther westward, softly falling into the dark——Shannon waves.*

My question is this: what word does Joyce use at the point left blank above? And if you do remember the correct word, do you regard this word as appropriate or expected? Is it clear why it has been chosen at just this point? (§)

ACTIVITY 6

Let us stay a little longer with Irish literature, to consider Seamus Heaney's poem, 'An Ulster Twilight', in terms of its narrative projections. Reconstruct 'what (has) happened' in the scenes Heaney depicts.

An Ulster Twilight

The bare bulb, a scatter of nails,
Shelved timber, glinting chisels:
In a shed of corrugated iron
Eric Dawson stoops to his plane

At five o'clock on a Christmas Eve.
Carpenter's pencil next, the spoke-shave,
Fretsaw, auger, rasp and awl,
A rub with a rag of linseed oil.

A mile away it was taking shape,
The hulk of a toy battleship,
As waterbuckets iced and frost
Hardened the quiet on roof and post.

Where is he now?
There were fifteen years between us two
That night I strained to hear the bells
Of a sleigh of the mind and heard him pedal

Into our lane, get off at the gable,
Steady his Raleigh bicycle
Against the whitewash, stand to make sure
The house was quiet, knock at the door

And hand his parcel to a peering woman:
'I suppose you thought I was never coming.'
Eric, tonight I saw it all
Like shadows on your workshop wall,

Smelled wood shavings under the bench,
Weighed the cold steel monkey-wrench
In my soft hand, then stood at the road
To watch your wavering tail-light fade

And knew that if we met again
In an Ulster twilight we would begin
And end whatever we might say
In a speech all toys and carpentry,

A doorstep courtesy to shun
Your father's uniform and gun,
But – now that I have said it out –
Maybe none the worse for that.

1 Would you agree that there are arguably two narratives here – a sequence of events in the distant past (probably more than twenty years earlier), and a contemporary second narrative sequence, of thoughts, in the speaker's head ('Eric, tonight I saw it all')? Or would it be better to say that the speaker's contemporary narrative sequence of reflections contains, embedded within it, a recalled earlier narrative?

2 The first five stanzas (and the first two lines of stanza 6) focus fairly straightforwardly on the distant, or embedded-- recollected, narrative. But what about the line *Where is he now?*: in Labovian terms, what functional element does this remark perhaps contribute to?

3 In lexical cohesion terms, you will have noticed the inventory of carpenter's tools and instruments, predictably co-occurring: *scatter of nails*, *shelved timber*, *plane*, *pencil*, and *spoke-shave*. (Incidentally, many of these are named in the order in which Eric would come to use them, in making the toy, so that they are not an unordered list but a narrative one.) Thus a large cluster of items, depicting tools and setting, fit unproblematically into a scene of 'toys and carpentry'. But one tool does not thus fit: the *cold steel monkey-wrench* weighed (or imagined being weighed?) in the speaker's (soft) hand. Why this mention of the cold steel monkey-wrench?

4 What poignant twist to this narrative (or narratives) is given by the late reference to Eric's father's uniform and gun? Assuming that this means that Eric's father is or was a member of the Royal Ulster Constabulary (which historically has always been overwhelmingly Protestant and Unionist), what complications – or clarifications – does this belated orientational material bring?

5 In the context of Northern Ireland, especially, all sorts of small details of the poem can be read as resonant. The fact that the toy is a battleship, an instrument of conflict and violence, is a straightforward enough marriage of war and peace. But battleships, as a product, are especially significant in Northern Ireland (by contrast with, e.g., tanks and machine guns) since for decades shipbuilding – including naval shipbuilding – was one of the major sources of employment, and the industry was notoriously discriminatory against Catholic applicants for work. Similarly, a *Raleigh* bicycle has a resonance in Ireland in a way a Motobecane does not: a Raleigh is a quintessentially *English* bicycle, and the brand name inevitably recalls the Elizabethan Sir Walter Ralegh, one of the colonizing ravishers

of Ireland (and other lands), to whom Heaney has referred in
other poems.

6   One of the finest attributes of this poem, to my mind, is the
    choice of title, which prompts the reader to find answers to the
    questions, 'Why specifically an *Ulster* twilight?' and 'Why an
    Ulster *twilight?*' The phrase appears again in the speaker's
    hypothesized meeting again with Eric, these many years later.
    Formulate, in your own words, reasons why the title is so fitting
    to the complex circumstances depicted. Would you agree, for
    instance, that there is a kind of parallel between doorsteps
    (which figure on two occasions in the poem) and twilight?

ACTIVITY 7

Let us turn now to an earlier poet, from the English tradition, and one
of his *Songs of Innocence*, 'The Chimney Sweeper':

When my mother died I was very young,
And my father sold me while yet my tongue
Could scarcely cry 'weep!' 'weep!' 'weep!' 'weep!'
So your chimneys I sweep & in soot I sleep.

There's little Tom Dacre, who cried when his head
That curl'd like a lambs back, was shav'd, so I said,
'Hush, Tom! never mind it, for when your head's bare,
You know that the soot cannot spoil your white hair.'

And so he was quiet, & that very night,
As Tom was asleeping he had such a sight!
That thousand of sweepers, Dick, Joe, Ned, & Jack,
Were all of them lock'd up in coffins of black;

And by came an Angel who had a bright key,
And he open'd the coffins & set them all free;
The down a green plain, leaping, laughing they run,
And wash in a river and shine in the Sun;

Then naked & white, all their bags left behind,
They rise upon clouds, and sport in the wind.
And the Angel told Tom, if he'd be a good boy,
He'd have God for his father & never want joy.

And so Tom awoke; and we rose in the dark
And got with our bags & our brushes to work.
Tho' the morning was cold, Tom was happy & warm;
So if all do their duty, they need not fear harm.

William Blake

1   Is this one narrative or two? Indicate how one might argue that in this poem we have one narrative embedded within another framing one. Or is one narrative conflated, or confused, with the other?

2   What is the resolution of (what finally happens in) Tom's story? Is there a clear resolution to the framing narrative? What is the framing narrative's coda? Is there a clear coda to Tom's narrative?

3   What do you think of the framing narrative's coda? Are you persuaded? Can the speaker be serious? Is Blake being serious (i.e., unironical)?

4   Is there a possible pun in the verb *want*, in the final line of the penultimate stanza?

ACTIVITY 8

The following passage is a brief account of the life and death of Frank Little, a leader of the syndicalist labour movement called the Industrial Workers of the World. The IWW, also known as the 'Wobblies', flourished for a short period in the United States in the early part of the twentieth century, organizing labourers to campaign for improvement of the appalling conditions they were driven to work under (note, for instance, the reference to 190 deaths in one industrial 'accident' below). The account is taken and abridged from Patrick Renshaw, *The Wobblies: The Story of Syndicalism in the United States* (New York: Doubleday 1967).

Apply Labov's narrative labelling scheme to this text, and comment on the ways in which orientation, complicating action and coda are extensive, but distinct from each other.

> Frank Little was probably the most courageous and impulsive leader the IWW ever had. He joined the IWW in 1906, was active in the free speech fights at Missoula, Fresno, and Spokane, and went on to organize the lumberjacks, metal miners, oil field workers and harvest bindlestiffs all over the West and Southwest. By 1916 he was a member of the General Executive Board and a powerful advocate of militant action. He favored the strong-arm methods employed by the AWO in the harvest fields and advocated sabotage of farming equipment in areas where the AWO met tough resistance from the employers. He was also a vehement opponent of the First World War . . .
>
> Although Little's antiwar attitude was very unpopular it was not super-patriotism that motivated his murderers. They were almost certainly agents of the copper trust who wanted to rid

themselves of a dangerous IWW agitator in a dangerous industry, where 190 men had died in a single industrial accident at the Speculator Mine in June 1917. Frank Little had been a tireless organizer in the metal mines of Arizona and Montana in 1916–17. He brought his own men out in protest against wartime wage cuts, which accompanied wartime increases in the price of copper. In July 1917 he was called into action again when 1200 Arizona metal miners, including 104 Wobblies, were rounded up by armed members of the Bisbee Loyalty League and shipped into the desert in cattle trucks before being imprisoned without charge.

Back in Butte, Montana, at the end of July, Little helped organize another strike of metal miners against the Anaconda Company. He had broken a leg in Oklahoma on his way back from Bisbee, but still managed to shout scorn and defiance at a threatening crowd of company guards. Later, in the early hours of August 1, 1917, the company guards were revenged. Six masked men, heavily armed, broke into Little's hotel room, beat him up, dragged him down in his pajamas to their car, tied him by a rope to the rear fender and dragged him along the dirt track to the Milwaukee Railroad trestle several miles out of town. There, in the harsh light of their car's headlamps, they hanged him, and pinned a notice to his lifeless body saying 'First and last warning.' This act of savage barbarity shocked Butte and the entire labor movement. The police kept up a pretense of looking for the man they called their prime suspect, a mentally deranged drug addict from the Western underworld, but no serious attempt was made to bring Little's murderers to justice. Frank Little's claims to be remembered by the Wobblies probably outstrip those of anyone else. He was a prominent member of the GEB, completely innocent of any crime save that of trying to organize his fellow workers, who was brutally killed by an armed mob. Yet for some reason Little is the least remembered of the IWW's martyrs. Perhaps that is because he was an extremist, an outspoken advocate of sabotage and opposition to the First World War, who died just as the IWW was trying to avoid persecution by playing down its revolutionary character and posing as nothing more than a militant industrial union. Perhaps it was simply that soon after Little's death the IWW found itself in court on trial for its very existence, so that the demands of this defense campaign took first place over any efforts to keep Frank Little's name alive.

ACTIVITY 9

As a final narrative poem, perhaps the most enigmatic of those presented here, consider Anne Stevenson's 'Utah':

> Somewhere nowhere in Utah, a boy by the roadside,
> gun in his hand, and the rare dumb hard tears flowing.
> Beside him, the greyheaded man has let one arm slide
> awkwardly over his shoulder, is talking and pointing
> at whatever it is, dead, in the dust on the ground.
>
> By the old parked Chevy, two women, talking and watching.
> Their skirts flag forward. Bandannas twist with their hair.
> Around them some sheep and a fence and the sagebrush burning
> and burning with its blue flame. In the distance, where
> mountains are clouds, lightning, but no rain.

What has happened here? If we cannot be entirely explicit about just what has happened, in what ways would you support the claim that this narrative, as presented here, is still tellable and interesting?

ACTIVITY 10

Finally, to the law. In any contested criminal action, it is reasonable to think of the trial as a struggle in which prosecution and defence vie in turn to persuade judge and jury of the plausibility of their version of a particular narrative of events, and the law's rulings on events of that claimed kind. Those accused are invariably central participants in this virtual narrative. The pressure, of course, is chiefly on the prosecution, to present evidence that will contribute to the construction of a narrative which seems valid beyond a reasonable doubt.

Who are the parties, then, to the narrative entailed in a criminal prosecution? In the first instance, the prosecuting lawyer, who is the teller, and the jury, who are his or her primary addressees. But there are clearly multiple ramifications from this simple nucleus, since defence lawyers will seek to unpick and re-interpret the prosecution's narrative; various witnesses may fleetingly 'take over the storytelling' from the prosecuting lawyer; and the judge may intervene to direct the jury or rule on matters of law and procedure. And what of those in the public gallery? Are they not addressees of a kind, of the legal narrative, albeit without the power, as a jury has, to ratify or dismiss the narrative they have heard?

This activity looks at those of us in a more distant public gallery, having relayed to us those parts of the evidential narrative that a courtroom journalist regards as most tellable. The following is a newspaper's report of one day's proceedings in a major recent trial, that of Mr Kevin Maxwell, for fraud. Kevin Maxwell is one of the sons of the media magnate Robert Maxwell, who disappeared from his yacht in the Atlantic in 1991 in mysterious circumstances.

Comment on the narrative, and the narrative within the narrative, to be found in the following passage, discussing the role that direct speech plays in unambiguously attributing particular narrative claims to Kevin Maxwell rather than Michael Horsnell (the journalist). As the familiar final phrase 'the trial continues' indicates, this is no more than the report of an instalment in an ongoing narrative production, which will continue at least until the jury delivers a verdict and (if applicable) the judge passes sentence; it may continue further if an appeal arises. So this is far from a complete narrative. Nevertheless, it is read (in *The Times*) as a complete instalment, and it is an incomplete narrative on the basis of which readers are likely to speculate about what the complete narrative 'really is' – e.g., whether or not Kevin Maxwell really did commit criminal fraud. On the basis of this re-telling (that is, Michael Horsnell's), are you inclined to judge Maxwell 'beyond a reasonable doubt' guilty, or not? Do you have a sense, from this re-telling, of Michael Horsnell's own opinions in the matter?

MAXWELL FELL OVERBOARD 'WHILE RELIEVING HIMSELF', SAYS SON
By Michael Horsnell, 21 October 1995

ROBERT MAXWELL probably fell overboard and drowned while urinating over the side of his yacht, *Lady Ghislaine*, his son told a jury yesterday.

According to Kevin Maxwell, the media tycoon's death was neither a case of suicide nor murder, but an accident in the Atlantic as the £10 million vessel cruised off the Canary Islands on November 5, 1991.

Mr Maxwell, 36, told the Central Criminal Court that his father was a light sleeper who would wake often. 'He found it more convenient, as a lot of men do on a boat, to relieve themselves over the side as it was moving.'

He said the spot next to the lifeboat from which his father chose to urinate was not guarded by a handrail and had only two thin pieces of wire across it. 'It was not the safest part of the vessel.'

The court has been told that the public perception that Robert Maxwell's death was 'suicide by a man who knew the game was up' caused a disastrous plunge in the share price of the Maxwell empire.

Mr Maxwell was giving his fifth day of evidence in the trial in which he faces two charges of conspiracy to defraud Maxwell pensioners in order to shore up his father's imperilled business empire. Describing his reaction when he learnt his father was missing at sea, Mr Maxwell said: 'It was a terrible feeling. I can't really explain it. It was the shock of thinking that he had fallen off the boat.'

'I was breathless. It was extremely hard to do anything . . . It was the physical loss and the fact he hadn't been found, it was a terrible burden.'

He realised after a few minutes that someone would 'have to stay and mind the shop' because of the business implications of his father's disappearance. He and his brother Ian decided to stay in London and send their mother to the yacht to supervise the search for her husband.

Pausing occasionally, he went on: 'It is very hard to explain the sense of panic . . . I consider myself to be quite a calm and solid individual, and I found myself almost unable to control myself physically, and I realised that if I didn't get a grip I would probably suffer some kind of breakdown. I literally pulled myself together on my own in that 20 minutes and realised that a hell of a lot depended on not losing control.'

Mr Maxwell said he prepared a list of the 'very urgent' steps to be taken, which included suspending the shares to prevent a 'disorderly' market. It took him some 45 minutes to convince the Stock Exchange to suspend the share price. It appeared that such a move, based on the disappearance of a company head, was not in their 'usual experience'.

As the day unfolded, a number of board meetings took place. Mr Maxwell said he was appointed chairman of MCC and that Ian was put in charge of Mirror Group Newspapers. By this time, a huge number of journalists had gathered outside the group's headquarters in Holborn, central London, and there was 'tremendous' pressure for a statement. 'We agreed to accept the inevitability of my father's death and we gave a statement in the entrance hall.'

From then on he worked long hours with little sleep, having meetings with bankers, accountants and businessmen. It was difficult to describe 'the intensity of the meetings and the phone calls and the amount of paper that was generated . . . and the confusion'.

He said he was particularly concerned to retrieve the certificate for 25 million Teva shares his father had taken with him to the boat. He denies conspiring to defraud the pension fund by misusing the Teva shares and pledging them as security for a loan.

He rang his mother on the yacht to ask her to look for the shares. 'I was extremely concerned. We had no idea how my father had met his death. It occurred to me it might be an accident, might be murder, there might be a robbery motive. It never occurred to me that he would have committed suicide, although that theory became popular as the days went by. I wasn't thinking on those lines and never did.'

His mother found the share certificate in a safe on board and he asked her to put it in one of several briefcases in the cabin. They were then flown in the company jet to London.

Mr Maxwell said it had been pointed out to him that a £23 million repayment was due on MCC's loan within the next few days and he was extremely concerned it should be paid on time.

He tried to arrange an eight-day loan with the National Westminster Bank, but it refused to give MCC an unsecured loan. He said there was no doubt MCC would be able to repay the loan as it was due to receive $157 million from the sale of an American subsidiary the following week. In the end the Teva shares were used as security.

Kevin Maxwell denies conspiring with his father to defraud pension funds of 5.4 million shares worth £100 million in the Israeli-owned Scitex Corporation. With his brother Ian, 39, and the former Maxwell financial adviser Larry Trachtenberg, 42, he also denies conspiracy to defraud by misusing shares in Teva Pharmaceutical Industries worth £22 million.

The trial continues.

Commentaries

ACTIVITY 2

4 Hamlet dismantled: a key.

1 (or, after 5' has been applied):
> A man murdered his brother and married the brother's widow.

2 (4'):
A man murdered his brother and married the brother's widow.
> The son of the murdered man killed his murdering uncle.

3 (3'):
In Denmark long ago, there was a king called Hamlet and his queen, Gertrude, and their philosophical son, Hamlet. King Hamlet also had a scheming brother, Claudius.
> Claudius murdered his brother and married Gertrude. Young Hamlet then killed his uncle.

4 (2'):
In Denmark long ago, there was a king called Hamlet and his queen, Gertrude, and their philosophical son, Hamlet. King Hamlet also had a scheming brother, Claudius.
Claudius murdered his brother and married Gertrude.
> ⇒ Young Hamlet was devastated; he became manic and obsessive.
> ⇒ The way he turned in on himself is really amazing.
Young Hamlet then killed his uncle.

5 (1'):
In Denmark long ago, there was a king called Hamlet and his queen, Gertrude, and their philosophical son, Hamlet. King Hamlet also had a scheming brother, Claudius.
Claudius murdered his brother and married Gertrude.
> ⇒ The dead king's ghost visited young Hamlet. He told young Hamlet of the murder.
Young Hamlet was devastated; he became manic and obsessive. The way he turned in on himself is really amazing.
Young Hamlet then killed his uncle.

6, 7, 8 (before any dismantling):

A PHILOSOPHER-PRINCE RELUCTANTLY ENACTS REVENGE

In Denmark long ago, there was a king called Hamlet and his queen, Gertrude, and their philosophical son, Hamlet. King

Hamlet also had a scheming brother, Claudius.

Claudius murdered his brother, apparently by poisoning him as he lay sleeping, and married Gertrude, even while by ordinary standards she should have been still mourning the death of her husband.

The dead king's ghost, a compelling and unquiet spirit lurking in the shadows of the castle, visited young Hamlet privately. He told young Hamlet of the murder and told him he must not fail to avenge his father.

Young Hamlet was devastated; he became manic and obsessive. The way he turned in on himself is really amazing.

Young Hamlet then finally killed his uncle, in the midst of such an orgy of pretend swordplay and real swordplay, switched goblets of wine and poisoned wine, intentional poisoning and accidental poisoning, everyone killing and then getting killed, that you're left appalled.

The story will always be powerfully affecting precisely because the final bloodletting and revenge feels so haphazard rather than predestined.

ACTIVITY 3

1   With Larkin's powerful little poem we are immediately reminded of how texts as finely wrought as poems are will depart in innumerable ways from the simplest 'default' system of narrative-construction that Labov has described. But this does not make the Labov system irrelevant to the Larkin poem; on the contrary, I would argue that Larkin's poem, like the other complex literary narratives looked at elsewhere in this chapter, *plays off* or exploits our 'default' constructional expectations about narratives which the Labov system describes. The key idea which Larkin's poem makes us consider is *inference* – our powers of inferring all kinds of reasonable connections between one sentence and following ones, even when there are no explicit cohesive links (of the kind described in Chapter 2) present. Thus we *know*, although nowhere is it acknowledged in so many words, that 'Mam' does indeed get 'us' one of the unaccommodated wretches described earlier, 'to keep'. We soon also know, again by inferring it rather than being told outright, that the wretch is not 'kept' but neglected, and dies. We infer too that the 'us' are children, that the 'living toys' are pets of some sort, mice or hamsters, perhaps. What helps us reconstruct the narrative and its key events (its complicating action and resolution) is that various other elements,

including the orientation and the evaluation, are extensively rendered.

3   While there is no genuine coda, the generic and cruelly casual observation 'Living toys are something novel, but it soon wears off somehow' could certainly stand as one.

ACTIVITY 4

The events in 'The Big Nose' comprise two simple pairs: the skeleton loses the nose and the vampire finds it, then the vampire loses the nose and the skeleton finds it again. But there are no motivations or explanations for these events: for example, the vampire doesn't find the nose in the course of actively *looking* for this or a similar tasty morsel. In short, events are temporally related but not causally so, and it is just this lack of motivation and causal connection between events that we can expect this child storyteller to amend as they become more adept in storytelling.

ACTIVITY 5

18   The missing word is *mutinous*: the snow is falling, among other places, into 'the dark mutinous Shannon waves'. But why or how are the dark Shannon waves *mutinous*? Against whom, and to what end? And while it is easier to conceptualize 'mutinous seas', which might wreck a ship, it is harder to see how an inland river, of the size of the Shannon, can easily do this. Is Gabriel obliquely equating the Shannon, from the west of Ireland, with Gretta; and is he, then, representing to himself Gretta's feelings for Michael Furey as a mutiny? There are no certainties beyond speculation here, but it is sufficient to note the resonance or 'provocation to thought' carried by such an unforeseeable word-choice as the one here.

7

A few well-chosen words

Of course word-choice (or lexis, or what used to be called 'diction') is central to whatever is distinctive about a particular literary text. Not for nothing did Coleridge talk about prose as words in their best order and poetry as 'the best words in the best order'. That is a brilliant formulation, practising what it preaches; today, oversensitive to heterogeneity of interests and readerships, we would probably ruin it with qualifications: 'the best words in the best order relative to particular purposes at a particular sociocultural moment'. Lexis (the words) and grammar (the order of those words), when broadly understood, are the purpose and the essence of verbal art.

There is a simple but highly effective way of sharpening our awareness of the importance to a text of the specific word-choices that its author has made. This involves using what is known as a cloze procedure. Cloze procedures are a widely used technique in language teaching, since they are often a good way of getting a student to display their level of fluency in the language. Basically, the student is presented with a text (usually written) which has certain words removed from it and replaced by gaps; the student then has to 'fill' the gaps with contextually relevant and grammatically appropriate ____ *Words*, yes; or *items*; *material* might perhaps be too vague; *stuff* would be too colloquial; *apples* would be contextually irrelevant; and *up* would be grammatically inappropriate.

This cloze procedure has the appearance of 'mechanicalness' and is therefore likely to encounter resistance from some devotees of *literae humaniores*. But though simple, it is not a trivial exercise, nor peripheral to matters of style and effective expression. What is one doing, as a teacher, circling various words and phrases in a native-speaking student's essay and scrawling w.w. (wrong word), or expr. (expression = awkward expression) or 'usage' in the margin, but responding to an internal cloze-assessing device, and judging that a fully proficient writer, in all the given circumstances, would have used a more appropriate word? The principle – of optimal contextual appropriateness of lexis – that underlies cloze testing is much the same principle which impels even gifted writers to thumb through a dictionary or a thesaurus in pursuit of the ideal wording. Writers frequently struggle to identify the most effective word or words, surfing a literal thesaurus or their metaphorical mental equivalent. The paradox, however, (to which I will return shortly) is that thesauri and dictionaries are almost invariably inadequate to the kind of task literary writing sets. Writers know, as Coleridge did, that it is axiomatic in literature that 'pretty good words in an OK order' is just not good enough. They know that the *mot juste* is the *mot* 'juiced'. The dedicated writer's goal is, in part, the following: that when the reader encounters the poetic text, and when they take due note of the discoursal situation (matters of tone, topic, characterization, etc.), there will be no points at which the reader is prompted to think 'interesting, but a pity they used *that* word when they might have used *this* one'. Does anyone hear Hamlet say 'How all occasions do inform against me!' and think to themselves '"*conspire* against me" would have been better'?

When we encounter a great poem, it seems that every *mot* is *juste*. But here lies a paradox: the words will sometimes seem absolutely right and fitting and at the same time not ones we might have predicted, nor ones to be found in a generalizing predictor such as a thesaurus or dictionary of usage. There are occasions in reading poems where you approve a poet's word-choice as being 'just what you had expected'; but far more typical is the situation in which you salute a word-choice which you had not expected at all.

Activities

ACTIVITY 1

Let us see to what extent cloze testing and the interplay of predictable and unpredictable word-choices are revealing, by 'filling the blanks' I have created in the following poem. The poem is 'La Belle Dame sans Merci' (the title might be translated as 'The Pitiless Beauty') by John Keats. Read through this poem a couple of times, and then make your best guesses as to which words Keats used at those places where I have substituted blanks.

La Belle Dame sans Merci

O what can ail thee, Knight at arms,
Alone and palely loitering?

The sedge has withered from the Lake
And no birds sing!

O what can ail thee, Knight at arms,   5
So ____, and so woebegone?
The squirrel's granary is full
And the ____ done.

I see a lily on thy brow
With anguish moist and fever dew,   10
And on thy ____ a fading rose
Fast withereth ____ .

I met a Lady in the Meads,
Full beautiful, a faery's ____,
Her hair was long, her foot was light   15
And her ____ were wild.

I made a Garland for her ____,
And bracelets too, and fragrant Zone;
She looked at me as she did love
And made sweet moan.   20

I ____ her on my pacing steed
And nothing else saw all day long,
For sidelong would she bend and ____
A faery's song.

She found me roots of relish sweet,   25
And honey wild, and manna dew,
And sure in language ____ she said
'I love thee ____ .'

She took me to her elfin grot
And there she wept and ____ full sore,   30
And there I shut her wild ____ eyes
With kisses four

And there she lullèd me ____,
And ____ I dreamed, Ah ____ betide!
The latest dream I ever dreamt   35
On the cold hill side.

I ____ pale Kings, and Princes too,
Pale warriors, death ____ were they all;
They cried, 'La belle dame sans merci
Thee hath in ____ !'   40

I saw their starved lips in the gloam
With ____ warning gapèd ____,
And I awoke, and found ____ here
On the ____ hill's side

And this is why I sojourn here,   45
Alone and _____;
Though the sedge is ____ from the Lake
And no birds sing.

And now here is Keats's complete poem, containing all the 'right' (or at least Keatsian) answers. You may prefer to consult it only after you have read the discussion on pp. 166–8.

La Belle Dame sans Merci

O what can ail thee, Knight at arms,
Alone and palely loitering?
The sedge has withered from the Lake
And no birds sing!

O what can ail thee, Knight at arms,   5
So haggard, and so woebegone?
The squirrel's granary is full
And the harvest's done.

I see a lily on thy brow
With anguish moist and fever dew,   10
And on thy cheeks a fading rose
Fast withereth too.

I met a Lady in the Meads,
Full beautiful, a faery's child,
Her hair was long, her foot was light   15
And her eyes were wild.

I made a Garland for her head,
And bracelets too, and fragrant Zone;
She looked at me as she did love
And made sweet moan.   20

I set her on my pacing steed
And nothing else saw all day long,
For sidelong would she bend and sing
A faery's song.

She found me roots of relish sweet,   25
And honey wild, and manna dew,
And sure in language strange she said
'I love thee true.'

She took me to her elfin grot
And there she wept and sighed full sore,   30
And there I shut her wild wild eyes,
With kisses four.

And there she lullèd me asleep,
And there I dreamed, Ah Woe betide!
The latest dream I ever dreamt   35
On the cold hill side.

I saw pale Kings, and Princes too,
Pale warriors, death-pale were they all;
They cried, 'La belle dame sans merci
Thee hath in thrall!'   40

I saw their starved lips in the gloam
With horrid warning gapèd wide,
And I awoke, and found me here
On the cold hill's side.

And this is why I sojourn here,   45
Alone and palely loitering;
Though the sedge is withered from the Lake
And no birds sing.

Every evidential clue at your disposal may be of help in performing this very high-level cloze test. Thus the French title, and its content, may put you in mind of medieval romance stories, the stanza pattern should remind you of medieval ballads, and yet you may know that Keats lived in the early nineteenth century. So you can infer some degree of artifice and unreality even before you come to the gothic and psychological pointers in the poem itself. But all such contextual knowledge is only of limited help when it comes to the very specific task of deciding on particular word-choices.

Students I have tried this exercise with have found it easier than expected in particular cases, but generally harder than they had expected. We should bear in mind the significance of some factors that seem obvious. One of these is that the task gets easier, the further one moves through the poem and the clearer one is about the possible point of the whole. This accords with the idea that a text is a microcosm, or at least a bounded construction, such that once one has developed some notions about the first half of the structure – its rhythm, its dynamics, its mood and tone, its likely point of closure – then intelligent predictions about the latter half are much more possible.

Thus, when you came to lines 44, 46 and 47, it is very probable that many of you 'retrieved' words from the opening stanza, and inserted them at the appropriate sites. But what I want to suggest is that more was involved than your simply spotting that lines 44, 46 and 47 were 'the same' as lines 1, 2 and 36. After all it is the knight who speaks the later lines, his questioner who speaks the first two; and in another context one can imagine replying with words which only partly echo, and also partly contrast with, a questioner's terms.

What additionally supports your judgement that the same words are used in lines 44, 46 and 47 as earlier is your confirmed sense, by the poem's close, of the theme of entrapment and enthralment, of the knight as enervated and immobile and therefore unlikely to be verbally innovative or progressive. At some level you will be aware of the medieval trappings, situation and language, and the ballad format, the simplicity of grammatical structure relying heavily on additive structures introduced by *and* or apposition (emphatically 'loose' rather than 'periodic' in structure), the pronounced metrical preference, in the final line of each stanza, for three stressed syllables preceded by a single unstressed one:

> *and no birds sing*
> *I love thee true*
> *on the cold hill's side*

You will also likely have found that, where the missing word came at the end of a second or fourth line, you were able to use its rhyming partner line to narrow down your word-search: on that basis, given the context, many of you may have correctly guessed *thrall* in line 40. Similarly, filling the gap in line 33 (judges predict *to sleep* more often than *asleep*) is relatively easy to do; and *woe betide* (line 34) is not difficult for those who know the idiom – and, presumably, still somewhat opaque even with the gap filled, to those who don't. Like *asleep*, *cheek* (l.11; some informants suggest *cheeks*, but one fading rose on two cheeks presents difficulties), and *eyes* (l.16) are highly predictable on physical and cultural grounds. What else but her eyes, by this stage, could possibly be wild, we ask ourselves. These cases point to the idiomaticity (*wild-eyed* is common usage, *wild-eared*, *wild-shouldered*, *wild-wristed* certainly are not), near-clichédness, of specific parts of this poem.

But a more interesting case may be one such as line 6: *So _____, and so woebegone*. Readers tend to be confident about the kind of word needed here, and its approximate sense, and the fact that it is likely to be disyllabic with stress on the first syllable. As a result certain candidates are widely supported: *lonely, wretched, friendless,* etc. But no reader in my classes, new to the poem, has hit upon Keats's choice, *haggard*. Again, readers often approximate Keats's choice in line 17, usually suggesting *hair*, but few guess *head*. Ironically and thought-provokingly, those missing words which readers most rarely guess correctly are the ones in lines 31 and 38, where the very token to be used is right there in the immediate co-text. In line 38, and contrary to our impulses to use varied language, Keats uses *pale* a third time in two lines, in the compound *death-pale*.

And faced with the task, in line 31, of filling the gap in *And there I shut her wild ____ eyes*, readers search among all kinds of variants, palpably intent on not repeating the word *wild*. But that is precisely what Keats did. And when readers discover this, they tend to see – after a fleeting reaction of having been 'tricked' – how contextually effective the choice is, and how inappropriate it would be to complain that Keats was 'lazy' and should have worked harder at finding a different descriptive adjective. Specificity of descriptive richness is not what the poem is about at all. And the second use of *wild* in line 31 is by no means redundant: many readers attest to the difference in tone and attitude attributable to the speaker who says *And there I shut her wild wild eyes* rather than merely *And there I shut her wild eyes*. The outcome of running a simple cloze test on line 31 speaks volumes about our conventional conditioning to 'vary our language', and the actual power and function of repetition as understood by a great artist.

ACTIVITY 2

This exercise focuses on some of the language effects in a short story achieved by use of certain words, phrases, and verbal stagings of the situation, and the absence of other, 'expectable' locutions. So at base, in the very different generic context of the contemporary short story, we are again considering, as in the case of 'La Belle Dame sans Merci', the power of well-chosen words. The story in question is told in the first person, so the viewpoint revealed or implied by all the language choices discussed can be fairly attributed to the story's narrator. In this way the style of a discourse can set forth the viewpoint, the values and attitudinal individuality, of that text's speaker.

I want to begin this exercise by asking you, the reader, to put yourself in an authorial-cum-narratorial position. Specifically, I would like you to write the beginning of story, one in which you will figure as both narrator and participant. What follows is the essential information you will need to complete this writing assignment.

(Imagine) you are male, white, American, aged around 30, working-class or 'blue-collar', and married. Your wife has an old friend, a blind person, whom she met when she worked for him one summer ten years ago (long before she met you). They became firm friends. Although he moved to a distant town, he was someone she could confide in, and they kept in touch by sending each other messages on audiocassettes. This friend's wife has recently died. And since he is visiting his in-laws, who live in Connecticut, 'just' five hours away from your town by train, the friend has telephoned your wife and arranged to visit you both, and spend the night.

That is the material with which I would like you to write the beginning of a story. Treat the information as setting the scene for the story; in other words, the above are not events in the story you are going to tell, but are the orientational background for the significant happening that you intend to narrate. As for your addressee, imagine you are telling the story to someone you don't know well, but a social equal, and someone you are able to be fairly informal with (perhaps someone you have got into conversation with in a bar or café). In a dozen or so fairly simple sentences in the past tense, write out this scene-setting introduction to your story, sticking closely to the information supplied in the previous paragraph. If this is an in-class assignment, you could work in small groups, to produce a single shared story-opening; or you could compare and contrast individual story-openings, when completed, in small groups.

When you have completed this writing assignment, turn to the Commentary on this Activity, at the end of the chapter, where you will find another version of this story-opening; this is the one that appears in Raymond Carver's story, 'Cathedral'. (§) Now itemize, as best you can, the main differences between the way you told the story-opening, and the way your alter ego, Carver's narrator, told it. Some of the specific differences between your version and the actual opening of 'Cathedral' are hard to predict. But the very fact of such differences, even within this relatively constrained task, highlights a principle which is foundational to stylistics, namely that writers always have choices to make between possible ways of putting things, and contrasting choices contribute to significant literary differences. Even with quite specific information and instructions – as supplied above – a writer (whether this happens to be you, or Raymond Carver) has numerous choices as to how to fashion their material, and the choices reflect and create differences of effect, emphasis, and interpretation.

1   Let us review a few of Carver's narrator's choices. He begins by saying

This blind man, an old friend of my wife's, he was on his way to spend the night.

Why does he choose to say the blind man was *on his way to* spend the night? What difference does that choice make? We often use the construction 'on one's way to' figuratively, as in *She is on her way to becoming Frankfurt's leading psychiatrist.* But here the usage is literal – the blind man really is travelling towards the couple. The chosen phrase also has the effect of bringing us readers to the very 'edge', the about-to-begin imminence, of the story of the visit. It is a simple but effective way for the storyteller both to get the story under way and immediately to create a notional span of time (the vague but delimited span of time between the beginning of the friend's journey and his actual arrival at the couple's house) which the teller can use in the immediately following paragraphs to fill in relevant background. The effect is therefore different (whether better or not is a matter to be decided upon) from both the simple past-tense version of the sentence, using *came*:

This blind man, an old friend of my wife's, he came to spend the night.

or the past progressive version, using *was coming*:

This blind man, an old friend of my wife's, he was coming to spend the night.

The simple past version doesn't enable the teller to generate any sense of 'imminence': the whole visit is already over and done with. The progressive version does convey the sense of 'in the process of happening' – but only in a general way. *On his way to* is closer to the progressive in meaning, but in addition is dramatically focused on the 'immediately about to happen'. Some of the difference in detail, between 'be coming to' and 'be on one's way to' can be tested out by comparing and contrasting sentences – always the grammarian's standby. Thus, notice that in the present tense with 'immediate/imminent' time-reference you can say either:

John is coming to see you right now.

or

John is on his way to see you right now.

But where present tense with future reference is intended, only 'be coming to' and not 'be on one's way to' sounds natural:

John is coming to see you tomorrow.

**John is on his way to see you tomorrow.*

From this we can conclude that, though quite similar in meaning, 'be on one's way to' is that bit more tied to immediate time-reference than 'be coming to' is.

2   *This blind man*, the storyteller begins, not *a blind man, a friend, an old friend of my wife's, this man called Robert*, or any other formulation. At least two questions are triggered by this: why *this*, not *a* or, possibly, *the*; and why the early mention of the blindness?

In fact the first two phrases of the story, describing the visitor, encode and rank a collection of 'charged' or evaluative characteristics, and it is useful to contemplate alternative formulations of those same characteristics. Thus, encoding just the same items of information supplied by the actual opening, but ordering them differently, the following alternative openings are possible:

This man, a blind old friend of my wife's, he was . . .

This old friend of my wife's, a blind man, (he) was . . .

An old friend of my wife's, who was blind, was . . .

A blind old friend of my wife's was . . .

Some alternative versions make less of the blindness, or of the person's gender. But you cannot, without distortion, get away from the narrator's assertion that the individual is specifically his wife's friend; now just how strongly and contrastively the teller wants to imply that the man is not his friend is something we can only infer at this point, although the covert hint is soon enlarged upon in subsequent paragraphs. Besides, we have the *This* to guide us.

As noted in Chapter 2, *this* is a deictic expression, one of those orientating words in the language which help a speaker to 'point' to a person, place or time from the assumed place and time which that speaker occupies. In order to make sense of any deictic expressions they use, you have to know or assume just where and when a speaker is positioned. Deictic terms also tend to come in pairs, with one term implying 'close to speaker', the other implying 'distant from speaker'.

Getting back to *this blind man*, what we can say is that the use of the deictic word *this* has the effect of pointing to the man as if he were close to the narrator and, possibly, close to the reader. But in fact this is a story-opening and we have no prior acquaintance with the blind man; besides, from other evidence in the sentence and the paragraph we can see that the man is not physically close to the narrator, nor emotionally close. One intertextual analogy to the usage here, I would suggest, is a somewhat comparable usage in jokes and stories:

'*This Englishman, Irishman, and Scotsman are painting this enormous bridge.*'

'I was just walking along the street when this police car screeches to a halt beside me.'

In examples like these, two effects seem to be sought for: (i) the addressee is projected into an experience of the story-events by having particular participants pushed, by the teller, into the foreground of the addressee's attention; (ii) the speaker projects intimations of teller–addressee solidarity, a co-opting of the addressee as in sympathy with the teller and distanced from or even opposed to the denoted participant. The latter amounts to a reverse-deictic effect: someone or something is both foregrounded and regarded with detachment – sometimes even with disfavour – at the same time, as when one disgustedly lifts a banana-skin off the piano keyboard and, holding it up, asks *Who left this here?*

Whatever is hinted at by the reverse-deictic use in *This blind man* is amply enlarged by the use of the distancing definite article in sentence 3, quoted below:

His wife had died. So he was visiting the dead wife's relatives in Connecticut.

Not that using the more natural *his* would entirely solve the problem: *So he was visiting his dead wife's relatives.* The *the* is jarring in its detachedness, especially coming after mention of *his wife*; but any mental correction from *the* to *his* only makes clearer to us, as readers, that there is something egregious and inappropriate about the redundant and graceless mention of the relatives as belonging to the dead wife. For what is more objectionable than *the* (instead of *his*) is the use of *dead* at all: in the context, it cannot be contrasting with, say, a new wife or a second wife. With our interpretive antennae alerted by now to off-colour or negative insinuations, we might also wonder about the cohesive conjunction selected here: *So*. Why the consequential conjunction *So*, rather than, say, the more 'general purpose' connector *And*? (Is the narrator suggesting that one's spouse's death 'naturally' *causes* one to visit one's in-laws?) Why, we should be wondering, did the narrator not simply state:

His wife had died. So he was visiting her relatives in Connecticut.

This would have been a more natural way of putting things. And yet the narrator has evidently gone out of his way to express things differently, with a detachment close to antipathy – and almost as if he thought we might have forgotten that the man's wife was dead, had he not reiterated the fact.

3   A third important feature of the narration in 'Cathedral' is really an extension of the tendency already noted. The narrator frequently includes words, or makes comments, of a kind which prompt the reader first to ask 'Why would he (think he needed to) *say* that at this point?', and then to answer that question in ways which pinpoint the narrator's preoccupations and prejudices. At numerous moments the narrator, on the basis of quite warped or blinkered assessments of what are relevant or likely expectations – thus, concomitantly, ill-judged assessments of what his addressee would expect – unwittingly reveals his prejudices, hostilities and insecurities concerning his subject-matter. Such 'showings' are particularly interesting to identify, since they have to do with presupposition and implicature in discourse (on which, see more in Chapter 9), rather than anything that is overtly and directly stated. Let us take one example. Before the visitor arrives, the husband quips that maybe he could take the blind man bowling. His wife asks him to show a little compassion:

> 'Goddamn it, his wife's just died! Don't you understand that? The man's lost his wife!'
> I didn't answer. She'd told me a little about the blind man's wife. Her name was Beulah. Beulah! That's a name for a colored woman.
> 'Was his wife a Negro?' I asked.
> 'Are you crazy?' my wife said.
> 'Have you just flipped or something?' She picked up a potato. I saw it hit the floor, then roll under the stove.
> 'What's wrong with you?' she said. 'Are you drunk?'
> 'I'm just asking,' I said.

Here, as elsewhere in the story, what is jarring in the man's question 'Was his wife a Negro?' – so jarring as to prompt the wife's outburst in response – is the occurrence of just this question here. The husband learns (and reports) that the woman's name is Beulah (we thus learn the name of the blind man's wife, from the narrator, and have it evaluated by the narrator, long before we discover the name of the blind man himself). He reacts to the name in a way that, from the exclamation point, we can infer is disapproving or scornful; and then appends his own stereotyping generic comment. This gives rise to his question 'Was his wife a Negro?', which, although relevant to his own line of thought (a line of thought which dwells on appearances and categories: the woman's name, her ethnicity) has slight relevance to his wife's reminders, which were to do with the blind man himself. In the specific context of the conversation between the husband and wife, how relevant is it whether Beulah was, or was not, black? Clearly, not at all. And yet, as revealed, the question is relevant to the husband's way of thinking – a way characterized by stereotypes and ignorance and negative presumptions.

Another of many examples of this, both comic and pathetic, occurs in the way the husband now proceeds to sketch out the life Beulah and the blind man had together, before she succumbed to cancer. He summarizes:

They'd married, lived and worked together, slept together – had sex, sure – and then the blind man had to bury her.

Again what jars is what the husband assumes to be in need of telling, on the presupposition that if he had not done so, we addressees might have assumed otherwise. Thus he judges that he needs to tell us that Beulah and Robert 'slept together – had sex, sure –' , believing that we wouldn't have expected such normal human behaviour from a couple that included a blind person. What the narrator does here is typical of what he does frequently in the story; and it may be characteristic of the narrators of Carver's acclaimed and allegedly 'minimalist' fiction: characters' values and preoccupations and kinds of hurt are not declared directly in what they say and do, but only indirectly, via what is presupposed by what they say and do.

4   Let us look again at the phrasing *This blind man, an old friend of my wife's*, since the order of words in phrases, and the order of phrases in sentences, commonly reflects an implicit evaluative ranking. Just as there may be considerable difference in

meaning between *an old blind friend* and *a blind old friend* (the former is advanced in age, the latter may not be), so there are glaring differences in implication between

This blind man, an old friend of my wife's

and, say,

This old friend of my wife's, a blind man.

The former quite clearly implies that the individual's maleness and, especially, his blindness, are more important character-istics – in the speaker's view – than the fact that he is an old friend of the speaker's wife. In what ways can we contrast these two descriptions (*is a blind man/is an old friend of my wife's*) as kinds of description?

5   The first sentence exhibits use of what is sometimes called a 'resumptive pronoun'. In standard written English, it is ungrammatical to append a subject or object pronoun to an already supplied NP; pronouns in English typically are 'eco-nomical' free-standing substitutes for other nominal expres-sions, thus not to be used together with the replaced form: that would be an extravagance, not an economy. On the other hand just this resumptive use of pronouns is common, like the use of *this* noted earlier, in partisan jokes and stories. And at the very least, the use here clearly signals narratorial inform-ality, colloquialism, and vernacular casualness. It is a marker of orality rather than written-ness. What consequences do such details construct and project? What kind of situation are we, the reader-addressee, being coaxed into by such language? At the very least, isn't it true to say that 'being addressed' in this way sketches in a role and status for us as a rather different audience in a rather different setting than those sketched for us by the narrator of a Nabokov novel, or a Margaret Atwood poem, or a Toni Morrison story?

6   How do we know, as we do know, that the blind man is going to spend the night *with the narrator and his wife* – when the opening sentence only states that the blind man was 'on his way to spend the night'? Here, as in many other points in the story, the reader has to make a reasonable inference, in order to make the text fully coherent. After all, in a sense, we are all always on our way to 'spending the night'. Here, reflecting his general colloquial informality, the narrator doesn't spell out the contextually inferrable fact that it was at the home of the speaker

that the blind man was going to spend the night. At the same time, perhaps the omission is not entirely accidental: just how participatorily active is the husband in the arrangement of this visit, according to the narrator's account? Look again at the relevant sentences:

He called my wife from his in-laws'. Arrangements were made. He would come by train, a five-hour trip, and my wife would meet him at the station.

It is the blind man who acts, involving the wife in his plans; certainly, there is no mention here of the husband facilitating the visit.

7   Keeping in mind this chapter's thesis, that every single language-choice made by the author of 'Cathedral' is potentially significant, assess how your version of the story-opening expresses the information which, in the Carver version, is cast thus:

They made tapes and mailed them back and forth.

Comment on what may be being insinuated by this phrasing, which would be absent if the sentence had run:

They made tapes and mailed them to each other.

8   The husband-narrator, from the beginning of this story and throughout, refers to his spouse as *my wife*, and their guest as *the blind man*. The narrator thus never introduces his co-protagonists, nor does he denote them by their proper names. What kind of attitudes might one suspect of a speaker who never denotes their spouse, in a story, by name, and who invariably uses the formulation *my wife*?

9   In view of the speaker's declining to name his wife or (with only very particular exceptions) the blind man, what sense can we make of his interjection in the following sentence, in the course of his rehearsal of his wife's earlier life with her first husband, a military officer?

Her officer – why should he have a name? he was the childhood sweetheart, and what more does he want? – came home from somewhere, found her, and called the ambulance.

10   Turns of phrase.
     (a) In the second paragraph of the story we are told how the blind man, on the last day she worked for him, asked if he

could touch the wife's face. The text continues: *She agreed
to this*. What construction might the narrator be suspected
of putting on this incident, by the narrator's choice of
these words?

(b) Similarly, consider some of the word-choices in the following section, and how they disclose the husband's
implicit suspicions of and lack of respect for his wife:

> So okay. I'm saying that at the end of the summer she
> let the blind man run his hands over her face, said
> goodbye to him, married her childhood etc., who was
> now a commissioned officer, and she moved away from
> Seattle. But they'd kept in touch, she and the blind
> man. She made the first contact after a year or so.

(c) Now consider these lines from the middle of the story,
where the husband reports the 'getting re-acquainted'
conversation between his wife and the blind man:

> They talked of things that had happened to them – to
> them! – these past ten years. I waited in vain to hear
> my name on my wife's sweet lips: 'And then my dear
> husband came into my life' – something like that. But
> I heard nothing of the sort. More talk of Robert.
> Robert had done a little of everything, it seemed, a
> regular blind jack-of-all-trades.

What emotions in the husband, not fully declared or acknowledged, do some of the turns of phrase here point to?

11 Besides the idea that 'style creates viewpoint', it is also clear
that, in some circumstances, content creates viewpoint. This is
what I conclude from my experiences when asking students to
create an introduction for the story. As here, I invited them to
construct a story-opening on the basis of the information
supplied earlier. But there was one further piece of information among those I provided them with, which I left out of the
version presented to you here. In the version of the 'docu-
mentation' I gave my own students, I asked them to imagine
they were 'male white, American, etc. and married *without
children*'. Rather to my surprise, a number of these students
commented on how the information that the narrator and his
wife are aged about 30 and without children was, for them, a
strong signal of dysfunction and 'trouble'. These students
took the information as a 'warrant' for starting the story as
one in which the couple are at odds with each other in some

way. Do you agree with those students? Is the inference they
drew, that to be married without children suggests some
problem in a partnership, a culturally specific one? Should I
have left out the information that the couple had no children?
A seemingly slight piece of orientational material, particularly
when compounded with the idea that the visitor is her friend
but not his, makes a considerable difference to the kinds of
stories students began to construct.

12   These questions only serve to initiate study of word-choice in
Carver's powerful story; in actuality the story is saturated with
resonant linguistic choices on every line. And the discussion
here has only begun to display some of the issues that the
story is about. My chief hope at this stage is that you will feel
impelled to find the story and read it through. If you do so, the
following exercise will make sense! The task, first, is to think
about the following set of English pronouns, *nothing*,
everything, *something*, *anything*, and to jot down a few ideas
about how they are used, and particularly how they are used in
everyday situations such as conversation. What do they mean?
What uses are they put to? Then I would urge you to scan the
entire 'Cathedral' story, noting all the uses of these words in
the narration, or in characters' speech. The prominence of
these pronouns, in the story, does not seem to me incidental;
but if that is the case, then what effects are they intended to
project? As two examples among many, notice how the narrator closes the discussion of cathedrals by saying to Robert

> 'The truth is, cathedrals don't mean anything special
> to me. Nothing. Cathedrals. They're something to look
> at on late-night TV. That's all they are.'

And consider also the story's end, where the narrator keeps
his eyes closed ('I thought it was something I ought to do')
rather than opening them to look at the picture he has drawn:

> My eyes were still closed. I was in my house. I knew
> that. But I didn't feel like I was inside anything.
> 'It's really something,' I said.

To repeat, it may be appropriate to argue that several distinct
effects are created by the prominent use of the 'something,
nothing, etc.' pronouns at major points in the narrative. But
one way to pursue the topic would be to relate these pronouns'
use to the suggestion, proposed by education theorist Basil
Bernstein, that a contrast exists between a more restricted and

a more elaborated way of using language description and self-expression, with the restricted 'code' sometimes being associated with disempowerment, marginalization, and inarticulacy, by comparison with the elaborated code. For a brief discussion of this topic, see Fowler (1977: 115ff.)

Metaphor

There have been several mentions of metaphor in these chapters, but it really needs an entire book for adequate treatment (an excellent recent contribution is Andrew Goatly's *The Language of Metaphors*, Routledge, 1997). Nevertheless a few more comments at this point may be in order, for metaphorical language – particularly *fresh* or creative metaphor – is often the most vivid example of word-choice that is at once both wonderfully fitting and wonderfully unexpected. As a result, metaphor can equally be thought about in relation to lexical collocation, as discussed in Chapter 2. For metaphorical language is the very opposite of collocation (expected and expectable congregation of particular words). In creative metaphor, words are put into the company of other words with which they never ordinarily associate.

It is also important to note that there are many kinds of metaphor or metaphorizing, and also that the broad domain of figurative language usually refers, in addition to metaphor, to irony, hyperbole, and understatement. There are equally numerous effects achieved by use of metaphors and figures. I will not go beyond preliminary comments here.

The first of these is that wherever a speaker says something, intentionally, which they know to be wrong or misleading if the utterance were to be merely interpreted literally or by the lights of ordinary meanings, then that speaker is speaking figuratively: they are 'gesturing towards' (but not spelling out) a related but more interesting and half-concealed meaning. And in metaphorical speech, specifically, the speaker often says something patently absurd, like the speaker below who says, in effect, 'I'm an elephant and a ponderous house and a strolling melon'. Our first reaction may well be that the speaker is lying, or can't be serious. But with a little further thought we may find that, in an out-of-the-ordinary sense, the speaker is not lying and is serious. If we use our pregnant imaginations, we may be able to conceive of a situation in which a speaker might, with an out-of-the-ordinary accuracy and insight, describe themselves as elephantine, house-like, and melon-like.

Metaphors

I'm a riddle in nine syllables,
An elephant, a ponderous house,
A melon strolling on two tendrils.
O red fruit, ivory, fine timbers!
This loaf's big with its yeasty rising.
Money's new-minted in this fat purse.
I'm a means, a stage, a cow in calf.
I've eaten a bag of green apples,
Boarded the train there's no getting off.

Activities

ACTIVITY 3

Consider the following remark:

> *That girl is a lollipop.* (Or, in American English: *That girl is a popsicle.*)

Outside of very special circumstances (e.g., a theatrical performance about animated sweets, in which some boys act as bars of chocolate, some girls perform as lollipops, etc.), this utterance is likely to be interpreted as a metaphor. But just what the intended or derived meaning is may be quite variable – particularly since no context is specified above. Note down some of the most sharply contrasting situations (different speakers, addressees, referents for the phrase *that girl*) in which the utterance might be used. Can you think up a parallel metaphorical sentence characterizing a male subject, that is, a sentence with the following blank filled: *That boy is a* ————? Is it as interpretively versatile as the *that girl* sentence?

ACTIVITY 4

Consider the following two sentences:

(a) Babar is a human elephant.
(b) Barry is a human elephant.

Although these sentences appear quite similar, your interpretations for them may be rather different. Explain the bases for the differences in your two interpretations. What might you conclude about the uncertainty an interpreter may experience whenever they encounter, out of context, phrases like a *human elephant, a talking machine, a resistance pulverizer?*

ACTIVITY 5

Often the best metaphorical language, as in Shakespeare, appears not as isolated equations (X is a Y) but in brilliant flows of vivid representation. Here are several from *Henry IV, Part One.* The first is spoken by the old and tired King Henry at the play's opening, hoping – rather than being in a position to ordain – that there will be an end to civil strife and bloodletting in England. Cloze-style, a key metaphorical term has been left blank to see if you can deduce what it is:

> No more the thirsty entrance of this soil
> Shall daub her ____ with her own children's blood,

Consider, now, Henry's immediately following words, which employ a different and only locally metaphorical picture, in which the land – now innocent victim – is churned and gouged by war. This is less metaphorical since, in war, the land is literally churned and disfigured.

> No more shall trenching war channel her fields,
> Nor bruise her flow'rets with the armed ____
> Of hostile paces.

Again, I have left blank a key word for you to guess at, given this context.

In the early ludic scenes between the young dissolute Hal and the old reprobate Falstaff, the pair take turns pretending to be the old king admonishing Hal for his wild conduct. Playing the king, Falstaff begins:

> Harry, I do not only marvel where thou spendest thy time, but also how thou art accompanied. For though the camomile, the more it is trodden on, the faster it grows, so——, the more it is wasted, the sooner it wears.

Again, in the given circumstances, decide on what word best fills the blank: what might it be that Henry/Falstaff would set up in contrast with the camomile lawn, and of specific application to young Hal's circumstances? (§)

Commentaries

ACTIVITY 2

Raymond Carver's story 'Cathedral' opens as follows:

> This blind man, an old friend of my wife's, he was on his way
> to spend the night. His wife had died. So he was visiting the
> dead wife's relatives in Connecticut. He called my wife from
> his in-laws'. Arrangements were made. He would come by
> train, a five-hour trip, and my wife would meet him at the
> station. She hadn't seen him since she worked for him one
> summer in Seattle ten years ago. But she and the blind man
> had kept in touch. They made tapes and mailed them back and
> forth. I wasn't enthusiastic about his visit. He was no one I
> knew. And his being blind bothered me. My idea of blindness
> came from the movies. In the movies, the blind moved slowly
> and never laughed. Sometimes they were led by seeing-eye
> dogs. A blind man in my house was not something I looked
> forward to.

ACTIVITY 5

The phrase *thirsty entrance* should make you think of mouths and
drinking, and the general figure is one of the land as monster, devour-
ing its own young, consuming its own progeny (in premature death
and burial), and drinking their blood. The missing word is *lips*. Like so
many Shakespearean figures it is suggestive and provocative in multiple ways: we may notice that Henry implicitly blames something as
vague as 'the land' as the monstrous agent of all the bloodletting; there
is no room, in his chosen figure, for any acknowledgement of his own
culpability.

The missing word from the second extract is *hoofs*, predictable if
one notes that, in medieval war, the chief participants who might
produce hostile *paces* would be men and horses, and that the weight
of the latter (particularly laden with armour and a rider) must have
wrought far more damage to the land than the weight of the former.

Falstaff's Henry upbraids Hal for wasting his *youth*.

8

Talking: acts of give and take

Talk: the basics

What are we actually *doing* when we talk to each other? And how many truly different things can we do in the course of talking to each other? In this chapter I would like to sketch a simple answer to these questions, and then use this answer in exploring some of the dynamics of passages of talk in plays. My sketched answer to the two questions heading this paragraph may well be flawed and inaccurate; it contains what amounts to a 'speech act' model of dialogue (I shall explain the term 'speech act' more fully below), and such models have come in for plentiful criticism over the years. Nevertheless I think such speech act models continue to be one among an array of analytical tools useful to the study of dialogue – real or fictional – and it is in that guarded spirit that I present it here. But those first two questions are my underlying interest: if we imagine a speaker saying each of the following remarks, in the typical kind of context in which that remark is usually heard, we know quite well that particular and different things are being done in each case:

Good morning, Mr Barnes.

I'm so sorry darling.

I love that coat on you.

Could you phone back before 5?

Does she have an email address?

These are, respectively and typically, a greeting, an apology, a compliment, a request, and a question. But just how long might be such a list of typical acts performed, each with its own distinct label? And are there any overlaps once a longer list is devised? Could it be that, even if we accept that there are hundreds of distinguishable acts performable through speech, nevertheless that diversity emerges from a quite delimited and systematic core set of speech functions? (You may have noticed that these are very similar questions to those I asked, in relation to the range of activities that English verbs can express, at the beginning of Chapter 4.)

Many analysts, including Halliday (1994), have suggested that the language of dialogue involves, in essence, acts of exchange: conversationalists typically use language in the exchanging of information or services. The term 'exchange' may not be entirely satisfactory, largely because it suggests that there is normally a return, from interactant B to interactant A, in compensation for whatever A has supplied. In actuality talk is often far less reciprocal than this, so that it might be better to say that talk involves transfer more consistently than exchange – although transfer doesn't seem quite the right word either! With that caveat lodged, I shall continue to use the term 'exchange' below. The following paragraphs adopt and elaborate a number of ideas which have their source in Chapter 3 of Halliday (1994), to which the reader is referred for further discussion of the grammatical roots of the different kinds of act. For an excellent introductory survey of the entire field of what is known as discourse analysis, Coulthard (1985) is recommended.

When individuals talk to each other, they are enacting exchanges, and these exchanged phenomena can be thought of as predominantly either mental or physical, and the grammar of English reflects this. If the enacted exchange is chiefly mental, the conversational contribution amounts to a giving of information or a seeking of information; if the exchange is chiefly physical, the contribution amounts to a giving or seeking of goods and services. The four core conversational moves, or acts, thus amount to the giving, or seeking, of either information or goods and services. These can be represented as in the table below, with example utterances:

	Goods & services	Information
Speaker is giving to addressee	*Can I give you a hand with that?*	*I mustn't do any heavy lifting*
Speaker is seeking from addressee	*Will you give me a hand with this?*	*Have you got a good hold at your end*

We can give familiar labels for the typical kind of conversational act performed in these four core categories:

	PROPOSALS Goods & services	PROPOSITIONS Information
Giving	offer	inform
Seeking	request	question

We can also group offers and requests together, and informs and questions: since offers and requests both concern future proposed action by one interactant or the other, they are called proposals; since informs and questions provide or seek information, they are called propositions. The future action that a proposal specifies is normally nonverbal (washing the dishes, closing the door, repaying a loan, etc.) although occasionally it can involve a verbal performance ('Billy, recite the present tense conjugation of *donner*, please'). The information sought or given in response to a proposition is normally verbal, but replies to propositions can be performed nonverbally (A: 'Where's the oilcan?' B: [points to far corner of garage]).

Each of these labels (offer, request, inform, and question) covers a range of utterances. For example, under the request category I include, as the figure above implies, any conversational act in which a speaker seeks goods or services from the addressee. Thus the request category includes commands, demands, requests, begging, much praying, and so on; for example:

> *Pull in to the side of the road, please.*
>
> *Could you pass the salad?*
>
> *Please don't tell Mummy.*
>
> *Shall we begin?*

At first glance one might be tempted to include threats within the offer category, since these sometimes promise to give some service to the addressee, even if they are intended to be damaging to that addressee. But threats are always implicitly or explicitly subordinate to some superordinate request which, in the threatener's view, is being unsatisfactorily addressed by the party being threatened: 'if you don't do/stop doing x I will etc.' Furthermore, the speaker's preference is for the request to be complied with and for the threatened consequence to be set aside, rather than for the request to be dismissed so that the threatened negative consequence has to be attempted. So threats are essentially requests, not offers.

Of the four primary classes, offers seem to be the least extensively used. But they are a relatively well-defined group: they are proposed future actions or services on the part of the speaker, ostensibly to the benefit of the addressee, the undertaking of which are, significantly, implicitly dependent upon the addressee's consent. This last point is arguably crucial, particularly for distinguishing offers from the kind of announcing utterance (*I'm going to reorganize our bookshelves into some sort of order*) which – depending on the addressee's response – can function as an inform rather than an offer. Grammatically, offers are usually in the first person, often with one of the modal verbs *shall, can*, or *may*, where these can be interpreted as contributing to a proposal which means 'Do you consent to me doing *x* for you?' A typical and expectable response to an offer is a reply expressing consent – *OK*; *alright* – or a declination with an appended reason – *No thanks, I've just had one*. Although offers often use the constructions *Can I . . . ? May I . . . ?* or *Shall I . . . ?*, it is important to note that this does not mean that all such constructions are invariably offers: *Can I fly there direct?*, for example, is clearly not an offer but a question.

Having said something about both requests and offers, the two basic act types which make proposals for action, the two proposition-conveying types of acts can be commented on more briefly. Informs include claims, warnings and compliments; they entail the imparting – at one level or another – of verbalizable information, and are broadly intended to be beneficial to the addressee. Whether or not the addressee finds an inform informative is a separate matter. And there are particular kinds of utterance that do not fit these criteria very smoothly. Thus if A tells B 'I'm bored', it is hard not to see this as some kind of inform; but how this information is beneficial to B is less clear. Perhaps the most straightforward of these four 'master' categories is that of questions: they are acts designed to obtain the kind of information that informs supply; they typically cast the addressee as 'knower', incurring the 'cost' involved in taking the trouble of informing the questioner, that is, giving something that is beneficial to the questioner.

Identifying acts functionally and formally

So far I have been calling this utterance an offer, and that utterance a request, as if the labelling were simple and invariable. But the situation is a little more complex. With suitably different contexts, the same string of words can easily function as a request in one dialogue and as, say, a question in another situation. Or, to give another example, consider the utterance you might hear when you phone the electricity company to complain about a bill:

Can you hold?

On functional grounds, since it is intended by the speaker to get the hearer to do something (and something more in the speaker's immediate interests than the hearer's), this is a request. But now consider the following invented exchange:

A: Can you guess the only words from a real human being that I got out of the electricity company this morning when I telephoned them to complain about the bill?
B: 'Can you hold?'
A: Exactly!

Here B's contribution serves as a question (similar to 'Would it have been 'Can you hold?' by any chance?'). Now consider an exchange between a switchboard supervisor and a trainee receptionist:

Supervisor: Now once you see that every adviser's line is busy, what is the first thing you must say to new callers?
Trainee: 'Can you hold?'
Supervisor: 'Can you hold, sir or madam.' Good.

Here the trainee's contribution is an elicited inform – no less an inform just because, like many responses to teachers' questions, it informs the instructor of something they know already.

I have supplied these examples to emphasize that the surface form of an utterance taken separately cannot tell us which speech act is performed by that sequence 'in all situations'. We have to look at utterances in context to do this (and my earlier examples, blithely labelled offers, informs, etc., have relied on your imagining the utterances in a *stereotypical* context of use). The examples also serve to underline that act-identification is guided by function, not form. This can seem troublesome, since functions are sometimes less tangible and explicit and more open to variant interpretation than forms. However, there are ways, outlined below, in which functionalist interpretation can be usefully underpinned, often with reference to formal and grammatical evidence. These confirmatory criteria help ensure that disputes where analyst A says 'That's an inform' and analyst B says 'No it's not, it's an offer' are actually quite rare. Similarly, in actual interaction, we are very infrequently forced to pause and wonder 'Is he asking me or telling me?', 'Was that an offer or a request?'; and the occasions when we do hesitate in this way are, clearly, worthy of attention for that reason alone.

The four-way system of contrasts outlined above, then, arguably 'pins down the four corners' of a schematic map charting the potential acts performed by interactants via language. And the four acts identified also seem supported by various kinds of linguistic evidence. The first kind of evidence to note is the established grammatical system of imperative, declarative and interrogative formats or moods:

Eat your spinach!

She ate her spinach.

Did she eat her spinach?

Often grammatical imperatives express discoursal requests, declaratives express informs, and interrogatives express questions. But on many occasions this simple matching is absent (to begin with, we have three grammatical sentence-types, but four act types). For example, despite being in the declarative, the following utterance in suitable context is more likely to be a request than an inform:

I want you to eat your spinach this minute!

How do we know that the above is a request, not an inform? What kinds of criteria, might justify describing it as a Request? Two criteria which may be particularly important here are:

1   '*please*-insertability' and

2   prospection.

With requests, unlike informs and questions (the third and fourth examples below), you can usually insert the word *please* before the verb denoting the action to be performed. This is true even in the case of 'indirect' requests like the present one:

Please eat your spinach!

I want you to please eat your spinach this minute!

?She please ate her spinach.

?Did she please eat her spinach?

The second criterion, prospection, refers to the kind of response – in terms of language behaviour – that we would expect to occur after the given act. For example, offers very often prospect 'Thank you', but requests and questions do not:

Take the rest of the day off, Mr Smith.
Thank you, Mr Soames.

Pick up your cards in Personnel and don't come back.
*Thank you, Mr Soames.

Instead requests standardly prospect some compliant action on the part of the addressee; and this may be optionally preceded or accompanied by a verbal acknowledgement of the request, such as 'OK', 'Sure', or a verbal declination, such as 'No!' Note that prospection concerns what you *expect* to see or hear after a question, offer, etc., rather than what you actually get. And these things vary culturally. Thus while offers in Britain between friends prospect *Thank you*, in America in similar circumstances you will quite often hear (just) *Okay*. This can be disconcerting to British ears! Here is a summary of act-prospection pairings:

Act type	Possible prospection
Offer	*Thanks/No thanks*
Request	*OK + action/No! (I can't/won't) + action*
Inform	*Oh*
Question	*Yes/I don't know*

The items listed here as prospections are not cited as necessarily the normal or most usual response to the given act, but rather as entirely possible responses for that act which are in addition highly implausible as responses for any of the other acts. Consider 'Oh', a legitimate response to informs. While this would be an awkward response to some kinds of informs it remains a coherent one; but 'Oh' as a complete and freestanding response to an offer ('I'll put the garbage out') or a request ('Put the garbage out, would you?') or a question ('Did you put the garbage out?') would be decidedly odd.

At the same time, a more likely response to some kinds of informs may well be 'Thanks' and not 'Oh'. Consider, for example, service-encounter enquiries in which you ask someone at an information-desk for a particular inform (the desk may be 'virtual', as when we phone directory enquiries). Here, a question (not a request, since the act is intended to secure the supply of verbal information, rather than a particular – usually nonverbal – behaviour) is, as is to be expected, followed by an inform and this inform is in practice much more likely to be responded to by 'Thanks' than by 'Oh'. But then this is a particular kind of inform, a contingent and non-exchange-initial one. It is a solicited inform. By contrast the specified prospections in the table above apply to exchange-initial acts, ones which initiate a round of talk rather than respond to another party's already initiated exchange. And when someone 'spontaneously' or freely provides you with information, via an inform, 'Oh' amounts to a default acknowledgement that you have heard and understood; 'Thanks', in the acknowledgement of an exchange-initial inform, amounts to treatment of that inform as exceptionally beneficial to the addressee, and a relatively 'unrecompensable' cost to the speaker. Imagine that, as you are walking away from your parked car, A says to you:

A: Excuse me sir, but you've left your headlights on.

You probably reply something like:

B: Oh yes, thanks very much.

That this is an exceptional situation, an unpredicted exchange outside the normal pattern, is perhaps signalled by the initial *Excuse me*.

Another way in which the core acts can be often be discriminated is by reference to the constrasting 'characterizing frames' into which the utterances instantiating them can fit. A useful 'characterizing frame' for requests is 'The speaker asked the addressee to (verb) ____' while, by contrast, that for questions is 'The speaker asked the addressee ____' where the blank element can be filled by *anything but* an immediate 'to + verb'. You will find that many utterances can be paraphrased using the latter frame; but where you find, in addition, that the former frame, for requests, is also a reasonable paraphrase, then this constitutes good evidence that the utterances is a request and not a question.

In short, with judicious consideration of verbal and behavioural prospections and formal tests like please-insertability, the basic four-way act classification can prove to be surprisingly reliable. It can also help us to re-think some of our expectations of particular kinds of language activity or genre. For example, the genre label 'service-encounter', may mislead us into thinking that these exchanges always involve a request for a material service. But in practice service-encounters may involve the seeking of either nonverbal goods and services (e.g., an airline ticket from a travel agency) or verbal information (e.g., a quoted price for a particular airline ticket, from the same agency); or, of course, a complex combination of both.

Complex acts, marginal cases, and phatic 'stroking'

While offers, requests, questions and informs as defined above are the canonical discoursal acts, there are invariably occasions of speech which seem to be intermediate between these categories. Consider, for example, the following utterances, from someone wishing to go out on a date with the person addressed:

1   *Would you be interested in going to a movie with me some time?*

2   *Can I offer you lunch?*

These are interrogative in form, but surely convey a proposal rather than a proposition, hence are either requests or offers. (1) is arguably a complex speech act, in which an underlying request (because a non-verbal action beneficial to the speaker is sought, whether or not it is also beneficial to the addressee) is wrapped in a question 'shell'. The question is enough of a real one to prospect 'Yes' as part of a possible compliant reply; by contrast a typical request – such as 'Please come to a movie with me' – never prospects the response 'Yes' as a sufficient reply. (1) is, then, an atypical request, with question-like trimmings. It is the kind of complexly designed utterance we can expect to find where a speaker wishes both to secure an addressee's cooperation and to minimize the sense of imposition or 'face-threat'. In other words, its complex exploitation of the basic system can be explained via recourse to politeness theory, on which a little more is said later in this chapter. The 'characterizing frame' test, mentioned above, can be useful here too. The question frame is applicable, although scarcely different from the source utterance: *The speaker asked the addressee if they would be interested in going to a movie with him/her some time.* But significantly, if we 'bracket out' the questioning element, *interested in*, the request frame is also appropriate –

> The speaker asked the addressee to go to a movie with him/her

– and this suggests that the utterance is indeed ultimately a request.

Sentence (2) is superficially a question checking the speaker's ability to do something – a question which the speaker is logically in a much better position to answer than the addressee; but the typical intent of this indirect formulation is to request that the addressee have lunch with the speaker. The act performed is therefore borderline between an offer and a request, but lying closer to the former prototypical category (it does not accept *please*-insertion – *Can I please buy you lunch?* – and, unlike a request, it seems to require some verbal response, of consent or declination). So (2) is an offer with overtones of requesting, and question-like trimmings! Such marginal cases show clearly enough how the specific dynamics of the situation of use, including the tenor of the relations between the parties involved, and the prosody adopted (the stress and intonation), are all crucial to the classifying of utterances as particular acts.

While offers, requests, informs and questions are argued here to be central to discourse, they are not the only acts involved. But they are the central ones, I shall hypothesize, in that just one among these four can occur as the nucleus of a first move in an interaction. But interlocutors' responses also merit classification. And in fact each of the canonical initiating acts strongly specifies a particular kind of response:

Offer   > Acceptance

Request   > (Acknowledgement +) Non-verbal performance

Inform   > Acknowledgement

Question > Inform

You will see that this elaboration introduces just two new kinds of act, acceptances and acknowledgements, of a quite secondary nature. Typical examples of acceptances are *thanks*, *ok*, and *very well*; typical examples of acknowledgements are *oh*, *thanks*, and *really?*; and non-verbal equivalents are often used instead. Acceptances and acknowledgements are secondary in that they are semantically attenuated, as the above examples suggest, and in that they are contingent upon some prior, exchange-driving act from among the set of four described above. Relatedly, while we have characterized talk as kinds of give and take, very little is given (back) when an acceptance or acknowledgement alone is made; and a bare positive acceptance is not very different from a bare negative one, i.e. a declination of an offer, even though the interactional implications and consequences may be great. Nor, taken as whole groups, are they profoundly different from each other in form or function. For these various reasons, I propose to treat all verbal acceptances/acknowledgements as members of a single secondary class of act, abbreviated as As, alongside abbreviations for the four other primary acts: O, R, I and Q.

The picture presented so far, of dialogue as a trading of offers, requests, informs and questions, seems to bias the picture towards a transactional view of talk, as if we were always intent on getting work done, of 'dealing', using our words and our physical capabilites. What about the interactional side to talk, where we give and take 'strokes' (or lashes)? Isn't verbal interaction peppered with greetings and partings, compliments, apologies, insults, acknowledgements, and so on, many of them traditionally classified as phatic communication? Where do these fit into a picture of offers, requests, informs and questions?

I shall argue that all these interactional manoeuvres can fit within the system sketched so far, even if they are atypical cases. The following apology is two informs – *I'm sorry; I shouldn't have done that* – even if the second of these is something the addressee knew already and the first is less than heartfelt. The compliments *What a fabulous jacket!* and *Sharp haircut!* are informs with evaluation and other-attentiveness uppermost. Greetings and partings are often the most mechanical and routine parts of interaction but they, too, can be characterized as in part informs, disclosing the speaker's wishes or disposition towards the addressee (as indeed do insults, also). Very many of our more interactional speech acts (compliments, greetings, and so on) are informs refracted by considerations of politeness. A compliment is an inform that is noticeably and excessively attentive to the addressee's positive face, while an insult is an inform designed to be abnormally threatening to the addressee's positive face. Since an inform is usually 'beneficial' to the addressee (see below), the insulting inform is sharply at odds with normal patterns in this respect too.

We can use additional, clarifying descriptive terms about the four core speech acts: giving or seeking goods and services are proposals, that something happen or be done; giving or seeking information are propositions, that something be known. A proposal involves a speaker intent on some act of doing, a proposition involves a speaker intent on some act of knowing. Furthermore, as should be clear from the examples of an offer, a request, an inform, and a question, the relations of dependence or obligation between speaker and addressee are sharply different in the four basic cases. Let us think of speaker and addressee as self and other respectively. Then, clearly, a rather different dependence-relation is implied when a speaker offers:

Can I give you a hand with that?

than when she requests:

Will you give me a hand with this?

In an offer, as the grammar reflects ('. . . *I give you* . . .'), the speech act is focused on the needs of the other, the addressee—or at least on what the speaker thinks are the other's needs. Other is cast as beneficiary, self is presented as the giver who, as in any genuine act of giving, is likely to incur some costs. Indeed it is hard to think of a genuine offer, a giving of goods and services, that doesn't involve one in some costs. Additionally, although less overtly, the speaker-self who makes an offer may be adopting a stance of deference or subordination to whoever the addressed other is.

In a request, on the other hand, the relations are broadly reversed: the utterance is self-oriented, imposes some cost on the addressee, and may cast that other in a subordinate stance. We can make similar characterizations of propositions, whether informs or questions. On the assumption that knowledge is desirable, informs involve a knowing self going to the trouble or cost of informing an other, primarily for the latter's benefit; and questions *typically* involve a not-knowing self imposing on an other-addressee, to self's benefit. So, unlike the cases in proposals, in which the subordinate-superior roles match up with those of cost-incurrer and beneficiary, in propositions the two pairs of roles diverge:

> **Offer**: speaker cast as subordinate and incurs cost, addresseee cast as superior and beneficiary
>
> **Request**: speaker cast as superior and beneficiary, addressee cast as subordinate and incurs cost
>
> **Inform**: speaker cast as superior (the knower) but incurs cost, addressee cast as subordinate but beneficiary
>
> **Question**: speaker cast as subordinate but beneficiary, addressee cast as superior (the knower) but incurs cost

The fifth and secondary category, acknowledgements, cross-cuts these, typically occurring as follow-up to a request–compliance pair, or a question–inform pair, or a free-standing offer or inform:

> **Acknowledgement**: speaker may be represented as subordinate, but is beneficiary of the preceding exchange, and incurs this minor cost of expressing thanks or acceptance

Let me emphasize again that these characterizations are tendencies, fitting canonical instances well and other instances more loosely. Thus in a canonical inform, the speaker is a cost-incurring knower, and the addressee is informationally subordinate but the beneficiary. But in an atypical inform, such as a compliment, these characterizations are obviously modulated: the superior–subordinate contrast is minimized, and speaker's cost is slight, and the extent to which the speaker is telling the addressee something they do not already know may range from great to small. Compliments are thus a kind of inform with some characteristics approaching those of an offer; nevertheless they are essentially informs and not offers. Propositions and proposals contrast in other interesting ways besides. Offers and requests specify actions scheduled to occur within a timespan that extends from the speaker's present into the future; their temporal reference is delimited to the non-past. Informs and questions, by contrast, are quite unrestricted in their potential temporal reference: a proposition can refer to a state of affairs sited in the distant past as easily as in the distant future.

On Cloud Nine

After that lengthy outline of the descriptive model, it is now time to look at some actual literary dialogue to see how the system works. The extract that follows comes from the opening of the second act of Caryl Churchill's play *Cloud Nine*, a farce-like overview of Anglo-Saxon attitudes 'then and now'. The play ranges freely among themes familiar and controversial: colonialism, sexism, feminism, marriage, family, racism, classism, sexuality, sexual-orientation, gender-bending, paedophilia, and so on.

Perhaps inevitably, many of the characters are, as a result, stereotypes, but they are interesting and funny rather than crude and boring. Their stereotypicality is shown rather than told. In addition, from Act One to Act Two there is a chronological leap of about 100 years, from Victorian colonial Africa to late 1970s London; so here at the opening of Act Two we effectively meet entirely new characters. My basic premise is that if we tag these characters' utterances in terms of the four speech act options – offer, request, inform, and question (and secondary acknowledgements) – we can proceed fairly speedily to a more detailed understanding of their different temperaments, interests, and goals. But first, the scene:

Winter afternoon. Inside the hut of a one o'clock club, a children's playcentre in a park, VICTORIA and LIN, mothers. CATHY, LIN's daughter, age 4, played by a man, clinging to LIN. VICTORIA reading a book.

CATHY: Yum yum bubblegum.
  Stick it up your mother's bum.
  When it's brown
  Pull it down
  Yum yum bubblegum.
LIN: Like your shoes, Victoria.
CATHY: Jack be nimble, Jack be quick,
  Jack jump over the candlestick.
  Silly Jack, he should jump higher,
  Goodness gracious, great balls of fire.
LIN: Cathy, do stop. Do a painting.
CATHY: You do a painting.
LIN: You do a painting.
CATHY: What shall I paint?
LIN: Paint a house.
CATHY: No.
LIN: Princess.
CATHY: No.
LIN: Pirates.
CATHY: Already done that.
LIN: Spacemen.
CATHY: I never paint spacemen. You know I never.
LIN: Paint a car crash and blood everywhere.
CATHY: No, don't tell me. I know what to paint.
LIN: Go on then. You need an apron, where's an apron. Here.
CATHY: Don't want an apron.

LIN: Lift up your arms. There's a good girl.

CATHY: I don't want to paint.

LIN: Don't paint. Don't paint.

CATHY: What shall I do? You paint. What shall I do mum?

VICTORIA: There's nobody on the big bike, Cathy, quick.

[CATHY *goes out.* VICTORIA *is watching the children playing outside.*]

VICTORIA: Tommy, it's Jimmy's gun. Let him have it. What the hell.

[*She goes on reading. She reads while she talks.*]

LIN: I don't know how you can concentrate.

VICTORIA: You have to or you never do anything.

LIN: Yeh, well. It's really warm in here, that's one thing.
It's better than standing out there. I got chilblains last winter.

VICTORIA: It is warm.

LIN: I suppose Tommy doesn't let you read much. I expect he talks to
you while you're reading.

VICTORIA: Yes, he does.

LIN: I didn't get very far with that book you lent me.

VICTORIA: That's all right.

LIN: I was glad to have it, though. I sit with it on my lap while I'm
watching telly. Well, Cathy's off. She's frightened I'm going to leave
her. It's the babyminder didn't work out when she was two, she still
remembers. You can't get them used to other people if you're by
yourself. It's no good blaming me. She clings round my knees every
morning up the nursery and they don't say anything but they make
you feel you're making her do it. But I'm desperate for her to go to
school. I did cry when I left her the first day. You wouldn't, you're
too fucking sensible. You'll call the teacher by her first name. I really
fancy you.

VICTORIA: What?

LIN: Put your book down will you for five minutes. You didn't hear a
word I said.

VICTORIA: I don't get much time to myself.

LIN: Do you ever go to the movies?

VICTORIA: Tommy's very funny who he's left with. My mother baby-
sits sometimes.

LIN: Your husband could babysit.

VICTORIA: But then we couldn't go to the movies.

LIN: You could go to the movies with me.

VICTORIA: Oh I see.

LIN: Couldn't you?

VICTORIA: Well, yes, I could.

LIN: Friday night?

VICTORIA: What film are we talking about?

LIN: Does it matter what film?

VICTORIA: Of course it does.

LIN: You choose then. Friday night.

[CATHY *comes in with the gun, shoots them saying Kiou kiou kiou, and runs off again.*]

Not in a foreign language, ok. You don't go to the movies to read.

[LIN *watches the childen playing outside.*]

Don't hit him, Cathy, kill him. Point the gun, kiou, kiou, kiou. That's the way.

VICTORIA: They've just banned war toys in Sweden.

LIN: The kids'll just hit each other more.

VICTORIA: Well, psychologists do differ in their opinions as to whether or not aggression is innate.

LIN: Yeh?

VICTORIA: I'm afraid I do let Tommy play with guns and just hope he'll get it out of his system and not end up in the army.

LIN: I've got a brother in the army.

VICTORIA: Oh I'm sorry. Whereabouts is he stationed?

LIN: Belfast.

VICTORIA: Oh dear.

LIN: I've got a friend who's Irish and we went on a Troops Out march. Now my dad won't speak to me.

VICTORIA: I don't get on too well with my father either.

LIN: And your husband? How do you get on with him?

VICTORIA: Oh, fine. Up and down. You know. Very well. He helps with the washing up and everything.

LIN: I left mine two years ago. He let me keep Cathy and I'm grateful for that.

VICTORIA: You shouldn't be grateful.

LIN: I'm a lesbian.

VICTORIA: You still shouldn't be grateful.

LIN: I'm grateful he didn't hit me harder than he did.

VICTORIA: I suppose I'm very lucky with Martin.

LIN: Don't get at me about how I bring up Cathy, ok?

VICTORIA: I didn't.

LIN: Yes you did. War toys. I'll give her a rifle for Christmas and blast Tommy's pretty head off for a start.

[VICTORIA *goes back to her book.*]

LIN: I hate men.

VICTORIA: You have to look at it in a historical perspective in terms of learnt behaviour since the industrial revolution.

LIN: I just hate the bastards.

VICTORIA: Well it's a point of view.

The scene begins with Cathy's racy rhymes, a series of provocative and unelicited – indeed, unwelcome – informs (themselves containing embedded fictional requests, such as 'Jack jump over the candlestick'). Lin's interjection, addressed to Victoria, is demonstrably not the kind of acknowledge that informs prospect; as her next utterance, a request, confirms – *Cathy, do stop* – she doesn't want to be in conversation with her daughter at all. But Cathy is not easily 'managed': Lin's next request to her is bounced straight back, to be returned again – all routine parent–child friction! When Cathy seeks guidance – via a question – on just what to paint (even though she has just implied she won't do a painting: such unannounced changes of attitude and compliance are not rare in natural discourse), Lin's suggestions (requests) are unsurprisingly rejected. In terms of the 'preferred' prospections of the four canonical acts, we have yet to encounter a single paired exchange in which a first act (of requesting, informing, etc.) has been compliantly responded to. Thus even our quite rudimentary speech act description highlights factors that one might certainly want reflected in the playing of this scene, and the interpretation of these characters, in an actual production. When Lin's exasperation point is reached, she resorts to grim humour with the suggestion that Cathy paint a car crash and blood everywhere. But more funny and ghoulish is Cathy's request reply, *No, don't tell me* – as if she wanted to have come up with this 'excellent idea' all by herself!

Activities

ACTIVITY 1

Not all the act-labelling of this scene will be as clear cut as it has been so far. Consider, for example, Lin's utterance 'There's a good girl' three lines further down. It follows her request that Cathy lift up her arms, evidently so that the apron can be put on her. But does the apron actually get put on? And relatedly, what act does 'There's a good girl' perform here? Does it approximate to 'please': is it thus a reiterated request? Or does it approximate 'thank you', and is hence an acknowledgement of performed requested behaviour? Both interpretations may be valid, and different productions of the play may select either one. Argue the case for your preferred interpretation.

ACTIVITY 2

With Cathy's resumed questions 'What shall I do? . . . What shall I do mum?' the tiresome prospect of another round of unproductive exchanges looms. How does this first episode, the badgering of Lin by Cathy, end? Comment in detail on how Cathy is finally placated. (§)

ACTIVITY 3

A little further into the scene, notice how Victoria responds when Lin encourages Cathy to 'kill' Tommy with the toy gun. Lin (requesting) says 'Point the gun, kiou, kiou, kiou. That's the way.' And Victoria informs Lin, 'They've just banned war toys in Sweden.' Would you agree that Victoria is here 'signifying' at Lin? What 'underlying' inform and request might we construct, and treat as implied by Victoria's neutral-seeming reporting inform? And what subsequent evidence do we have to suggest that Lin has indeed 'heard' Victoria's underlying speech acts? §

Thus the specificities of how characters interact – how Lin requests and Cathy requests or questions back, and of how Victoria implies proposals by actually uttering mere informs – provide a rapid and revealing illumination of their contrasting natures. Even this early some patterns are beginning to emerge. Working-class and less-educated Lin tends to interact via proposals (offers and requests), which also means she is intent on doing things and (trying to) get things done; middle-class educated Victoria tends to interact via propositions (informs and questions), even when particular proposals are her goal; so on the latter occasions, there is inevitably an indirectness and subtlety, and a 'non-face-threatening' politeness to her discourse.

ACTIVITY 4

In the next exchanges between Lin and Victoria it is reasonably clear that Victoria is a reluctant conversationalist: Lin wants to be talking with Victoria, while Victoria would evidently rather be reading. Comment on how the contrasting nature and extent of Victoria's turns of speech, by contrast with those of Lin, confirm these impressions.

ACTIVITY 5

Would you agree that Lin's announcement *I really fancy you* is almost entirely unprospected? Comment on how this utterance, and those that follow it, might need to be performed. In short, what does this unexpected inform contribute to the dynamics of this scene and our sense of these characters? (§)

ACTIVITY 6

There is not enough space here to look at length and in appropriate analytical detail at how humour is created in the passage. Some comments on just one instance will have to suffice. For example, what factors contribute to the humour to be found in both Lin's and Victoria's final turns in the reproduced passage?

1 LIN: I hate men.
2 VICTORIA: You have to look at it in a historical perspective in terms of learnt behaviour since the industrial revolution.
3 LIN: I just hate the bastards.
4 VICTORIA: Well it's a point of view.

Here, too, act analysis seems relevant. Turns 1, 3 and 4 are informs, while in turn 2 Victoria produces a modalized request concerning how we 'have to' understand the historical basis of men's behaviour. But Lin will have nothing to do with this suggestion, as her use of *just* announces to us. We can also sensitize ourselves to the importance of just how 3 is phrased by comparing it with other possible responses which Lin could have used but did not (this way of proceeding is very much the approach taken in the previous chapter). In place of the actual turn 3, Lin might have replied to Victoria with any of those listed below:

LIN: I hate men.
VICTORIA: You have to look at in a historical perspective in terms of learnt behaviour since the industrial revolution.
LIN: I hate men.
  – I just hate men.
  – I just hate them.
  – I loathe the bastards.
  – I just loathe the bastards.
  – I hate the way that they blame you for everything wrong with their lives and claim all the credit for everything that's right with their lives.
  – No I don't.
  – Why should I?
  – What's that got to do with my ex-?

And so on. Arguably, none of these is as funny or works quite the same effect as Lin's actual reply. And those alternatives which are closest to the actual reply, such as *I just loathe the bastards*, may be the most illuminating of what sets the actual reply apart. Do you agree that, given what we can infer of Lin's character and Victoria's character, and given what Lin has said in utterance 1 and Victoria in utterance 2, that *I just hate the bastards* is indeed the best choice among those listed? How is it contextually more appropriate or effective than either *I just loathe the bastards* or *I just hate them*? Make the case in support of *I just hate the bastards* if you prefer that formulation, or make the case for an alternative utterance if that is your preference. (§)

The reader will find many other ingenious exploitations of speech-act sequences and presuppositions (on which, see the next chapter) in *Cloud Nine*. Clearly the model sketched here should be useful in analysis of a range of fictional and actual dialogues. Some readers may still be wondering: Why should we bother with all this laborious and fallible classification? And why, in particular, should it be thought that this has any relevance to the reading and appreciation of literature? A decent reply to these doubts should begin by considering how one might proceed to study drama dialogue without recourse to systems, methods, and inventories. What is likely to happen is that, on a step-by-conversational-step basis, you notice how Lin 'shares' while Victoria is more reserved; how Lin tells her child to do things while Victoria barely does at all, and quickly gives up the effort; how Lin pesters and prods Victoria. But what you would be unable to do would be to locate these tendencies – however acutely recognized and described in their particularity – within a general scheme of interactional possibilities. It is one thing to note that one character makes a series of impositive requests of another character; but we cannot grasp the full significance of this unless we have a clearer understanding of the complete range of possible discourse acts that an interactant could perform; this is what any general description of discourse acts attempts to articulate. By analogy, to describe a shirt as 'cyan' is only fully understood if speaker and addressee have a shared grasp of the full set of colour terms, and in particular the set of terms for shades of blue, that is being assumed. Our general description of discourse acts attempts to map, in themselves and relative to each other, the foundational colours to be found on the spectrum of interactional possibilities.

Literal and figurative

So far, the presented examples of offers, commands, etc. have been relatively straightforward requests. But we should now add to our account a complication of very much the same kind that is evident in process and participant analysis: the complication is, broadly, that a speaker can cast their language as if one kind of process (or, here, interactive act) were involved, and yet really intend to express a rather different process (or interactive act). A speaker can do this because the English language – perhaps to a degree rivalled by few other languages – has innumerable well-established practices of metaphorizing, saying things indirectly, and so on, which exist alongside previously established and still recognizable 'nonmetaphorized' or direct expressions. Thus we saw, in the transitivity section of this workbook, that many clauses invite a 'double' analysis for one of several reasons: the expression used may be metaphorical (*That album really blew me away*), where what viewed literally would be glossed as a material process is clearly mental, with the album as phenomenon, not force; or the expression may involve a participant which, being a nominalization, itself entails a backgrounded process.

Just as there are indirect and reconfigured ways of expressing various processes in the language, there are similarly indirect and reconfigured ways of performing offers, requests and so on, so that, as in the case of processes, a 'two-level' analysis is possible, with the underlying level similarly being more crucial. Thus if someone says, 'I've just baked a Victoria sponge, if you'd like a piece', this might superficially look like a statement, with the interactive function of an inform; but in context it is very much more likely to function as an offer, and it prospects the kind of response that offers typically do ('Thanks, that sounds lovely'; 'Oh, no thank you, I'm trying to avoid cakes and sweets'). Or if a parent says to a child 'How many times am I going to have to ask you to pick your coat up off the floor?', this is only at the most superficial level a question: functioning in context it is almost certainly *not* looking for an informative answer such as 'Twenty-three times' or 'Until thy visage is azured o'er'. The 'enquiry' is underlyingly a directive request, and a noticeably forceful one at that, and it prospects prompt compliant behaviour or some accounting for why that behaviour cannot be forthcoming. On this point notice that a reply like 'But you told me to bring the shopping in from the car!' is a much more acceptable reply than 'Twenty-three times', although the former is no kind of direct answer to the construction 'How many times?'

The point to take away from this brief discussion of 'figurative' speech acts is that, in looking at moves in talk, you will often need to think about the underlying purpose or function of the utterance, rather than its surface form and content. Very many times, we give and take in talk in ways that veer away from the simplest formats. The cover term for those factors that lead us to make simple acts more verbally complex is affect: considerations of politeness (or face), deference, affection, antipathy, anger, exuberance, guardedness, and so on, are the major sources of our recastings of direct offers, informs, questions and requests. Indeed a rich analytical literature has emerged in recent years, exploring these issues, and in particular exploring how each of us projects and protects our own sense of self, and respects other people's sense of their identity, via various politeness strategies. This mutual awareness of our fragile selves is also known as 'face attentiveness'. This may seem somewhat abstract, but consider our everyday lives, and the role of requests within them: to the extent to which we interact with others at all, we are constantly imposing on them, asking them to do things for us, and expecting them to appreciate things we do for them. (Children are inducted into the fundamentals of 'face attentiveness' when their caregivers drill them with the injunction 'Always remember to say *please* and *thank you*'.) Face and politeness are usually characterized as having two fundamental aspects, called 'positive face' and 'negative face'. Positive face covers all the ways in which, when interacting with someone else (and particularly, when placing any imposition on them), we indicate that we are approving of them, are complimentary or sympathetic, or in other ways effectively say 'I like you, you're like me': in positive face we project ourselves as close to our addressee. Negative face covers all the ways in which, again during acts like offers and requests, we indicate that we defer to them, respect them as above us, as they are more talented or important or busy, or in other ways effectively say 'I acknowledge you, you are unlike (better than) me': in negative face we project ourselves as humbly distant from our addressee. Space limitations forbid further discussion of politeness here, but see, especially, Leech (1983), and Simpson (1989).

Activities

ACTIVITY 7

Those interested in teasing out the range of acts performable with a single, variously inflected and variously contextualized utterance, can cut their analytical teeth on the following utterance:

> *Can I help you?*

Sketch in at least three different scenes of human interaction, in which this formulation is used with quite distinct intonation, emotional colouring, speaker intent, impositiveness, and so on. In sketching these contrasting scenes indicate, among other things, the plausible verbal or non-verbal response of the addressee(s).

ACTIVITY 8

Some of the most versatile and problematic of utterance-constructions are those which begin with *Let's*:

> *Let's take a taxi.*
>
> *Let's not quarrel.*
>
> *Let's be perfectly frank.*

Where does each of these examples fit into this chapter's categorizations? Is *Let's not quarrel* a blend of request and offer, with a phatic element to it? And what is the functional difference which *sometimes* emerges to distinguish utterances beginning *Let us* from utterances beginning *Let's*? Why do religious figures usually say *Let us pray* but not *Let's pray*, while at a party you might say *Let's dance* but not *Let us dance*? What are the contrasting normal contexts of use of *Let's go!* and *Let us go!*?

ACTIVITY 9

In the run-up to the Republican party's selection of a candidate for the US presidential election of 1988, CBS aired a series of interviews with the chief candidates, in January 1988. The front runner at the time was President Reagan's vice-president, George Bush, although something of a question-mark hung over him concerning the degree of his knowing involvement in the 'arms for hostages' Iran-Contra scandal. In a live, nationally broadcast news interview, lasting nine minutes, veteran CBS presenter Dan Rather attempted to draw out Vice-President Bush on his role in the Iran-Contra affair, while Bush, for his part, offered various kinds of rebuttal and pressed for the interview to focus on his platform on education, the economy, and so on. Even in its dysfunctionality, that nine-minute interview became famous or infamous, a high point in the clash of the press and the candidates in the 1988 campaign. Arguably the encounter was enormously face-threatening (here in the large sense of 'career-threatening') for both parties. Mr Bush went on to secure the Republican nomination, and then to be elected president that November. Here is a transcript of the final moments of the interview. Note that, on any impartial assessment, it would be hard to describe Mr Bush's contributions to the interview, often interruptions or lengthy tangential responses, as 'straightforward'; and note, too, that Rather's closing remarks appear to have been rushed by the network requirement to 'go to commercials' at particular rigid time allocations.

Comment on the acts being performed by each participant, and on how these may have been evaluated by the viewing and listening audience:

> Rather: Mr Vice President, I appreciate you joining us tonight, I appreciate the straightforward way in ah – which you've engaged in this exchange. (There're) clearly some unanswered questions here –
> Bush: Fire a- another
> Rather: Are you willing . . . Are you willing – to go to a news conference before the Iowa caucuses and answer questions from all come – all comers?
> Bush: I've been to 86 news conferences since March – ah – 86 of em since March –
> Rather: I gather that the answer is no. Thank you very much for being with us Mr Vice President. We'll be back with more news, in a moment.

ACTIVITY 10

Discuss the kinds of offers, informs, questions and requests carried in the following supermarket encounter, taken from Don DeLillo's novel *White Noise* (New York: Penguin, 1986, pp. 39–40). Consider the content and sequencing of Murray's remarks in relation to the notions of imposition, and positive and negative face.

> Before Murray went to the express line he invited us to dinner, a week from Saturday.
> 'You don't have to let me know till the last minute.'
> 'We'll be there,' Babette said.
> 'I'm not preparing anything major, so just call beforehand and tell me if something else came up. You don't even have to call. If you don't show up, I'll know that something came up and you couldn't let me know.'
> 'Murray, we'll be there.'
> 'Bring the kids.'
> 'No.'
> 'Great. But if you decide to bring them, no problem. I don't want you to feel I'm holding you to something. Don't feel you've made an ironclad commitment. You'll show up or you won't. I have to eat anyway, so there's no major catastrophe if something comes up and you have to cancel. I just want you to

know I'll be there if you decide to drop by, with or without kids. We have till next May or June to do this thing so there's no special mystique about a week from Saturday.'

'Are you coming back next semester?' I said.

'They want me to teach a course in the cinema of car crashes.'

'Do it.'

'I will.'

ACTIVITY 11

The following dialogue is taken from Scene Six of David Hare's play, *The Secret Rapture* (New York, Grove Weidenfeld: 1989), pp. 64–6. Even without having seen or read the previous scenes, you should be able to glean a considerable amount about the main characters – Isobel, Marion, and Tom – by closely attending to their talk here, and their patterns of questioning, informing and offering. Draw up a profile of these three characters, on the basis of their tendency here to give or take proposals or propositions.

[*At once* ISOBEL *comes warmly across the room, smiling and embracing* MARION *when she reaches her*].

ISOBEL: Marion. Hello. How are you? I've missed you terribly.

TOM: Hello.

ISOBEL: Tom. How are you? [*She goes over to kiss him.*] It's such a lovely day out there. It's incredible. I've never seen the sun so high at this time of year. It's beautiful. I've spent half an hour in the park. Have you seen?

TOM: No.

MARION: No, actually. We've been too busy.

ISOBEL: I'm sure.

MARION: I'd love to spend my day just staring at the sun.

[ISOBEL *catches her tone, but tries to ignore it, keeping cheerful.*]

ISOBEL: I've never been here. What a nice office!

MARION: Isobel. Please.

ISOBEL: Yes?

MARION: Could you just tell us what's going on?

[ISOBEL *smiles at* MARION, *who is looking at her unforgivingly.*]

ISOBEL: Of course. I'm sorry we can't have a proper board meeting. At the moment it's difficult between Irwin and me. It'll get better.

MARION: Now listen . . .

ISOBEL: Forgive me, I don't want to talk about it. Shall we talk about business?

[*She smiles cheerfully at* TOM, *trying to make interruption impossible.*]

TOM: Of course.

[ISOBEL *is suddenly decisive.*]

ISOBEL: You want to sell the firm because it's not profitable and sack all the staff, is that right?

MARION: [*Rising at once*] Now that isn't fair.

ISOBEL: Please. I'm not judging, Marion, I'm just asking the facts.

[ISOBEL *sits opposite* TOM *at the desk.*]

We redecorated the premises you bought us. They're now commercially very attractive. You can make a profit by selling them. You can double your money. But then of course there's nowhere for us to go.

TOM: That isn't quite it. [*He smiles.*] There is also the point you are losing money. Sadly, the expansion hasn't really worked.

ISOBEL: Well, no. I did warn you.

TOM: I mean, any responsible businessman would tell you at this point he has a duty to his own survival. We have no real choice. We have to get out.

[ISOBEL *smiles.*]

ISOBEL: With a little profit?

TOM: Well, certainly.

ISOBEL: Is it true we didn't cost anything in the first place?

MARION: Isobel . . .

[*But* ISOBEL, *who is quite calm and gentle, puts up her hand to stop* MARION's *indignant interruptions.*]

ISOBEL: Look, I'm just asking. Someone said you wrote us off against tax. Is that right?

[*She has to put her hand up again to quell the next interruption.*]

Marion, please. I'm not criticizing. Is it true, because of tax, we cost you nothing?

TOM: In a sense.

MARION: Why apologize?

ISOBEL: No, I don't expect it.

TOM: It is legitimate business practice.

ISOBEL: Of course.

[*She smiles a moment at* MARION, *calming her down.*]

And now I imagine your tax position has changed.

TOM: Exactly.

ISOBEL: Selling is now advantageous.

TOM: Yes, that's right.

ISOBEL: And the extra workers we took on?

TOM: They would be compensated.

ISOBEL: How much?

TOM: Three weeks' wages.

[*There's a pause, while* ISOBEL *thinks this over.*]

ISOBEL: Uh-huh.

[*There's a silence as* ISOBEL *nods slightly, not moving. Then she sweeps her hand across Tom's desk.*]

MARION: Now, look, Isobel . . .

ISOBEL: Well, I guess that's it.

MARION: I wouldn't call them workers. Ex-students, more like. And ex- is being kind. They've had six months' fun at high wages. Now they're back on the market. I don't think they'll want to complain.

ISOBEL: No. [*She shrugs slightly.*] Then it's done.

TOM: What d'you mean? Let's be clear. Are you agreeing? [*He is disturbed at the ease of his own victory, puzzled now.*] Isobel?

ISOBEL: Why even ask me. I'm only one vote. [*She smiles as if that were the end of it.*]

ACTIVITY 12

The following are poems by W. B. Yeats, from his 'Crazy Jane' sequence, written rather late in his life. Comment on the part played in these poems by generic sentences (review the discussion of these in Chapter 3, if necessary), and discuss also the contribution made by the various kinds of speech act (informs, questions, requests and so on) that occur here. In the second and third poems reproduced, note the status and apparent assumptions of the respective speakers producing them, before drawing conclusions about what has been 'given', what 'taken', in these scenes.

V
Crazy Jane on God

That lover of a night
Came when he would,
Went in the dawning light
Whether I would or no;
Men come, men go;
All things remain in God.

Banners choke the sky;
Men-at-arms tread;
Armoured horses neigh
Where the great battle was
In the narrow pass:
All things remain in God.

Before their eyes a house
That from childhood stood

Uninhabited, ruinous,
Suddenly lit up
From door to top:
All things remain in God.

I had wild Jack for a lover;
Though like a road
That men pass over
My body makes no moan
But sings on:
All things remain in God.

VI
Crazy Jane Talks with the Bishop

I met the Bishop on the road
And much said he and I.
'Those breasts are flat and fallen now,
Those veins must soon be dry;
Live in a heavenly mansion,
Not in some foul sty.'

'Fair and foul are near of kin,
And fair needs foul,' I cried.
'My friends are gone, but that's a truth
Nor grave nor bed denied,
Learned in bodily lowliness
And in the heart's pride.

'A woman can be proud and stiff
When on love intent;
But Love has pitched his mansion in
The place of excrement;
For nothing can be sole or whole
That has not been rent.'

VII
Crazy Jane Grown Old Looks at the Dancers

I found that ivory image there
Dancing with her chosen youth,
But when he wound her coal-black hair
As though to strangle her, no scream
Or bodily movement did I dare,

Eyes under eyelids did so gleam;
Love is like the lion's tooth.

When she, and though some said she played
I said that she had danced heart's truth,
Drew a knife to strike him dead,
I could but leave him to his fate;
For no matter what is said
They had all that had their hate;
Love is like the lion's tooth.

Did he die or did she die?
Seemed to die or died they both?
God be with the times when I
Cared not a thraneen for what chanced
So long as I had the limbs to try
Such a dance as there was danced –
Love is like the lion's tooth.

Commentaries

ACTIVITY 2

Victoria – nice, polite, middle-class, un-self-critiqued Victoria (as becomes clear later in this scene) – diverts Cathy's attention by way of an inform. Is there an explicit request in Victoria's words at all? Only the fact that the inform is explicitly directed at Cathy (since Victoria names her), together with the appended *quick*, overtly convey that the inform entails a suggestion. And clearly Victoria's instincts are right: anything more direct in the way of a proposal to Cathy, we suspect, would be sure to receive nothing but some such reproof as 'No, don't tell me!' (of requests) or 'I can do it myself!' (of offers). All this reflects the fact that there is a stage in child language development – early on – when only quite overt and direct requests and offers to children are understood and responded to by them; and there is a later point, in relation to some children at least, where *in*direct requests and offers are likely to be much more successful with them than direct ones!

ACTIVITY 3

The first thing to notice about this putative inform, *They've just banned war toys in Sweden*, is that it is not directly relevant to the ongoing interaction between the two children and the two mothers. That is, neither 'Sweden' nor 'war toys' nor banning things nor

'They' has been the explicit or implied topic of the foregoing interaction. So the listener, like Lin, has to assess in what way, if at all, Victoria's contribution here is indirectly relevant to the situation. In the established context, it is clear that Victoria doesn't wish to turn the conversation to Sweden, as such; the link, rather, is with the 'war toy' that Cathy is playing with, and the focus of Victoria's remark is on the banning of such toys in another country. So we can begin an appropriate interpretation of what Victoria's remark conveys by recognizing that it must be delivered with the dominant intonational emphasis on the word *banned* – perhaps a pronounced falling tone on *banned* and a low rising tone on *in Sweden*.

A significant interpretive step clearly remains to be taken: why does Victoria here invite mutual attention to the banning of war toys in Sweden? She might wish to suggest that she finds this deplorable, or ridiculous, or problematic, or admirable: it is difficult to decide which attitude is intended, if the utterance is viewed removed from its context. Perhaps the strongest clue within the utterance is the description *war toy* which, for detailed lexicogrammatical reasons I lack room to explore here, arguably treats the item referred to as more to do with real war, and less to do with toys and play, than do the descriptions like *toy gun* or *toy weapon* (compare *war toy* with *car toy*, used to describe a mobile phone: the mobile phone is actually real rather than a toy, and the car in which it sits is also real rather than pretend). But more important than any utterance-internal clues are the indications we gather from the surrounding co-text and context, which cumulatively suggest not merely that Victoria approves of Sweden's banning of war toys but also that, in approving that ban, she herself disapproves of such toys. Hence Victoria's remark is a good example of what in politeness theory is called an 'off-record' or pronouncedly indirect speech act. There is no overt request here, and any implicit request we might postulate ('You shouldn't encourage children to play with toy weapons') is so 'off-record' that we cannot be sure it is intended: what Victoria actually intended might have been a much stronger or much weaker imposition – that is the beauty of indirect hinting speech acts. None of this complexity is lost on Lin, whose immediate inform rejoinder is certainly worth considering. That is to say, well beyond the confines of this scene, it leads to such questions as the following: 'Is it better for children to really hit each other than to play at killing, if this leads them to grow up still hitting but not killing?'. At the same time, Lin does not ignore the unspoken request we have suspected in Victoria's inform: much later in the scene she breaks away from the current topic (men) to make the blunt request *Don't get at me about how I bring up Cathy, ok?*, and is undeflected by Victoria's denial. Thus the specifities of how characters interact – how Lin requests and Cathy requests or questions back, and of how Victoria implies proposals by actually uttering mere informs – provide a rapid and revealing illumination of their contrasting natures. Even this early a broad pattern is beginning to emerge: working-class and less-educated Lin tends to interact via proposals (offers and requests), which also means doing things and (trying to) get things done; middle-class educated Victoria tends to interact via propositions (informs and questions), even when particular proposals are her goal; so on the latter occasions, there is inevitability an indirectness, subtlety, or 'non-face-threatening' politeness to her discourse. These systematic contrasts, which are part off what characterize Lin and Victoria, persist and are exploited in later scenes.

ACTIVITY 5

Lin's *I really fancy you* is not prospected by immediately preceding utterances, but the very unresponsiveness of Cathy's previous remarks, in a sense, may have provoked Lin to this outspokenness. Lin's daring and amusing rupture of conventional talk, which also resets the interactional footing for the two women, comes at the end of a lengthy rehearsal of her anxieties about Cathy. That rehearsal is evidently wasted on Victoria since she neither expresses sympathy nor even pays attention; that is, Victoria provides no attending acknowledgement acts (and this, in turn, helps clarify how Lin's long turn of talk needs to be played: it needs to be delivered with enough time between its informs so that Victoria's lack of supplied acknowledgements can be noticed).

But different things can be made of Lin's frank inform. In response to Victoria's checking question (*What?*), Lin does not repeat or reformulate this inform (as usually happens following checking questions). This may leave us uncertain as to whether *I really fancy you* was said only as a joke, as an attention-getter; and uncertain whether, if sincere, the declaration is unrepeated due to some lapse in Lin's confidence. But like any 'powerful' speech act (by which I mean, broadly, any act with the potential to trigger multiple significant interactional consequences) that *I really fancy you* resonates long after in this scene and beyond it, long after its lack of local uptake has been forgotten.

ACTIVITY 6

I just hate them, as a rejoinder, says nothing that was not already said by Lin's *I hate men*; it therefore does not move the discourse forward, and does not so much reply to Victoria's qualifications as ignore them, returning the discourse to the point reached previously, in Lin's former inform. *I just loathe the bastards*, on the other hand, perhaps 'goes too far', in not only introducing a new claim (that men are bastards) but in also amending the previous assertion about hating (correction: I don't hate them, I loathe them). Lin would in effect be distancing herself from her earlier claim, and that is very unlike Lin. Furthermore, she would lose the forceful and humorous effect to be derived from repeating (partially, significantly), without detraction, what she announced previously. The actual utterance 3 goes 'just far enough': it introduces a powerful description of men, one that serves to rebut all Victoria's liberal understanding (Men are bastards), and embeds this within the repetition as a compelling *reason* for hating men. So if Lin's utterance 1 seems irrational or unreasonable, utterance 3 counteracts this by providing a reason!

We can also note, concerning 3, that in the context of 2, it is thoroughly unprospected. But it would not be both unprospected and funny if it did not exploit (a) speech act logic and (b) cohesion logic in quite the way it does. In terms of speech act logic, 3 is unexpectedly redundant, and therefore significant in its redundancy: it is an inform which is virtually a copy of a prior inform, 1. In terms of cohesion logic, where it does not link to 1 by means of simple repetition it links by means of substituting a general term for an evaluative epithet, introduced by the definite article. The effect of this is that speaker (and attending listener) skip over an intermediate proposition, that 'men are bastards', which is then 'taken as read'. Lin's 'point of view', as Victoria gamely calls it (doing more of the middle-class relexicalizing of abuse as 'opinion', to which she is prone), is thus all the more succinctly encapsulated. And Lin's succinctness in comparison with Victoria's lengthy and wordy abstraction is already a source of humorous contrast.

9

Presupposition

Presupposition vs. assertion: foreground and background again

Take this section title, and the way that 'foreground and background *again*' implies that foreground and background have been considered on at least one previous occasion: that is what presupposition is. It is the label for all the linguistic constructions that prompt us to note some further claim or point, behind those explicitly made in a text.

In a number of situations in this book, the value of a foreground/background distinction has been emphasized. In narratives, we have seen how the bare and essential event-sequence gets foregrounded by virtue of being expressed, typically, in the simple past tense. Alongside such simple past tense verbs, verbs in present tense, with or without progressive or perfective aspect, are treated as carrying accompanying or background information (often orientational or evaluative). We have also seen, in sentence structure, how whatever comes first in the sentence (which may well not be the subject) is by that means alone foregrounded. Recall how, in Auden's 'Musée des Beaux Arts', suffering itself is foregrounded at the peom's opening: 'About suffering they were never wrong, the old masters'. Intonationally, of course, whatever word contains the tonic syllable in a tone group – the syllable with the most striking pitch-change – is foregrounded relative to the surrounding and back-grounded syllables. Narratologically, one might argue that within passages which are predominantly narration, any lexical-sequential level of discourse-construction, those lexical selections which are least predictable and therefore, in a sense, most distinctively informative, are moments of foregrounding (it was suggested that a version of cloze-testing can sometimes sensitize us as to what words are least predictable, therefore most 'original' or 'creative', and therefore most telling). Thus the foreground–background principle operates at many levels, in literary composition and analysis.

At this point I want to introduce another version of the background–foreground contrast, namely the semantic contrast between presupposition and assertion. Although these terms are sometimes used rather broadly (for example, to refer to such things as 'cultural presuppositions'), I shall use them here in a relatively 'narrow' or directly linguistic sense. I shall use them to refer specifically to textually encoded assumptions which are directly retrievable from analysis of the sentence or sentences under discussion. This notion of linguistic presupposition should become clearer once the difference between presupposition and assertion has been explained.

A typical declarative sentence represents, as a new claim, that such and such is or was the case, or that such and such is or has happened or was done, or that this thing has that quality or identity. The content of such a declarative 'new' claim is called the sentence's **assertion**; the things about which the sentence makes whatever claim it makes, are called the sentence's **presuppositions**. For example, in the sentence

My neighbour smokes

what I am asserting is that my neighbour smokes: that my neighbour smokes is what I claim. But involved in making that assertion is an assumption or presupposition, namely that I have a neighbour. That I have a neighbour is presupposed by the sentence, and not asserted by it. That I do indeed have a neighbour is not the point of the sentence at all (that s/he smokes is), but instead is here cast as 'understood', or uncontroversial background. Assertions 'impose' on us rather differently than presuppositions: they impose less. That is to say, you can contest or 'grapple with' an assertion much more straightforwardly than with a sentence's presuppositions. Consider again *My neighbour smokes*. An interlocutor can accept or reject the assertion here quite directly, for example with any of the following four rejoinders:

True.

Wrong!

Yes she does.

No she doesn't!

Each of these is very directly, semi-automatically, linked to the given sentence. But now consider how one might contest that sentence's presupposition:

But you don't have a neighbour (so it can't be true that s/he smokes).

At the very least, this is more convoluted, involves more 'verbal effort' on the part of the interlocutor, and is in no sense 'semi-automatic'. I will return to these points later.

The simplest examples of sentence contents which carry simple presuppositions tend to be sentences which include proper names and definite noun phrases – e.g., *Bill Clinton* and *the President of the United States*. Thus in the sentence

Bill Clinton is the President of the United States

the assertion is that Mr Clinton is the US President. But the sentence also presupposes at least two propositions, namely that there *is* some individual named 'Bill Clinton' and that there *is* some role or office called 'President of the United States'. It doesn't **assert** those propositions (it implies that they are much too obvious to warrant asserting), it **presupposes** them and proceeds to weave them into the asserting of something slightly more interesting.

So, typically, whatever in a discourse is likely to be common knowledge, or is too basic to justify being talked about, will usually be presupposed. (It's hard to think of an addressee to whom it would feel reasonable to assert all of the following: 'There is a person called Bill Clinton, and there is an office called "President of the United States", and he holds that office.') But other material besides that which is deemed basic or common knowledge also gets presupposed: if information is assumed to be known in the given situation, or has been mentioned in recent prior discourse, then that too tends to be presupposed.

With the above guidelines in mind, we can see why sentence 2 below is rather odd, while sentence 1 is not:

1 The Rolling Stones' lead singer Mick Jagger was at school with me.

2 My former schoolmate Mick Jagger is the Rolling Stones' lead singer.

Sentence 2 is odd because it is cast in such a way that it *presupposes* uncommon and possibly interesting knowledge (namely, that Mick Jagger is my former schoolmate), which more naturally ought to have been asserted, as in sentence 1; and it *asserts* what is very old news, that Mick Jagger is lead singer with the Stones, which should have been presupposed, as in 1.

A variety of lexical or grammatical elements create or 'trigger' presuppositions. We have mentioned one already, namely the use of the definite article in a noun phrase, which almost invariably triggers the presupposition that the thing denoted did, does, or will actually exist (on this basis, note that both sentences 1 and 2 above presuppose that something called *The Rolling Stones* exists). Bear in mind that the question is not whether the claim in the presupposition is true or not in fact: the issue is only about whether the claim is truly presupposed. Thus, concerning 1 and 2 above, it happens not to be true that I was at school with Mick Jagger (he's much much older than me). Nevertheless 1 asserts I was at school with him, and 2 presupposes I was. In 1 the falsehood is in the assertion, in 2 it is in the presupposition and, as indicated earlier, it is considerably harder to 'catch' or challenge the falsehood as it scoots past you in sentence 2: 'Wait a minute: was Mick Jagger really a schoolmate of yours?' And the presupposition-triggering power of the definite article is not even blocked in highly fanciful and hypothetical sentences. Thus in

> 3   The scientist who discovers how to reverse ageing will transform human life.

the sentence does indeed – absurdly, you may feel – presuppose, thanks to the definiteness of the noun phrase *the scientist who . . .*, that some day a scientist will discover how to reverse ageing. It then proceeds to assert that such a person will transform human life. Compare 3 with 4:

> 4   A(ny) scientist who discovers how to reverse ageing will transform human life.

Here there is no presupposition that such a genius will ever appear. It may be worth mentioning odd sentences such as *The king of France is bald*, over which philosophers of language have torn their hair – some arguing that the invalidity of the presupposition (since there is, in fact, no present king of France) has the effect of rendering the framing assertion void. From our discourse-analytic perspective it will be enough to note that in this and similar cases the speaker has cast things as if it were reasonable to presuppose that the king of France exists. Everything will then depend on an addressee's resources – e.g. in co-textual evidence – for assessing the 'reliability' (in a legal-evidential sense) of this claim in the relevant discoursal world that the addressee has committed themselves to. Just what the 'discoursal world' is that the utterance inhabits is crucial: rather than appearing in the Court Circular from Versailles in today's *Le Monde*, is this sentence part of a science-fiction text, or of a medieval romance, or is it being used figuratively, as a description of the latest haircut of Gerald Depardieu?

Below I list some of the commonest linguistic items or structures which 'trigger' presuppositions, together with examples of them in use. These items are called presupposition triggers since you cannot use them in a sentence, normally, without the addressee inferring that some related idea, not directly asserted in the present sentence, also holds. In the examples below, the sign >> stands for 'presupposes'.

Lexical presupposition triggers: *again*; *nearly*; *try to*; *X managed to Y* >> *X wanted to Y*; *stop, start, continue, resume, begin, return* (+ (*to*) verb or noun)

> Our boiler has broken down again.
> >> Our boiler has broken down before.

Adverbial clauses of time, place, reason, manner, etc.

> Because I could not stop for Death, Death kindly stopped for me.
> >> I could not stop for Death.

> When the spring rains came, his shoes let in water.
> >> The spring rains came.

But think carefully about hypothetical or conditional clauses; usually the subordinate clause here is not presupposed:

> If I won the Nobel prize, I'd give all the money to charity.

and, reverse-wise, of condition:

> If/when you walk to the end of this corridor, you will find an elevator.
> >> You have not just walked to the end of the corridor.

Note, however, that where *if* approximates in meaning to *whenever*, in generic uses, both the antecedent and the consequent seem to be presupposed to have happened at least once:

> If you insist on putting your hands into the fire they will get burnt.

> If I pressed Control and the F9 key together, the screen froze.

'Factive' verbs: verbs that can take, as a full-clause complement, something which has the status of a fact and not a guess or hypothesis: *realize, know, discover, grasp, regret*, etc.:

Archimedes realized that bodies displace their own weight in water.
>> Bodies displace their own weight in water.

I regret that I didn't refinance my mortgage in 1992.
>> I didn't refinance my mortgage in 1992.

I've just realized we will be on half-term holiday next week.
>> We will be on half-term holiday next week.

But notice that, where the complement clause has future reference, as in the example immediately above, the degree to which the speaker really is presupposing its content may be variable, and the chief effect may be rhetorical:

I know the Ecology party will form the next British government.
?>> the Ecology party will form the next British government.

In such cases, context and co-text can make a substantial difference. Compare these two situations (~>> means 'does not presuppose'):

I know the Ecology party will form the next British government. I just know they will. It's vital for the planet.
~>> The Ecology party will form the next British government.

I know the Ecology party will form the next British government. But will business and the unions work with them? That's what I worry about.
>> The Ecology party will form the next British government.

The reason why, in the former of these, there seems to be no genuine presupposing that the Ecology party will be the next government, arguably has to do with modality. Specifically, it has to do with what has been called a 'metaphorized' way of expressing modality (see Chapter 3). For the speaker is using the 'I know' formulation as a 'metaphorically' variant way of saying 'For sure, in my view, the Ecology party. . . etc.'. That is, the *I know* in that utterance does not encode the assertion of a genuine and distinct process of cognizing; it expresses the speaker's modality, of subjective certainty, about the asserted process of the Ecologists forming the next government. Because the *I know* in the former sentence does not amount to a genuine process of cognizing, you cannot rephrase the sentence as 'I recognize the Ecology party will form . . . etc. I just *recognize* they will.' Whereas in the latter sentence you certainly can: *I recognize the Ecology party will . . . etc . . . but will business and the unions work with them?*

We can also compare the verbs above, in their factive non-modalized use, with 'non-factive' ones such as *think, guess, suspect, believe* – none of which cause their complement clause to be taken as presupposed. Thus

I thought we had an appointment

does not presuppose 'we had an appointment'.

Implicative verbs (*forget*, *manage to*)

Did you forget we had an appointment?
>> We had an appointment.

Restrictive relative clauses

The man who robbed the bank is my uncle.
>> Someone robbed the bank.

WH-questions

What is the capital of Washington state?
>> Washington state has a capital.

Why did you put maple syrup in my shampoo bottle?
>> You put maple syrup in my shampoo bottle.

It cannot be emphasized enough just how tricky and unpredictable presupposition can turn out to be. In such cases as that of *before*, used to introduce temporal clauses, even if the subordinator normally triggers the presupposition that the embedded clause is true (*He fell asleep before the guests left* >> *the guests left*), co-text and context can cancel the normal pattern (*He apologized before she got upset*; compare *He had started being quite insulting before she got upset*). To give another example, consider the verb *keep*, which in many ways seems like the verb *continue*, listed above among the 'lexical trigger' items. Literally, it would seem that *keep* is a straightforward alternative to *continue* (in its literal sense):

Keep/continue taking the medication.

Why do you keep/continue saying that I'm misogynist?

The presupposition in each of these is that the proposition in the verb complement has persisted in happening across a span of time which has *continued* from an earlier time to a later one. But on the other hand there seem numerous situations in which *keep* (and *continue*) is used in directives, where the presupposition is that something that was the case formerly has more recently ceased to be the case:

Keep turning the handle!

Keep tabbing to the end of the file.

Here, part of the point of casting the directive in quite the way it is cast is that the once-valid state of affairs has ceased to obtain at the time of speaking. In various cases it is fairly clear which reading (continuation vs. resumption) must be involved. In other cases it seems impossible to predict, outside the specific situation. Consider Annie and Betty, both trying to finish their first marathon: Annie, labouring but still moving at a fast jog, turns towards Betty and says:

> Keep going, Betty!

If Betty has actually stopped moving, we might say Annie's injunction is for Betty to *resume* running; but if Betty is still moving, the directive can only be that Betty *continue* running.

So far we have talked about presuppositions as the enabling background propositions without which the given constructed sentence would not properly signify. In a way presuppositions are the guaranteed background propositions which the very use of particular words or structures necessarily projects. Thus you cannot use the structure 'stop V-ing' without projecting a background in which the V-ing was formerly going on:

> Have you stopped burning your rubbish?
> >> Formerly you were burning (or used to burn) your rubbish.

An extremely useful diagnostic of 'presuppositionhood' we should now mention is the idea of 'constancy under negation'. This is a rather condensed way of saying that presuppositions hold true (are constant) even when the given sentence is directly negated. Thus, both

> Have you stopped burning your rubbish?

and

> Haven't you stopped burning your rubbish?

presuppose:

> Formerly you burned your rubbish.

Only presuppositions hold good whether the whole sentence is positive or negative. So if you say *He didn't realize she was a genius* rather than *He realized she was a genius* you are asserting quite different things (about what the 'he' realized); but the presupposition remains unchanged: the speaker (not the *He*) still presupposes she was a genius.

Presupposition vs. entailment

In order to be even clearer about just what are and are not presuppositions, we also need to distinguish presuppositions from the more directly semantic property of sentences, entailments. Consider the following sentence (taken from Levinson, 1983: 178):

> 5   John managed to stop in time.

This has the entailment

> 6   John stopped in time.

Time Out: entailment: the basic definition

An entailment of a sentence is a paraphrase of at least part of a sentence, such that in any situation in which the source sentence is true the paraphrase is also necessarily true, but if the source sentence is false the original paraphrase may or may not be false.

If 5, 'John managed to stop in time' is true then 6, 'John stopped in time' is also necessarily true. And if 5 is false then 6, also, would be false. Therefore we say that 6, 'John stopped in time', is an entailment of 5, 'John managed to stop in time'.

Sentence 6 cannot be a presupposition of sentence 5, since it does not hold true when 5 is negated, in the way that a presupposition should ('John didn't manage to stop in time' certainly does not presuppose 'John stopped in time'). In principle, at least, entailments and presuppositions are really quite distinct.

We can characterize a sentence entailment as a partial paraphrase of a sentence's assertion(s): an entailment is a stating, in different words, of part of what is actually stated by the sentence. I mention the 'partial' nature of entailments since linguists sometimes like to list all the potentially distinct propositions entailed by a particular sentence, so that one sentence can have numerous entailments.

In the case of sentence 5, for example, two more entailments are:

> John stopped

and

> Someone stopped in time.

That these are rather uninteresting, and are actually entailed by the first entailment mentioned, is neither here nor there. What is of significance is that they are indeed partial paraphrases of the assertion in the first sentence, and must be true if the source sentence is true. Notice, however, that if the first sentence is negated –

John didn't manage to stop in time

– then none of the three cited entailments of the positive form of the sentence holds true. Neither that 'John stopped in time', nor that 'John stopped', nor that 'Someone stopped in time' is now valid. There is no 'constancy under negation' in the realm of entailment.

Activities

ACTIVITY 1

Now consider again the sentence we have just examined in relation to entailment:

John managed to stop in time.

Can you identify one of its presuppositions? Bear in mind that the confirmatory test is 'constancy under negation'; therefore we are looking for a backgrounded proposition which underwrites and 'enables' both *John managed to stop in time* and *John didn't manage to stop in time* to assert what it is they assert.

The solution emerges from the verb *manage*, which is a typically lexical 'trigger' of a presupposition: whether you 'manage' or 'do not manage' to do something, the verb *manage* presupposes that you *tried* to do that something. In this case, the presupposition is:

John tried to stop in time.

So using the structure 'X (did or did not) manage to V' projects the presupposed background that that X tried to V, and presumably that X intended to V.

Irony, humour and presuppositions

I have already mentioned various ways in which constructions which usually carry a particular presupposition have to be 'handled with care'. This is quite generally the case whenever language is being used with ironic or humorous intent. This can be demonstrated with the construction, ordinarily presupposition-triggering, just discussed (*X managed to V* >> X *tried* to V). Consider the following sentence, uttered sarcastically:

> Rodney managed to smash our cherished Royal Doulton condiment set when he was 'helping' with the washing up.

Although the speaker superficially describes Rodney's deed as if it were intentional, it is clear that in actuality they know Rodney did not try to smash the condiment set; whereas if the speaker *really* believed that Rodney tried and succeeded in smashing, etc., then there would be no irony here, but simply a factual report. Evidently, in cases of irony or sarcasm such as this, presuppositions do not hold in the ordinary way.

In the face of this we can either revise our whole conception of presupposition, or treat irony as a special situation. The latter course seems preferable; we shall say that in cases such as that of a speaker saying *Rodney managed to smash our cherished Royal Doulton condiment sets*, 'manage to V' does still trigger, in the usual way, the presupposition that Rodney 'tried to (smash)', and that the speaker appears superficially to be committed to that presupposition. In typical more fully specified contexts, however, the addressee is expected to infer that Rodney's damage was accidental and that the presupposition is not entirely serious. Nevertheless it sits there, quietly perpetrated by the speaker, and – we inferentially calculate – expressive of the speaker's upset, irritation, disapproval of Rodney's clumsiness, and so on. It is as if the speaker thinks: 'Someone this prone to causing damage, one is half-inclined to assert (or inclined to half-assert), would almost seem to be doing it on purpose.' Or, 'he might as well have done it on purpose, so negligent was he'. Incidentally, it is worth noting that here, as in irony quite often, we do not infer the direct negation of the ironically intended presupposition: we do not derive the presupposition 'Rodney tried to smash the china', negate it, and assume that the speaker wished to convey 'Rodney did not try to smash the china' (or 'Rodney tried not to smash the china'). Actually the message the ironist wishes to convey is somewhere between the 'he tried to' and the 'he didn't try to' readings: 'Rodney didn't intend to smash the china, but at the same time he didn't try hard enough not to!'

In summary, we will not take ironical uses of *Rodney managed to get his leg broken* and other such cases as instances of presupposition-failure. Rather the standard presupposition is triggered, and then set aside as playful, or malicious, or an emotional exaggeration or whatever – i.e., its figurative import is calibrated relative to the assessed context. Similarly, if you say *When I joined the discussion group, I felt as welcome as a pacifist at a regimental dinner*, I would argue that the 'as [adjective/adverb] as Y" construction triggers the presupposition that pacifists are welcome at regimental dinners, as with this construction generally (*She's as clever as her sister* ordinarily presupposes that her sister is clever). But in the regimental dinner case, drawing on real-world knowledge and the semantic 'clash' between regiments and pacifism, we conjecture that the speaker cannot seriously intend the conventional meaning, and does not intend to say that 'I was very welcome'. Rather they intend us to assume irony, and that some variant of the triggered presupposition – perhaps in this case, its very opposite – is actually intended to serve as measure of just how welcome they felt.

Before we leave *manage to X*, one further frequent use of it may be mentioned. As we have noted, *manage to X* means to attempt and succeed at doing X, while *not manage to X* means to attempt but fail to do X. Either way, attempting is presupposed. In the white lies of everyday conversation speakers often trade on the presupposed 'attempting to' carried by the verb *manage*, even when no real effort has been made; and, in certain circumstances, that dissembling is challenged by sceptical interlocutors:

A: I didn't manage to get to the bank this afternoon.
B: Did you even try?
A: Er, well I was feeling a bit exhausted actually.

Given the presupposition, A's first remark amounts to saying 'I tried but failed to get to the bank'. In the given situation, this latter formulation would be an outright lie, and it is striking how speakers who wouldn't dream of such blatant dishonesty will without embarrassment use the presupposition-embedding version, as A does.

Activities

ACTIVITY 2

The following is a satirical report on one day's proceedings in the British parliament, including 'PM's questions': a ritualized cross-questioning of the prime minister by the leader of the Opposition. A number of the presupposition-triggering words and phrases within it have been highlighted in bold face. Express, in sentence form, each of the presupposed facts or ideas, which form such an enabling background to the mockery displayed here. Some of the phrases I have highlighted in bold work in mysterious ways upon us. Consider, for example, the allusion to seeing a Tony Banks joke coming **from the other end of Victoria Street**. What does this presuppose about the deictic location of the utterer of the joke, and perhaps about the location of the British parliament?

SPEAKER CHOKES ON A DIET OF PICKLES AND BEETROOT
By Matthew Parris, 25 February 1994

In a prepared statement, Madam Speaker yesterday **begged MPs to grow up and ask proper questions.** Her appeal had been utterly vindicated by **the pantomime that went before.**

One does not wish to be thought a killjoy. We can, at a stretch, allow Tony Banks (with a question about promoting British vegetables) **his joke about the Tories.** As Chris Patten once observed, you can see a Banks joke coming from **the other end of Victoria Street.**

And, allowing Banks **his tomfoolery,** we must allow the minister, Michael Jack, **his riposte:** about a new vegetable promotion campaign featuring Captain Carrot and Sergeant Strawberry. Banks, a socialist, he thought would have to take the role of Private Beetroot 'because he is red all the way through'.

Allowing Mr Jack **his merriment,** we cannot wonder at MPs' wild hilarity when the next thing to loom into Miss Booth-royd's weary vision was the vast hulk of Eric Pickles.

Mr Pickles wanted to ask about lettuce, so we cannot **deny** the minister **his fun:** 'My hon. friend is a perfect advertisement for lettuce.'

Mr Pickles is about as good an advertisement for lettuce as Kate Moss is for suet.

So let us allow all that.

But not PM's questions. The session was preceded (as it increasingly is these days) by **the infantile ritual surrounding the entry into the chamber of the two principal combatants, Mr Major and Mr Smith.** Each side tries to give its own hero the louder cheer. As with those Christmas pantomimes when the children in the audience are divided into two teams and invited to out-sing each other, the next logical step must be to ask Major and Smith to withdraw, then come back in, for each side to have another go.

The questions lived up to the overture. Mr Smith and Mr Major locked horns in a juvenile contest over whether 'all sections' of Britain were richer than before.

As this depends on how narrowly you define your sections, Major could correctly assert that even the bottom 25 per cent were richer, while Smith could correctly reply that the bottom 10 per cent were not.

This piece of vacuity was pursued with passion for a while, both sides cheering their own, each side shouting 'reading! reading!' when the opposing leader looked at his notes.

Dennis Skinner scowled silently, the Fall of the Beast of Bolsover still fresh in Tory hecklers' minds. But the beast beside him, Bob Cryer (Lab, Bradford South) could not remain silent.

In reply to a taunt about Tory place-men on quangos, the PM had cited Cryer, appointed to a film industry quango, as an unlikely Tory. Fall of the second Beast. Cryer's embarrassment was evidenced by the length of **his subsequent question, which was not a question**.

Then a Tory lap-dog asked Major if he was aware of the latest piece of 'good news' about this or that; a Labour MP asked the PM if he would meet the widow of a murder victim.

Another piece of Tory plankton rose with **further good news**, barely remembering his own script.

Perhaps, as with real pantomimes, someone in a fairy costume could dance in with the words written up onto a big board?

If **these noodles** could at least keep their questions short, we should achieve pace if not wisdom. But, as Madam Speaker pointed out, questions are rambling affairs, often prefaced by lengthy statements. Answers are even longer. In future, she said, she expects single, snappy questions and brisk answers.

Madam Speaker is an irresistible force. But the Commons is an immovable object.

The collision could be fun.

ACTIVITY 3

Whenever we encounter language, we are invariably involved in a complex task of contextualizing, involving the making of inferences, noting of presuppositions, assessment of situation, and so on. How easy – or hard – is it for you to contextualize (and thus, adequately interpret) the following sentence?

> After three hours' kip and a dollop of burgoo, this time with bacon in it as well as dried fish and schnapps, I took off the cylinder-head covers of the Coventry Vixen twin cylinder horizontally opposed London fire-brigade ex-trailer-pump diesel engine, to find that both big ends had finally given way. (§)

ACTIVITY 4

This activity, together with a subsequent one, looks at journalistic analysis of South Africa from the recent but somehow distant past. Recent, in that, for example, the following article was published only seven years ago; but dated in that South Africa and the world seem to have moved on so far in the interim (Mr Mandela has moved from being prisoner to president, and South Africa is emerging as a multi-racial democracy). In fact for such reasons these texts may be all the more instructive to us, as reminders of how the representations of the world that we derive from very well-informed top-class journalists may nevertheless render the world as more settled and unchanging (within the swirl of slight or inconsequential developments) than it really is. We tend to read newspaper articles today about Northern Ireland or Burma (or, one might add, about the British House of Lords and monarchy) as if movement out of the gridlock of current entrenched political arrangements is almost unimaginable. And yet we have seen in the recent histories of South Africa and Eastern Europe that the general assumption that 'things will never really change' can be quite mistaken. The following article therefore, and the subsequent book review about Africa, are particularly instructive viewed from this middle-distance, since it is only at this distance that their discourse of pessimism and, more specifically, of anti-reformism, is really apparent. (Back in 1990, the typical reader of the Mandela article would surely be forgiven for thinking that the *Economist* article was sheer pragmatic description, of the 'incontrovertible fact' that the peaceful future of South Africa would require Mandela to compromise with de Klerk, failing which the white ascendancy would not entertain power-sharing at all; only at this distance can we see that the underlying presupposition that *thoroughgoing* reform was impossible was, as events have shown, false, and that the presupposition is a construction of the writer's own anti-reformist assumptions.)

Analyse and discuss the transitivity choices, and their effect, in the following article from the *Economist* of 6 January 1990, which is about Nelson Mandela and his (at the time) impending release from prison.

South Africa
AWAITING MANDELA

The release of Mr Nelson Mandela will almost certainly be heralded when President F. W. de Klerk opens the new session of South Africa's Parliament on February 2nd. The man jailed a quarter of a century ago on sabotage charges now holds the key to peaceful resolution of his country's racial conflict: almost all black leaders regard his freedom as the absolute precondition for negotiations with Mr de Klerk's government. But once he is free, black organisations will have to show a flexibility to match that of their white opponents.

Eleven months after his election as leader of the ruling National party, and less than four months after taking office as president, Mr F.W. de Klerk has thrown to the winds his reputation for caution. He succeeded Mr P.W. Botha after an election at which the National party suffered its worst setback since it won power in 1948, and lost 30 parliamentary seats. Mr de Klerk mght merely have crawled forward. Instead he astounded most South Africans.

The president has sanctioned peaceful protest marches, released eight prominent political prisoners (including five of those jailed for life with Mr Mandela) and turned a blind eye to speeches and flags boosting the outlawed African National Congress. He has dismantled Mr Botha's 'national security management system', which gave great power to army and police officers, scrapped apartheid on beaches and halved the period of conscription for white men from two years to one. He has promised that the Separate Amenities Act, a chief pillar of apartheid, will soon be scrapped, and faltered only in refusing a judicial inquiry into alleged murders by policemen.

In December Mr de Klerk met Mr Mandela, and reportedly discussed ways to remove 'obstacles in the way of meaningful dialogue'. Several impediments are still in place. The ANC demands complete repeal of the government's state of emergency; Mr de Klerk says it may go, but only when violence in black areas – or the threat of it – abates. The ANC also insists that the government must lift its ban on outlawed organisations, of which it and its rival, the Pan-Africanist Congress, are the most significant. Mr de Klerk says that this will be done only if the black organisations formally renounce violence.

The main underlying difference concerns the concept of 'group rights', which black people regard as a politer term for apartheid. Mr de Klerk has shifted enough to concede that the idea is negotiable. Similarly, the ANC and its more-than-allies in the Mass Democratic Movement (MDM) have circulated a document commending the need for elasticity in negotiations.

Mr de Klerk and Mr Mandela are likely to meet again before Parliament reassembles. Meanwhile Mr Mandela, from his prison bungalow in Paarl, has been allowed, under supervision, to confer with his comrades in the ANC and the MDM who, in turn, have travelled to Lusaka in Zambia to consult the exiled leaders of the ANC; Mr Mandela has spoken by telephone to the acting leader of the exiles, Mr Alfred Nzo.

The gap between the government and the blacks seems to have narrowed. Mr Mandela may not be 'orchestrating' the liberation movements' change of tone, but he is clearly being consulted about it. There are, indeed, signs of anxiety among his colleagues that, as a prisoner, he may be outmanoeuvred by Mr de Klerk. Mr Cyril Ramaphosa, the mineworkers' leader and a pillar of the MDM if not of the ANC, has stated that Mr Mandela's status is 'no different from any other member of the ANC'. Prestige apart, this is true: when arrested 25 years ago Mr Mandela was merely one of the party's four provincial leaders.

1   Using the process-and-participant analytical system of Chapter 4, identify the main clause processes and participants throughout this article. Do you notice any tendencies here, in terms of which individuals are regularly a particular kind of clause participant? What kind of 'do-er' (and how often) are Mr de Klerk and the government; what kind of 'do-er' (and again, how frequently) are Mr Mandela and the ANC?

2   Are there any interesting patterns of contrasts in the naming of participants? Do not look only at how the main protagonists, Mr de Klerk and Mr Mandela, are named, but analyse also the naming(s) of those groups that de Klerk and Mandela are said to represent. Be alert to doubtful or inacurate namings: for example, when the text asserts that, by his reforms, Mr de Klerk *astounded most South Africans*, is it possible that *South Africans* here actually denotes 'enfranchised South Africans' rather than 'all South Africans, regardless of race'?

3 Comment on the use and effect of any instances of probability or obligation modality in the passage.

4 The article is accompanied by a photograph of a political banner, evidently held aloft by unseen protestors. On the right side of the banner is a picture of Nelson Mandela as he looked in the early 1960s, and to the left of this in large print the banner proclaims:

> NELSON
> MANDELA
> LEADER OF
> THE NATION

Beneath the picture, is one of the *Economist*'s hallmark 'clever' but worldly wise captions, sited to the left so as to catch the eye immediately after the printed words of the banner:

But still locked up.

What do you make of this configuration? Would you agree that, alongside an innocent, 'face-value' reading of this picture and caption, there may be a more ironic and caustic interpretation? (§)

5 State the English idom that involves the words *throw* and *reputation*.
   State the (quite separate) idiom that involves the words *throw, caution* and *winds.*
   Now look again at where the text asserts that Mr de Klerk *has thrown to the winds his reputation for caution*. What might this imply? (§)

6 Using the speech act labels introduced in Chapter 8 – offers, requests, informs, etc. – compare and contrast the verbs describing Mr de Klerk's speech act moves, as reported here, and those used to describe the ANC's moves. (§)

7 Falling partly under naming and partly under presupposition, it is interesting to notice that the phrase *the government* is used on two occasions in paragraph 4, the paragraph in which the ANC's demands are rehearsed. And, furthermore, the phrase is used within sentences indirectly reporting those ANC demands. E.g.:

> The ANC demands complete repeal of the government's state of emergency

The ANC also insists that the government must lift its ban on outlawed organisations.

What difference is there between the second of these, and the alternative version below:

The ANC also insists that the ban on outlawed organisations be lifted? (§)

ACTIVITY 5

Consider the following book review, published in the *Daily Telegraph* (London) in 1984. Identify those words or phrases in it which trigger specific presuppositions, and comment on those presuppositions which strike you as most controversial. Be careful to distinguish dubious presuppositions from dubious assertions. Sometimes the dubious assertions are themselves qualified or conceded to be less than certain. At the close of the article, for example, the author embeds the dubious claim that *'One man, one vote' however worthy in principle, would plunge southern Africa into ruin and civil war*, inside a hedged assertion: *Experience suggests (this)*. What can be said of the modality of *Experience suggests* compared, say, with *It is a fact that* or *History demonstrates that* on the one hand, or *We all know that* on the other? Like the former, you have to contest the dubious embedded claim by rejecting and negating the framing clause:

No it is *not* a fact that

History does *not* demonstrate that

Experience does *not* suggest that

So you are left negating the introducing clause rather than the really offensive embedded assumption directly. In addition, that introducing clause is quite hedged in itself: Experience *suggests*, it does not guarantee or ordain. By contrast if the author had written *We all know that [universal suffrage would precipitate civil war]*, contesting and negating the introducing clause would leave the embedded clause (in this case a factive presupposition) intact, and this would have the consequence of drawing our attention *to* the objectionable embedded clause quite directly.

STILL DARK, RICHARD WEST

The Africans: Encounters from the Sudan to the Cape by David Lamb, Bodley Head, 363pp, £12.50.

It is 20 years since Sir Alec Douglas-Home, becoming confused with the terms 'underdeveloped' or the 'developing' countries, came up with his own phrase 'under-developing countries'.

Perhaps he was not far wrong. During the subsequent 20 years, almost every country in Africa has been 'underdeveloping' steadily. In *The Africans: Encounters from the Sudan to the Cape*, an American journalist, David Lamb, has produced such facts as these:

> Zaire, at independence in 1960, had 31,000 miles of main roads; twenty years later, only 3,700 miles of usable road remained. Uganda at independence had 48 hospitals and several hundred rural dispensaries. Now two-thirds of the doctors have either been killed or gone into exile, and virtually no medical services exist outside the capital.
>
> The Tanzanian Investment Board has admitted that during the decade from 1969, the productivity of the workers dropped by 50 per cent, while the State bureaucracy rose at a rate of 14 per cent a year. A decade ago a Zambian farmer needed to produce one bag of maize to buy three cotton shirts; today that bag of maize buys only one shirt.

During his stint in Africa Mr Lamb succeeded in visiting some of the Left-wing countries. He is both perceptive and funny about the way that Socialism produces lethargy in Africans. '"Angola, Angola, Angola!" a navy lieutenant exclaimed, throwing up his hands in exasperation one day when most of his men didn't show up for a training exercise.' A Tanzanian student, attending an all-African party in the United States, 'headed directly for two young men, sitting morosely and alone in a corner. "As soon as I saw them there with long faces, I knew they were Tanzanians," he said.'

This book was written for an American readership; hence the constant references to 'Ohio-sized' Liberia, 'California-sized' Zimbabwe or the 'Montana-sized' Ogaden plateau. This would not matter, except that Mr Lamb, while explaining a continent of which the Americans know little, intrudes some very American prejudice.

He is shocked by the ignorance and the poverty that he saw

in Africa. The Europeans with long experience of the continent tend to expect it . . . He seems to believe that, before the slavers and then the colonialists, black Africa had enjoyed political institutions, even in places civilisation, much like the rest of the world's.

It is true there were patches of civilisation in places reached by Islam, like the Mandingo country, or by Christianity, like Ethiopia. Yet even these were frail and primitive civilisations compared with those of ancient China, India, Egypt, Greece, Rome, European Christendom and Islamic North Africa. I fear Mr Lamb is misleading his countrymen as he writes:

> And when we criticise Africa for stumbling we never mention that the United States in, say, 1796 was a country where corruption was rampant, political unity and national prosperity were distant goals and a civil war lay half a century down the road.

It is absurd to say of Africa that 'the colonialists designed the scenario for disaster.' It is absurd and mischievous to say: 'If any country needed a revolution, Ethiopia did.' It is absurd and illusory to suggest that if only South Africa were a multi-racial State it would become the happiest place on the continent. It is a nice idea. But harsh experience suggests that 'one man, one vote,' however worthy in principle, would plunge southern Africa into ruin and civil war.

ACTIVITY 6

The following passage is the opening of Chapter V of *Frankenstein*, by Mary Shelley. It comes at the point where, after extensive studies, having 'succeeded in discovering the cause of generation and life' and having become 'capable of bestowing animation upon lifeless matter' Victor Frankenstein sets about creating his first human being. Discuss the ways in which the presuppositions contained in the phrasing of these sentences, and the background assumptions they disclose, contribute to the telling of unforeseen developments in the story at this stage:

> It was on a dreary night of November, that I beheld the accomplishment of my toils. With an anxiety that almost amounted to agony, I collected the instruments of life around me, that I might infuse a spark of being into the lifeless thing that lay at my feet. It was already one in the morning; the rain pattered dismally against the panes, and my candle was

nearly burnt out, when, by the glimmer of the half-extin-
guished light, I saw the dull yellow eye of the creature open;
it breathed hard, and a convulsive motion agitated its limbs.

How can I describe my emotions at this catastrophe, or
how delineate the wretch whom with such infinite pains and
care I had endeavoured to form? His limbs were in propor-
tion, and I had seen his features as beautiful. Beautiful!
Great God! His yellow skin scarcely covered the work of
muscles and arteries beneath; his hair was of a lustrous black,
and flowing; his teeth of pearly whiteness; but these luxur-
iances only formed a more horrid contrast with his watery
eyes, that seemed almost of the same colour as the dun white
sockets in which they were set, his shrivelled complexion and
straight black lips.

The different accidents of life are not so changeable as the
feelings of human nature. I had worked hard for nearly two
years, for the sole purpose of infusing life into an inanimate
body. For this I had deprived myself of rest and health. I had
desired it with an ardour that far exceeded moderation; but
now that I had finished, the beauty of the dream vanished,
and breathless horror and disgust filled my heart. Unable to
endure the aspect of the being I had created, I rushed out to
compose my mind to sleep. At length lassitude succeeded to
the tumult I had before endured; and I threw myself on the
bed in my clothes, endeavouring to seek a few moments of
forgetfulness. But it was in vain; I slept, indeed, but I was
disturbed by the wildest dreams. I thought I saw Elizabeth,
in the bloom of health, walking in the streets of Ingolstadt.
Delighted and surprised, I embraced her; but as I imprinted
the first kiss on her lips, they became livid with the hue of
death; her features appeared to change, and I thought that I
held the corpse of my dead mother in my arms; a shroud
enveloped her form, and I saw the graveworms crawling in
the folds of the flannel. I started from my sleep with horror;
a cold dew covered my forehead, my teeth chattered, and
every limb became convulsed; when, by the dim yellow light
of the moon, as it forced its way through the window
shutters, I beheld the wretch — the miserable monster
whom I had created. He held up the curtain of the bed;
and his eyes, if eyes they may be called, were fixed on me.
His jaws opened, and he muttered some inarticulate sounds,
while a grin wrinkled his cheeks. He might have spoken, but
I did not hear; one hand was stretched out, seemingly to
detain me, but I escaped, and rushed down the stairs. I took

refuge in the courtyard belonging to the house which I
inhabited; where I remained during the rest of the night,
walking up and down in the greatest agitation, listening
attentively, catching and fearing each sound as if it were to
announce the approach of the demoniacal corpse to which I
had so miserably given life.

ACTIVITY 7

The next paragraph comes from the opening chapter of Ian McEwan's
novel, *Black Dogs*. The chapter introduces us to Jeremy, who, writing
autobiographically, is looking back on his late teenage self, when as a
young adult without parents he was finding his way in the world – and
often doing so by 'grafting himself' on to the parents of his friends. In
the passage below, Jeremy refers to his passive teenage self in line 5,
and contrasts himself with his 'normal' peers, such as Toby and Joe.
Comment on how irony, presupposition, and modality are interwoven
in these lines:

> I realize that much of the above tells against me, that it is Toby
> pursuing in impossible circumstances a beautiful crazy young
> woman beyond his reach, or his and Joe's and the Silversmith
> kids' excursions in to the neighborhood, that display a proper
> appetite for life, and that a seventeen-year-old's infatuation
> with comfort and the conversation of his elders suggests a dull
> spirit; and that in describing this period of my life I have
> unconsciously mimicked not only, here and there, the super-
> ior, sneering attitudes of my adolescent self, but also the rather
> formal, distancing, labyrinthine tone in which I used to speak,
> clumsily derived from my scant reading of Proust, which was
> supposed to announce me to the world as an intellectual. All I
> can say for my younger self is that although I was hardly aware
> of it at the time, I missed my parents terribly.
>
> Ian McEwan, *Black Dogs*, xvi (Doubleday, 1992)

ACTIVITY 8

What follows is one of the most compelling brief articulations of the
case for freedom of religion and freedom of expression ever written –
certainly, ever written in English.

A BILL FOR ESTABLISHING RELIGIOUS FREEDOM

Well aware that the opinions and belief of men depend not on their own will, but follow involuntarily the evidence proposed to their minds; that Almighty God hath created the mind free, and manifested his supreme will that free it shall remain by making it altogether insusceptible of restraint; that all attempts to influence it by temporal punishments, or burthens, or by civil incapacitations, tend only to beget habits of hypocrisy and meanness, and are a departure from the plan of the holy author of our religion, who being lord both of body and mind, yet chose not to propagate it by coercions on either, as was in his Almighty power to do, but to extend it by its influence on reason alone; that the impious presumption of legislators and rulers, civil as well as ecclesiastical, who, being themselves but fallible and uninspired men, have assumed dominion over the faith of others, setting up their own opinions and modes of thinking as the only true and infallible, and as such endeavoring to impose them on others, hath established and maintained false religions over the greatest part of the world and through all time: That to compel a man to furnish contributions of money for the propagation of opinions which he disbelieves and abhors, is sinful and tyrannical: that even the forcing him to support this or that teacher of his own religious persuasion, is depriving him of the comfortable liberty of giving his contributions to the particular pastor whose morals he would make his pattern, and whose powers he feels most persuasive to righteousness; and is withdrawing from the ministry those temporary rewards, which proceeding from an approbation of their personal conduct, are an additional incitement to earnest and unremitting labours for the instruction of mankind; that our civil rights have no dependance on our religious opinions, any more than our opinions in physics or geometry; that therefore the proscribing any citizen as unworthy the public confidence by laying upon him an incapacity of being called to offices of trust and emolument, unless he profess or renounce this or that religious opinion, is depriving him injuriously of those privileges and advantages to which, in common with his fellow citizens, he has a natural right; that it tends also to corrupt the principles of that very religion it is meant to encourage, by bribing, with a monopoly of worldly honours and emoluments, those who will externally profess and conform to it; that though indeed these are criminal who do not withstand such temptation, yet neither are those innocent who lay the bait in their way; that the opinions of men are not the object of civil government, nor under its jurisdiction; that to suffer the civil magistrate to intrude his powers into the field of opinion and to restrain the profession or propagation of principles on supposition of their ill tendency is a dangerous fallacy, which at once destroys all religious liberty, because he being of course judge of that tendency will make his opinions the rule of judgment, and approve or condemn the sentiments of others only as they shall square with or differ from his own; that it is time enough for the rightful purposes of civil government for its officers to interfere when principles break out into overt acts against peace and good order; and finally, that truth is great and will prevail if left to herself; that she is the proper and sufficient antagonist to error, and has nothing to fear from the conflict unless by human interposition disarmed of her natural weapons, free argument and debate; errors ceasing to be dangerous when it is permitted freely to contradict them.

We the General Assemby of Virginia do enact that no man shall be compelled to frequent or support any religious worship, place, or ministry whatsoever, nor shall be enforced, restrained, molested, or burthened in his body or goods, nor shall otherwise suffer, on account of his religious opinions or belief; but that all men shall be free to profess, and by argument to maintain, their opinions in matters of religion, and that the same shall in no wise diminish, enlarge, or affect their civil capacities.

And though we well know that this assembly, elected by the people for the ordinary purposes of legisiation only, have no power to restrain the acts of succeeding Assemblies, constituted with powers equal to our own, and that therefore to declare this act irrevocable would be of no effect in law; yet we are free to declare, and do declare, that the rights hereby asserted are of the natural rights of mankind, and that if any act shall be hereafter passed to repeal the present or to narrow its operation, such act will be an infringement of natural right.

Thos. Jefferson, 1777

The bill comprises one long first paragraph, by way of preliminary rehearsal of principles and 'background'; a brief second paragraph containing the key ordinance (*We do enact that* . . .); and a third coda-like paragraph, asserting that what has gone before is a statute 'above ordinary statutes' and beyond orthodox lawmaking, being a matter of natural rights.

1   On what grounds might you argue that *all* of the long first paragraph is, as presented, a network of presuppositions, while all the key claims in paragraph 2 are assertions (so that all of this bill, save the short final paragraph, amounts to a single 'sentence' with the format presupposition + assertion)?

2   Within the postscript-like final paragraph, what key existential presupposition is made which, to the ears of many late-eighteenth-century rulers, might have seemed a highly improper – indeed revolutionary – notion?

3   Can you find a single presupposition within Jefferson's bill which (a) you regard as false and (b) the falsity of which tends to undermine the case for freedom of religion and freedom of expression? (The *combination* of criteria (a) and (b) is important: for instance, many readers may reject the presupposition that *Almighty God hath created the mind free*, on the ground that they do not believe that any Almighty God exists; but is the second criterion also met?)

4   Why is truth (presupposed to be) female (at the close of paragraph 1)?

5   Would you agree that Jefferson brilliantly demonstrates that insisting upon freedom of religion also requires an 'unprivileging of religion', and that this blueprint, ostensibly a protection of religion, also argues for a set of conditions in which an entirely secular and non-religious society can flourish?

6   And would you agree that most questions that begin with 'Would you agree' are usually leading questions? What is the name given in this chapter to the kind of presupposition-trigger that *agree* is, when it is used in a leading way?

7   As noted in passing in this chapter, more radically backgrounded than presupposed information is that information which is not mentioned at all (in neither the asserted foreground nor the presupposed background). In light of this, consider the descriptions of himself that Jefferson chose as his own epitaph:

> Author of the Declaration of American Independence, of the Statute of Virginia for Religious Freedom, and Father of the University of Virginia.

Discuss any controversial silences 'audible' in that epitaph.

ACTIVITY 9

The following passage is the opening to Malcolm Bradbury's novel, *The History Man*:

> Now it is the autumn again; the people are all coming back. The recess of summer is over, when holidays are taken, newspapers shrink, history itself seems momentarily to falter and stop. But the papers are thickening and filling again; things seem to be happening; back from Corfu and Sete, Positano and Leningrad, the people are parking their cars and campers in their drives, and opening their diaries, and calling up other people on the telephone. The deckchairs on the beach have been put away, and a weak sun shines on the promenade; there is fresh fighting in Vietnam, while McGovern campaigns ineffectually against Nixon. In the chemists' shops in town, they have removed the sunglasses and the insect-bite lotions, for the summer visitors have left, and have stocked up on sleeping tablets and Librium, the staples of the year-round trade; there is direct rule in Ulster, and a gun-battle has taken place in the Falls Road. The new autumn colours are in the boutiques; there is now on the market a fresh intra-uterine device, reckoned to be ninety-nine per cent safe. Everywhere there are new developments, new indignities; the intelligent people survey the autumn world, and liberal and radical hackles rise, and fresh faces are about, and the sun shines fitfully, and the telephones ring. So, sensing the climate, some people called the Kirks, a well-known couple, decide to have a party.

1   Lack of modality can sometimes be as revealing as copiousness of modality. What effects do you sense are achieved, in part, by the relative *absence* of modality in the passage?

2   What do you make of the juxtapositions of diverse topics, from one sentence to the next and even in the course of sentences? What effect does all this have?

3   On the basis of your interpretation of the content of the entire passage except the final sentence, what sense do you have of the climate or atmosphere in which these people are currently living? And in view of your sense of the climate, do you see a party as a reasonable response? With the exception of the *But* of sentence 3, the final sentence's *So* is the only cohesive conjunction (causal) in the paragraph. Comment on the appropriateness, or the effect on the reader, of this resultative *So* used here.

Commentaries

ACTIVITY 3

This sentence comes from Tristan Jones's *Saga of a Wayward Sailor* (New York: Avon, 1980).

ACTIVITY 4

4 It is certainly possible to argue, concerning the banner and caption, that the *Economist* is simply stating what was, in January 1990, the rather obvious. But in the context, a more suspicious reading seems warranted. In particular, the *Economist* subeditor has phrased the caption as if it were simply a neutral continuation of the proposition asserted by the banner. And yet few readers will be unaware that two rather different voices are involved here: one voice says 'Nelson Mandela is the leader of the nation'; the other comments 'but he's still locked up'. As a result a somewhat different exchange of propositions is hinted at: 'Your demo banner claims Mandela is the leader of the nation, but in fact he's still locked up isn't he; and what kind of leader can a person be when imprisoned in such a way?' The use of the contrastive or adversative conjunction *but* certainly contributes to the suspicious interpretation. What difference of impression would have been created if the text had run:

> NELSON MANDELA
> LEADER OF THE NATION.
> And still locked up

Some might also question the word-choice of *lock up*, to denote a period of imprisonment spanning twenty-five years. In the spirit of Chapter 7, one might argue that *lock up* has a much wider range of uses, and hence a less focused set of implications, than verbal adjectives like *imprisoned*. In particular, various things can be 'locked up' without their being any sense of punitive imprisonment: things that are locked up may be simply 'out of circulation', disabled (e.g. a computer), or rendered inaccessible (as when someone is 'locked up in a meeting'). Imprisonment is always an undesirable state of affairs when applied to humans (however necessary in particular cases); locking up is not. In fact the choice of verb in the caption may have been prompted by the surrounding text, in which it is asserted that Mandela 'holds the key to peaceful resolution of his country's racial conflict'. The fact that the key Mandela allegedly holds is not the key to the lock that still imprisoned him, in January 1990, is a textual incongruity which the *Economist* swiftly passes over. Incidentally, we should note the important presuposition in the sentence just quoted, namely that the conflict in need of resolution (by Mandela, de Klerk, etc.) in South Africa is a racial conflict. Is this tenable? If so, can we name the distinct races which constitute the distinct parties to the conflict? Analogously, it is one thing to call a conflict between one group, entirely Catholic, and another group, entirely Protestant, a religious conflict; but supposing the 'Catholic side' actually has a number of Protestants aligned with it, and vice versa? The *Economist* has 'racialized' what might in another light be seen as a political struggle for equal rights and democracy; that is, the multiracial ANC is campaigning for enfranchisement of black South Africans not because they are black, but because they are disenfranchised. Similarly, multi-gender movements for women's rights were not involved in a 'sexual conflict', and were not asserting those rights because the claimants were women, but because they had been denied them.

5   The phrase strikes me as an extraordinary conflation of *throwing caution to the winds* and *throwing away one's reputation* (whether or not it is a conscious conflation is secondary). It insinuates that de Klerk has been daring and venturesome, but also that he has possibly also triggered his own downfall, through 'loss of reputation'.

6   Mr de Klerk is represented as *promising*, *saying*, and *discussing*, while the ANC *demands* and *insists*. In this picture, de Klerk's patriarchal and benevolent reasonableness, cast in offers and informs, is set beside the ANC's insistence, its 'rebellious teenager' role, of other-costly proposals: de Klerk is giving, the ANC is taking.

7   Again arguably – these points are undoubtedly controversial besides of considerable importance – the *Economist* text is exploiting the maxim that to name something in a certain way is to legitimize it in a certain way. And what the phrasing of the text suggests is that the ANC recognizes the legitimacy of the South African government *qua* government, and that it is in the business of 'petitioning the government for a redress of grievances', as the first amendment to the American Con-

stitution puts it. The idea would then be that, with demands and conflicts resolved, the continuously legitimate government could run smoothly on. The model is one of a centre, permanently occupied by the government, and a periphery, occupied by various coalitions of factions and advocates of change. Or, even more explicitly, the Nationalist party government is and remains in charge, after the grievances of reformists like the ANC are met. That, I would suggest, is the narrative that is projected by the *Economist*'s way of representing the world of South African politics in January 1990. Clearly, the ANC and others might represent matters differently. Incidentally, even in the reformulated version – with its reference to lifting the ban on outlawed organizations – there is a glaring redundancy involving the terms *ban* and *outlaw*. These are variant labels for the same status. The ANC was not banned because it was outlawed; it was banned (or outlawed) because it would not *renounce* a military campaign. The key process is that of renouncing, a verbal one. Here questions about language interestingly merge with ethical and jurisprudential ones (as the phrase 'freedom of speech' reflects). You might review, at this point, whether it is ever justifiable to attempt to suppress or silence others on the grounds that they have said, or failed to say, any particular things. (You might want to address exceptional cases, such as obscene speech addressed to children, or deliberately and falsely provoking alarm and chaos by crying 'Fire!' in a crowded theatre, where there might be a clear and present danger of mayhem ensuing.) Whatever you conclude, compare your views with those of Jefferson, in the Bill for Establishing Religious Freedom given in Activity 8.

References and recommended further reading

CARTER, R. 1997: *Investigating English Discourse*. London: Routledge.
CARTER, R., GODDARD, A., REAH, D., SANGER, K., and BOWR-ING, M. 1997: *Working with Texts: A Core Book for Language Analysis*. *London: Routledge.*
FOWLER, R. 1977: *Linguistics and the Novel*. London: Methuen.
FOWLER, R. 1981: *Literature as Social Discourse*. London: Batsford.
FOWLER, R. 1986: *Linguistic Criticism*. Oxford: Oxford University Press.
GOATLY, A. 1997: *The Language of Metaphors*. London: Routledge.
HALLIDAY, M.A.K. and HASAN, R., 1976: *Cohesion in English*. London: Longman.
HALLIDAY, M.A.K. 1994: *Introduction to Functional Grammar*. 2nd edn. London: Arnold.
HASAN, R. 1985: *Linguistics, Language, and Verbal Art*. Deakin: Deakin University Press.
KENNEDY, C. 1982: 'Systemic grammar and its use in literary analysis.' In R. Carter, ed., *Language and Literature: An Introductory Reader in Stylistics*. London: Allen & Unwin. pp. 82–99.
LEECH, G. 1983: *Principles of Pragmatics*. London: Longman.
LEECH, G. and SHORT, M. 1981: *Style in Fiction*. London: Longman.
LEVINSON, S. 1983: *Pragmatics*. Cambridge: Cambridge University Press.
LYONS, J. 1978: *Semantics*. Vols. I and II. Cambridge University Press.
SHORT, M. 1996: *Exploring the Language of Poems, Plays and Prose*. London: Longman.
SIMPSON, P. 1989: 'Politeness phenomena in Ionesco's *The Lesson*.' In R. Carter and P. Simpson, eds., *Language, Discourse and Literature: An Introductory Reader in Discourse Stylistics*. London: Unwin Hyman. pp. 171–94.
SIMPSON, P. 1993: *Language, Ideology and Point of View*. London: Routledge.
SIMPSON, P. 1996: *Language through Literature*. London: Routledge.
TOOLAN, M. 1988: *Narrative: A Critical Linguistic Introduction*. London: Routledge.
VERDONK, P. 1993: *Twentieth Century Poetry: From Text to Context*. London: Routledge.

VERDONK, P. WEBER, J.J. 1995: *Twentieth Century Fiction: From Text to Context*. London: Routledge.

WALES, K. 1989 *A Dictionary of Stylistics*. Harlow: Longman.

WEBER, J.J. 1996: *The Stylistics Reader: From Roman Jakobson to the Present*. London: Arnold.

Index